LEONARD COHEN
Everybody Knows

Harvey Kubernik

Backbeat
Books

An Imprint of Hal Leonard Corporation

Published in 2014 in the United States by
BACKBEAT BOOKS
An Imprint of Hal Leonard Corporation
7777 West Bluemound Road
Milwaukee, WI 53213
Trade Book Division Editorial Offices
33 Plymouth St., Montclair, NJ 07042
www.backbeatbooks.com

Design and layout © 2014 Palazzo Editions Ltd
Text © 2014 Harvey Kubernik
Please see picture credits on page 223 for image
copyright information.

Created and produced by
Palazzo Editions Ltd
2 Wood Street,
Bath, BA1 2JQ,
United Kingdom
www.palazzoeditions.com

Publisher: Colin Webb
Art Direction: Extra Strong
Editor: James Hodgson
Production Manager: Andy Hannan

ISBN 978-1-4803-8628-0

Library of Congress Cataloging-in-Publication Data
is available upon request.

10 9 8 7 6 5 4 3 2 1

Printed and bound in China by Imago.

Endpapers: Palau Sant Jordi, Barcelona,
October 3, 2012.

Page 1: Portrait by Alain Denize, 1983.

Pages 2-3: Portrait by Antonio Olmos, 1994.

CONTENTS

"The artist, and particularly the poet, is always an anarchist in the best sense of the word. He must heed only the call that arises within him from three strong voices: the voice of death, with all its foreboding, the voice of love and the voice of art."

– Federico García Lorca, c. 1933

"I studied the English poets and I knew their work well,
and I copied their styles, but I could not find a voice. It was
only when I read, even in translation, the works of Lorca that
I understood that there was a voice. It is not that I copied
his voice; I would not dare. But he gave me permission to find
a voice, to locate a voice, that is to locate a self, a self that
is not fixed, a self that struggles for its own existence."

— Leonard Cohen, 2011

INTRODUCTION

It was a most peculiar voice I heard late one night in January 1968 on the "underground" FM radio station KPPC-FM (106.7) broadcasting from a church in Pasadena, California. My transistor radio in West Hollywood could pick up the faint signal, especially after the midnight hour. The DJ, probably B. Mitchell Reed or Charles Laquidara, back-announced "Suzanne" by Leonard Cohen from Canada, "a poet who has just cut his debut for Columbia Records." And then he proceeded to recite the matrix number, as jazz DJs used to do, and spun the entire album. It was sort of scary, a dirge-like grumble sequenced between the blue-sky harmonies of *Magical Mystery Tour* and the Byrds' *Younger Than Yesterday*.

The next day, in Mr. George Schoenman's English class at Fairfax High School, Leonard made his presence felt again. Mr. Schoenman, who worshiped Ernest Hemingway, did not dislike rock 'n' roll music like some of the other teachers on campus. His summer job was ushering baseball games at Dodger Stadium, where the Beatles performed their penultimate concert in 1966. Schoenman was assigned to "protect" the group in the dugout and aid in their great escape from frenzied fans, past center field into Elysian Park.

That semester we were assigned term papers on contemporary modern literature. Some of the "hipper" kids placed dibs on Bob Dylan; I countered with my way cooler discovery, the brooder from north of the border. And besides, half the kids in my class were named Cohen, a couple of 'em even claiming blood relation, which was a laugh because any Ashkenazi could claim kinship with the Cohen tribe. Schoenman applauded my adventurous choice and put Leonard's name on the chalkboard next to mine.

After the school bell rang, I raced across Melrose Avenue to Aaron's record shop and bought the album. My parents couldn't complain – this was homework! I subsequently received a C on my paper with a notation to pay stricter attention to what was happening between the words – *metaphor* and *allegory* being difficult new terms to swallow. But I was hooked, a witting draftee into Field Commander Cohen's company.

How could I have imagined that years later I would sit across from him at Canter's Delicatessen, which I could see outside that classroom window; that over the course of my journalistic career I'd also interview him by phone and while sitting at his kitchen table; that I would talk to the players and engineer of that first album; or shake hands with the fabled Columbia Records executive John Hammond, who signed him to the label? Or that I would visit Cohen recording sessions and provide hand claps on a couple of tracks on his *Death of a Ladies' Man* collaboration with Phil Spector at Gold Star recording studio in Hollywood?

Leonard encouraged me to stay in the music journalism and poetry game. One memorable night in the mid-seventies we went to see Allen Ginsberg read at the Troubadour in West Hollywood. I stayed the course; in 2006 I wrote the liner notes to the first CD release of Ginsberg's *Kaddish* album originally issued on the Atlantic label overseen by producer Jerry Wexler. The eighty-eight-year-old Wexler was rather amused when I called him in Florida to chat about this unearthed gem. "Hey kid, who's the next *alter kaker* [Yiddish for a crotchety old person] you're gonna talk to? Leonard Cohen? He's working and doing quite well."

With *Everybody Knows*, I set out to explore Leonard's oceanic body of work. But this book is not a monologue. It is socially constructed, meaning that it is a conversation among many of his professional and personal confederates – band members, producers, engineers, DJs, academics, filmmakers, authors, photographers, previous biographers, well-informed pundits and fan(atic)s – who have had decades to think about and reflect on the role Leonard has played in shaping their space. He is Whitmanesque in his reach, a welter of contradictions, simmering with multitudes.

My hope is to add some clarity and context to this most extravagantly lived, most solitary of public lives. Leonard is a man of simple gifts, an aspiring country-and-western singer turned clarion voice to multiple generations of disciples, who hang on his every utterance like he's the oracle of Delphi.

This book is neither definitive nor encyclopedic; the subject's quicksilver nature puts paid to that. If anything, the multi-voiced approach is the most reliable path to Leonard's indeterminate location. He has transformed uncertainty into a personal mantra – part physics, part poetry, part promiscuous imbibing of life. It is enough for his friends and colleagues to say, "I heard him, I worked with him, I felt I knew him … until I didn't."

I also emphasize the importance of the West Coast in Leonard's life and times. It continues to surprise many that such a well-traveled, Eurocentric figure has called Los Angeles home

since the late seventies. Because he hails from Montreal and the literary center of America is still on the East Coast, Leonard is often associated with tweedy, Ivy League types. But, without grabbing a longboard, Leonard has shown himself to be a true California dreamer. He is, of course, a great many things other than that – the consummate hyphenate: poet, novelist, songwriter, singer, guitarist, traveler, Buddhist, Jew, thinker, healer …

I've tried to frame this panoramic life, aided by the terrific visuals which illustrate his inexhaustible trek into a ninth decade. I hope you find pleasure in the vivid recollections of those articulate witnesses who opened up to me, to both correct the record and, in the words of the teacher and spiritualist Ram Dass, honor the incarnation.

Leonard Cohen remains, at age eighty, a masterly recording and performing artist; in his sharp-suited elegance, a seductive fedora adorning his noble head, he has achieved an "Elder Cool" street cred to which I suspect he never paid the slightest attention. Leonard learned very early on that the music business was a racket rendered moot by committing to a work ethic and immersing himself in daily toil.

As a youth he was disciplined, invested in the pursuit of an ideal that he inherited from his learned grandfather. Later, he found that he could record the ideal and perform it on stage to an audience who would share his resolve. It is this very conversation, the struggle to share something so intimate with so many, which provides the spine of this story.

It is hard to explain, dissect, and tout the mysteries of charisma. But you sort of know it when you hear it, see it, or feel it.

This is not a history report on the life of Leonard Cohen. I tried that a long time ago and was told to stop talking and start listening. There's *a lot* of listening in this book.

Harvey Kubernik, Los Angeles, California

This iconic 1973 portrait by Sam Tata, taken outside Leonard's duplex house in Montreal, was used in some countries for the back cover of his fourth album, New Skin for the Old Ceremony (1974).

1. COMPARING MYTHOLOGIES

"If you happen to be born Jewish and have been formed by Jewish sensibilities, then it's wholly appropriate that you look to the past through your own tradition, which is often very hospitable to your own kind of vision. So, in that sense, I could describe myself as a traditionalist."

— LC, 1975

TIMELINE

1934
September 21:
Leonard Norman Cohen born, Royal Victoria Hospital, Westmount, Montreal

Lives with his mother and father, Masha and Nathan, and his elder sister, Esther (born January 14, 1930), at 599 Belmont Avenue, Westmount

1944
January 14:
Death of father, Nathan Cohen, aged fifty-two

1948
September:
Joins Westmount High School

1950
Has a short story, "Kill or Be Killed," published in the school yearbook, Vox Ducum

Discovering The Selected Poems of Federico García Lorca helps inspire him to start writing his own poetry

Buys a Spanish guitar and is taught how to play it by a Spanish flamenco player

Second marriage of mother - to Harry Ostrow

1951
June:
Graduates from Westmount High having become president of the Student Council and served on the publishing board of the school yearbook

September:
Enrolls at McGill University, Montreal, to study general arts, then maths, commerce, political science, and law

Wins the Bovey Shield for excellence in the university Debating Union and later becomes president of the society (in his fourth year)

1952
January:
Elected president of his fraternity house, Zeta Beta Tau

Summer:
Forms country and western group, the Buckskin Boys, with Terry Davis and Mike Doddman

1954
At McGill, meets and becomes friends with the "Montreal Group" of poets, including Louis Dudek, F. R. Scott, and, in particular, Irving Layton

March:
Has some of his poems published for the first time in a journal called CIV/n

1955
Wins first prize in McGill's Chester Macnaghten Literary Competition

October:
Graduates with a BA from McGill

This page: Scenes from 1950s Montreal (left). Six Montreal Poets (1957) was Leonard's first appearance on record (above left). The twenty-five lessons in hypnotism he absorbed as a teenager continue to serve him well (above right).

Pages 12-13: Portrait by Ann Johansson, 2001.

1956

May:
Publication of Let Us Compare Mythologies, his first collection of poems, which wins the McGill Literary Award

Fall:
Enrolls as a graduate student at Columbia University, New York

Experiences his first bout of serious depression

1957

Release of the spoken-word album Six Montreal Poets, on which he reads eight of his poems – his first appearance on record

While in New York, frequents clubs and cafés of Greenwich Village, attending performances by leading Beat writers

Also in New York, founds a short-lived literary magazine called The Phoenix

Falls for Georgianna (Anne) Sherman, and moves into her Manhattan apartment, but breaks off the relationship when marriage is mentioned

Breaks off his studies at Columbia and returns to Montreal, initially moving back into the family h

1957-1958

His first novel (working title "A Ballet of Lepers" is rejected by publishers

Works at family firms W. R. Cuthbert, a brass found and Freedman, a clothing company

1958

April 8:
Appears on stage at Dunn's Birdland with jazz pia Maury Kaye and his band, performing his poetry/l in an improvisational style influenced by the Be

Summer:
Works as a counselor at Pripstein's Camp Mishmar a children's summer camp in the Laurentian Moun

"Some say that no one ever leaves Montreal,
for that city, like Canada itself, is designed to preserve
the past, a past that happened somewhere else."

– LC, The Favourite Game, 1963

Great cities are invariably founded beside great rivers. Montreal, Quebec's rich cosmopolitan center, draws its vitality from the mighty St. Lawrence, a fabled thoroughfare along which sailed the most intrepid early adventurers from Europe to explore the possibilities of the North American interior. By the first part of the twentieth century, Montreal teemed with a polyglot of British, French, Italian, and Eastern European cultures, all vying to harness and shape the burgeoning city they now called home.

Leonard Norman Cohen, born September 21, 1934, in Montreal's Westmount district, a prosperous Jewish enclave, was nurtured in this lively climate of Old World (and Old Testament) influences, seasoned by the arrival of modernism's clamorous achievements. Leonard's family was a not uncommon mashup of intellectuals and industrialists. The family's patriarch, Lazarus Cohen, Leonard's great-grandfather, parlayed the scholarly training he had received in his homeland of Lithuania into a successful engineering enterprise in Canada, winning contracts from the government to dredge the St. Lawrence between Lake Ontario and Quebec. Lazarus's younger brother, Hirsch, became the Chief Rabbi of Montreal. Leonard's grandfather on his mother's side, Solomon Klonitzki-Kline, was another rabbi and a renowned authority on the Talmud; he lived intermittently in the Cohen household. Leonard would spend countless hours imbibing philosophy and biblical insights from Rabbi Kline, a towering influence on the young and impressionable boy.

It was, however, the absence of Leonard's father that played the largest role in shaping his childhood. Nathan Cohen, grandson of the imperious Lazarus,

presided over his own family with a stern formalism and sense of social propriety that bordered on the Prussian. Resplendent in vested suits and spats even on vacations to Florida, Cohen *père* was the soul of discretion, a man whose temperament reflected a nagging melancholy brought about by a lifetime of poor health. His death in 1944 at age fifty-two cast a pall that would shadow all of Leonard's subsequent endeavors; the "poet laureate of pessimism" was born here.

"The most significant incident of Leonard's childhood happened when he was nine years old. His father died. It left a scar that runs through a great deal of his work. But it also freed him up to become a poet and a musician. Had his father lived, and had he not been raised in a house of women – his doting mother, Masha, and his elder sister, Esther, with whom he is still close – he might well not have been indulged in following this path."

– Sylvie Simmons, 2014

Being a dutiful Jewish son, Leonard strived to meet the demands of his mother, Masha, for academic and artistic excellence. He took piano lessons, played clarinet in the high school band, and became chairman of the drama club and a member of the student council, all of which enhanced both his

With a portrait of his father, Nathan, 2003.

"I first wrote when I was nine. My father died and I wrote this little thing and sewed it into his bow tie and buried it in the garden where the pansies grew. He always used to wear a pansy in his lapel. That did something good for my head so I kept on writing."

– LC, 1972

At McGill Leonard participated in debating, theater, and music. He made a return visit to the university Debating Society in 1957 (left).

CV and his mother's sense of pride. There were also private pursuits; he began to express the bewildering thoughts of adolescence in journals and poetry. At the age of fourteen, he discovered the great Spanish poet and playwright Federico García Lorca, who would become his most enduring literary influence. It was around this time that he started to play the ukulele and then the guitar. Leonard's first guitar teacher was a Spanish flamenco player he encountered one day in a park near his home. After only three lessons, tragically the young man was to commit suicide.

Leonard also demonstrated an interest in somewhat darker pastimes, dabbling in hypnosis and magic. Perhaps he was drawn to the idea of exerting control over other people at a time in his life when he felt powerless; or maybe he saw a way of transcending his daily routine, a fraught state to be resisted with every fiber of his being. These teenaged proclivities shine a light on the conjuring he would later perform before witting audiences the world over.

Sylvie Simmons: Leonard Cohen is quite the magician. He was drawn to smoke and mirrors as a young boy and never completely let them go. As a child he'd been a keen amateur magician – no great surprise there; children are drawn to magic, and magic kits back then were a popular toy. But he took it further. By his early teens he had developed an interest in closely studying and/or taking lessons in whatever subject interested him – everything from poetry to fasting to playing a guitar. He acquired a book on hypnotism, set about

learning it from chapter to chapter and, in a famous incident, having successfully hypnotized his dog, Tinkie, he tried his skills on the family maid. Once he had her in a trance, he instructed her to undress – an incident he fictionalizes in his first novel, *The Favourite Game.* What was fascinating to me, having found the actual book – *25 Lessons in Hypnotism* – in his archives, were the subsequent chapters, teaching how to hypnotize a room full of people, how to modulate your voice and tone, let it become deeper and slower. That mesmerizing quality is an important part of Leonard Cohen's music and his personality. *(2014)*

By the time Leonard was a senior at Westmount High School, the tug of a bohemian lifestyle, filled with artistic and amorous pursuits, chafed against his family's bourgeois aspirations for him – college and then a position in the family business. He applied to and was accepted by McGill, the preeminent English-speaking university in Quebec, a long-distinguished training ground for Canadian elites in the fields of law, medicine, and commerce. Leonard shouldered the intellectual challenges of a general arts course with a certain amount of haughty disdain – "paying off old debts to my family and society," he told Canada's *Saturday Night* magazine years later.

Sandra Djwa: McGill was the major Canadian university next to UOT [University of Toronto] in international considerations for a great many years. McGill was very traditional, very English, very WASP-ish, and, of course, in the forties there

<u>Left</u>: The Buckskin Boys, 1952 (Leonard is kneeling).

<u>Above</u>: Among friends at Le Bistro in Montreal, where on the wall behind him he would write his celebrated poem "Marita / Please Find Me / I Am Almost 30."

was a Jewish quota. For a bright boy it was very important to get into McGill. By the time Leonard had got there it was the fifties. So things were loosening up. *(2014)*

If Leonard didn't exactly rise to the top of the Dean's List, he did manage to engage in enough off-campus activities to build a reputation as something of a provocateur. He was a leader in his fraternity, became a vibrant presence in the Debating Union (winning the prestigious annual Bovey Shield in his freshman year, as well as representing McGill in a host of national and international debating competitions), bantered with Hillel, the Jewish students' society, where he teamed with his friend Robert Hershorn in some theatrical folderol, and formed the Buckskin Boys, an ad hoc country-and-western trio that fueled Leonard's appetite for live performance while improving his modest guitar chops.

Leonard's time at McGill was ostensibly a path to middle-class respectability. It was to his great good fortune, however, that his instincts to swim against the current were recognized by a formidable literary faculty that cultivated his raw, often impolitic talent. Hugh MacLennan's course in creative writing introduced students to the loquacious surrealism of James Joyce, another profound influence on Leonard's writing. The poet Louis Dudek guided Leonard's first published work in *CIV/n*, an Ezra Pound–inspired literary journal. Leonard garnered a prize for his poem "The Sparrow" sponsored by the school's newspaper, the *McGill Daily*. Energized by the attention, Leonard became a constant if contentious participant in the flourishing poetry scene in Montreal, which was displacing Toronto as Canada's center of intellectual foment.

Above all others, however, it was Irving Layton who attracted Leonard's most rapt admiration. Layton's poetry crackled with a zealot's fury; like a Hebraic John Brown, he brooked no compromise in his writings, mixing sex, politics, and iconoclasm into a pungent, intoxicating brew that proved irresistible to his young protégé. Layton was a shaman, a seer, and a showman, intoning his incantatory cadences before an audience eager to take the plunge into a metaphorical abyss with him. Leonard quickly positioned himself as Layton's steadfast companion, traveling to conferences and readings with him, locked and loaded for action.

LC: In the early days I was trained as a poet by reading poets like Lorca and Brecht, and by the invigorating exchange between other writers in Montreal at the time. E. J. Pratt. A tremendous influence. Robinson Jeffers. His poetry has always been especially important to me.

You may be writing a song or a poem about something personal, but, more deeply, there's sometimes another cry. Many men to be at home need certain channels to the past, just as they need certain indications of the future. And heritage or history are all techniques with which you can touch the past, and these are important because then and only then does a man feel more at home within himself. *(1975)*

"Yeats's father said poetry is the social act of a solitary man – we all find ways of bridging that isolation. For writers it is words, but for the cabinet maker it is the presentation of the finished bureau. I don't think the act of writing is especially significant. I think a man or a woman lays their work at the foot of their beloved. We do everything for love."

– LC, 1997

Sandra Djwa: The McGill English department was very important to Cohen. Frank [F. R.] Scott was a thin, very witty man. Louis Dudek had studied under Lionel Trilling and he was very conscious of the significance of the intellectual in society. Irving Layton had a tough time getting himself established and he took up a pose as the poet against the bourgeoisie. Determined to get in the way. He loved to shock. *(2014)*

Sylvie Simmons: The Canadian writer who had the biggest effect [on Leonard] was Irving Layton. He was much older than Leonard – who has tended to befriend a lot of older men – but he didn't appear to be a father figure. I spoke to Layton's widow, Aviva, also a writer, and she insisted that Layton never saw himself as Leonard's mentor, and neither did Leonard. They were equals. Irving Layton was a very interesting man, a Jew who lived in a far more downscale neighborhood than the Cohen family, but in a way he was what Leonard wanted to be. Leonard was playing this kind of downwardly mobile role, distancing himself from his family not as people but as a lifestyle and a system he wanted no part of. Layton was much less shy, much more outspoken and showier than Leonard, especially when it came to sexuality. He was something of an enfant terrible of poetry. Leonard was drawn toward that. He also, like Dudek, took Leonard under his wing and, in Layton's case, helped introduce Leonard as a performing poet. *(2014)*

Ira Nadel: Leonard was a presence in the Canadian poetry scene following the footsteps of Irving Layton. Why, here was a young poet who wore a leather jacket and was absolutely cool! *(2013)*

Leonard's time at McGill concluded with a blast of literary acclaim: the Chester Macnaghten Prize for Creative Writing, the Peterson Memorial Prize in Literature. He dallied with the idea of law school after graduating in 1955, a writer's life still an uncertain, bedeviling prospect. But the die had been cast: *Let Us Compare Mythologies*, a compendium of poems written in his late teens and early twenties featuring line drawings by his first significant girlfriend, Freda Guttman, was published in May 1956, the first volume in the McGill Poetry Series. The entire run quickly sold out.

Ruth R. Wisse: I met Leonard Cohen in 1954 when I was a student in "Great Writings of European Literature," the only undergraduate course at McGill University that satisfied my idea of the intellectual life.

I believe it was Louis [Dudek] who introduced me to Leonard. He had decided to launch the McGill Poetry Series with a volume of Leonard Cohen's verse, to be published while its author was still in college.

Appointing myself head of Dudek's sales team, I went down to the nearest Woolworth's, bought a couple of receipt books, and lickety-split sold over two hundred advance copies. My work as feature editor at the *McGill Daily* had brought me into contact with so many students and teachers that I was able to sell my quota strictly on campus among people I knew. Anyway, the name Leonard Cohen was already a draw. *(1995)*

Ira Nadel: [*Let Us Compare Mythologies* is] an odd, early effort, very romantic and certainly a beginner's book. Other than unrequited love and constant self-reflection, it is not a very rigorous work. A delicate foray avoiding the more substantial themes presented in *Death of a Lady's Man*, *The Energy of Slaves*, and *Book of Mercy*. *(2013)*

For all its youthful impetuosity, *Let Us Compare Mythologies* touched on some of the subjects that have preoccupied Leonard throughout his career – Judaism, political and social upheaval, self-actualization, self-immolation, and most inescapably, the gravitational pull of sex, the tango between Eros and Thanatos, love and death.

LET US
COMPARE
MYTHOLOGIES

Leonard Cohen

Summer 1957: Vacationing in the Laurentians in Quebec with his
girlfriend Anne Sherman and Irving and Aviva Layton.

"I was always on the fringe. I liked the places they gathered, but I was never accepted by the bohemians because it was felt that I came from the wrong side of the tracks. I was too middle class ... I didn't have the right credentials to be at the center table in those bohemian cafés. Maybe it was the tailored suits?"

– LC, 1996

ROCKHEAD PARADISE

Like countless aspiring artists before and since, Leonard succumbed to the temptation of the Big Apple. Columbia University, where Lorca and Dudek had plied their craft, offered him a spot as a graduate student, enabling him to further both his academic credentials and his status among the postwar cognoscenti. Suddenly, Montreal appeared wan and hopelessly retrograde. New York was beckoning, the Mount Parnassus of the rising hip-oisie, and Leonard wanted in.

Ira Nadel: Columbia was just a distraction. It allowed him to explore New York and meet a few of the Beats, but he did not click with them. *(2013)*

Soon after Leonard arrived in New York in late 1956, the Canadian Broadcasting Company invited him and five other poets – Louis Dudek, A. M. Klein, Irving Layton, F. R. Scott, and J. M. Smith – to contribute to a spoken-word album called *Six Montreal Poets*. Leonard read poems from *Let Us Compare Mythologies*. The album was issued in America in 1957 on the respected Folkways label.

By the late 1950s, New York had solidified itself as the center of Bohemian chic. The abstract expressionists – Pollock, de Kooning, Rothko – had become the blazing stars in the visual arts. Bebop, that bumptious rhythmic religion practiced at the after-hours churches along Fifty-Second Street, was in full swing. And the Beats – Kerouac, Corso, Ginsberg, Burroughs, names that read like a degenerate law firm – held sway as the final word in Coolsville. Leonard moved fluently within these crowds, eager to experience the energy coursing through this demimonde. He remained wary, though, stifled by his Canadian sense of rectitude, that northern otherness at odds with the anarchic streak running through this playground of dharma bums.

Robert Inchausti: In 1956 Leonard Cohen heard Jack Kerouac read at a jazz club in New York. Kerouac was thirty-four years old, and *On the Road* had yet to be published.

After the reading, Leonard went to the party at Allen Ginsberg's apartment, where he saw Kerouac lying beneath the dining-room table "pretending to listen to jazz." Looking back on that night fifty years later, Cohen said that he had found in the Beats a confirmation of his own antiestablishment attitudes – although "they never really accepted him."

The historian Douglas Brinkley has written that Kerouac "inspired an entire generation to look for holiness in the mundane, God in oneself, and beauty in every shard of broken glass of a bottle in the street." If this is true, and I think it is, then it was

Above: "André Gideian sophisticate" William Burroughs lecturing "earnest Thomas Wolfean All-American youth" Jack Kerouac, as photographed (and described) by Allen Ginsberg in Ginsberg's living room, New York, 1953.

Right: Back in Canada and attending the 1963 Foster Poetry Conference, left to right, Irving Layton, Milton Wilson, Leonard, Eli Mandel, and Aviva Layton.

Kerouac who found the heroes in the seaweed. And Leonard Cohen blossomed within that discovery – as a renegade golden boy of means and connections – playing Shelley to Kerouac's Wordsworth and Ginsberg's Blake.

Cohen has told us that it was the delicate, imperious Lorca who gave him his voice and an angelic flamenco suicide who gave him his song. But it was the Beat Generation that provided the context and community capable of receiving his gifts.

Cohen's yoking of sin and salvation was more erotic than Kerouac's and more heterosexually focused than Ginsberg's, but it reflected the same postwar longing to move beyond ideological divides to celebrate beatific outcasts, holy goofs, desolation angels, and beautiful losers. *(2013)*

Like most middle-class Jewish boys of his generation, Leonard viewed university life as an opportunity to explore his unrequited sexual and emotional longings. He was ripe for a deep connection and found it in the alluring form of Georgianna Sherman, a striking, dark-haired beauty who would invade Cohen's heart and mind for years following their brief courtship at Columbia. Anne, as he called her, was older, more centered than Leonard. She was strong and sensitive, passionate and compassionate. Although their

relationship was short-lived, it left a lasting impression on Leonard, who wrote about Anne in a number of his poetic and prose works, including *The Spice-Box of Earth* and *The Favourite Game*.

Leonard returned to Montreal in the summer of 1957, spending the next two years at loggerheads with his own creative instincts. He divided his time between working in the family business and furthering his literary aspirations. A conversation with F. R. Scott, one of his mentors from McGill, helped to redouble his artistic resolve.

Sandra Djwa: Cohen was having a hard time trying to decide and he felt a real pull to go on with the family clothing business. He didn't know whether he could be a success as a poet. But Frank apparently told him to go for it, you know. What Cohen said to me was that, "Frank gave me the courage to fail." Frank had given him the kind of assurance that you need when you are young and unsure, "Gosh, what should I do?" *(2014)*

Leonard fell back in with Irving Layton's crowd, impressing his friend with vivid readings of his latest writings, set to hip jazz accompaniment. Words and music were swirling around him; it was only a matter of time before he made the leap to priestly singer-songwriter.

23

2.
CAME SO FAR
FOR BEAUTY

> "The years are flying past and we all waste so much time wondering if we dare to do this or that. The thing is to leap, to try, to take a chance."
>
> – LC, c. 1960

TIMELINE

1959
Spring:
Receives a grant from the Canada Council to fund a writing trip to Europe

December:
Travels to London

1960
January-March:
Completes first draft of another novel, provisionally titled "Beauty at Close Quarters"

March:
In search of warmer climes, travels first to Jerusalem, then to the Greek island of Hydra

Becomes friends with members of the island's colony of expat writers and artists

Meets Marianne Ihlen, and falls in love with her

September:
Buys a house on Hydra

October:
Drives Marianne and her young son Axel to Oslo to finalize her divorce from Norwegian writer Axel Jensen, then travels back to Montreal to try to make some more money - applying for another Canada Council grant and co-writing scripts for TV plays with Irving Layton

Marianne and Axel (junior) join him in Montreal soon after

1961
March-April:
Visits Cuba, deciding to leave shortly after the unsuccessful US invasion attempt at the Bay of Pigs (April 17)

May:
Having rejected "Beauty at Close Quarters," Leonard's Toronto-based publishers McClelland & Stewart publish his second poetry collection, The Spice-Box of Earth

August:
Secures another grant from the Canada Council and returns to Hydra

1962
March:
Back to London to revise "Beauty at Close Quarters" (which ends up as The Favourite Game)

July:
Returns to Hydra and receives a month-long visit from his mother

1962-1965
Divides his time between Hydra and Montreal and his drug intake between pot, hash, acid, and speed

1963
September:
Publication of The Favourite Game in the UK (not published in the United States until 1964 and in Canada until 1970)

December:
At a Jewish symposium in Montreal, his address –
"Loneliness and History" – in which he accuses
the Jewish community of prioritizing commerce
over spirituality, creates a national controversy

Winter:
Meets dancer Suzanne Verdal, inspiration for
the song "Suzanne"

1964
Fall:
Publication of his third poetry collection,
Flowers for Hitler

Receives Prix Littéraire du Québec for
The Favourite Game

Winter:
Back to Hydra to write Beautiful Losers, after which
a combination of exhaustion, excessive drug intake,
and fasting causes him to be admitted to hospital
and put on a protein drip

1965
Confined to bed and in a hallucinatory state after
his hospital stay, his thoughts turn increasingly
to music

Release of Ladies and Gentlemen ... Mr. Leonard Cohen,
a forty-five-minute documentary by Don Owen and
Donald Brittain for the National Film Board of Canada

1966
Spring:
Publication of Beautiful Losers

Composes instrumental music for Angel, a short film
by his Montreal friend Derek May

Publication of fourth poetry collection, Parasites
of Heaven

THE FAVOURITE GAME

A NOVEL BY LEONARD COHEN

Scenes from Hydra, 1960. At the back of the Katzikas grocery
store and taverna with Marianne Ihlen, her husband, Axel
Jensen, and their baby son, Axel Joachim (left) and on th...

"Discovering Leonard occurred through his poetry and prose fiction, not his music. His music was not a draw at first. Of course, that's changed dramatically."

– Ira Nadel, 2013

In early 1959, Leonard received a Canada Council grant that would subsidize his maiden voyage to Europe. In December he touched down in London and began work on what was to become his first published novel, *The Favourite Game*. Having produced a draft, with the working title "Beauty at Close Quarters," he turned to a final edit of *The Spice-Box of Earth*, a second poetry collection. Clearly, the damp English air had inspired a rush of words. (It also inspired him to buy a blue Burberry raincoat, later immortalized in song.)

Still too, the gunmetal-gray skies took their psychic toll; sunshine was the necessary tonic. The Greek islands enticed Leonard with their glistening idylls, as they had legions of London-dwellers before him. In April 1960 he flew to Jerusalem, spending a few days exploring the Holy City before transferring to Athens and setting sail for the island of Hydra. It was here, in the windswept, whitewashed southern Aegean, he found his true North.

Sylvie Simmons: Leonard has always courted discipline, and probably this was his most disciplined existence outside of life in the Zen Buddhist monastery on Mount Baldy, where he would one day be ordained a monk. In the simplicity of these surroundings, he established a daily routine, getting up early, swimming in the sea, going back home to write, stopping for a long lunch down by the port, then back to work again. He learned some Greek, and for many years carried Greek worry beads in his pocket.

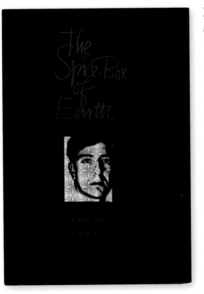

Greece was also where he met Marianne Ihlen, a beautiful Norwegian model with a young son by her soon-to-be-ex-husband, a writer. She was very important in Leonard's life and work. Not just because of the famous song. It was one of his longest and most meaningful relationships. *(2014)*

Hydra, ablaze in Homeric heat and light, provided the mythic setting for Leonard to write, ruminate and find spiritual succor. A bequest of US$1,500 from his recently deceased grandmother enabled him to purchase a house on the island; a three-story, whitewashed residence, unprepossessing in its austerity, but a grounding influence for his wandering soul.

With his Olivetti typewriter at the ready, he dived into creative activity. He also dived into a relationship that would figure prominently in the Leonard Cohen mystique. Marianne Ihlen, mid-twenties, of Norwegian extraction, instantly captured Leonard's vagabond heart. She was living with another writer, Axel Jensen, and their young son, also called Axel. But she soon succumbed to Leonard's mesmeric presence, and moved into the poet's spartan home. Leonard, with a genteel aplomb, allowed the relationship to grow organically, with Marianne providing a kind of motherly ballast which gave him the psychic space to write. Over time, though, their partnership would ripen into a full-blown love affair.

"His friends say that Leonard took a lot with him from his life on Hydra. He loved the simplicity of his life there, in a small white house on a hill with no running water and electricity."
— Sylvie Simmons, 2014

Greece in the early sixties was incredibly cheap. Not surprisingly, a great many writers, musicians, and artists found the Aegean islands an enticing alternative to the indignities of the rat race. Beat reprobates like Allen Ginsberg and Gregory Corso, authors John Knowles and the Australian George Johnston (who chronicled Hydra's white mischief in his loosely fictional account *Closer to the Sun*), were often shoulder to shoulder with a movable feast of cinematic glories: Brigitte Bardot, Melina Mercouri, Tony Perkins. Perhaps the 1957 movie *Boy on a Dolphin*, starring the alluring Sophia Loren, which was shot primarily on Hydra, made an impression on Leonard when he was sending grant applications to the Canada Council.

While on Hydra, Leonard met fellow poet Steve Sanfield, whom he immortalized in the poem "I See You on a Greek Mattress." It would be at Sanfield's wedding in 1969 that Leonard would first encounter Zen master Roshi Joshu Sasaki, who would become his most trusted spiritual guide, teacher, and confidant.

These were wild days and wilder nights; Leonard dabbled exhaustively in hashish and other exotic combustibles. He was beginning to fray around the edges, the bell tolling on his apparent domestic bliss. Like an earlier imprudent high-flyer, Leonard was circling an unforgiving sun and was in danger of crashing.

"When I got to Greece I felt warm for the first time in my life. I remember I was lying in the sun for a couple of weeks - on a rock, doing nothing, feeling all the ice that had built into my bones over many cold Canadian winters melt."

– LC, 1985

<u>Above</u>: Playing guitar for friends Charles Heckstall (far left)
and Charmian Clift (right). Hydra, 1960.

<u>Opposite</u>: Dining by the harbor with Marianne, Norwegian
artist Berentz Pedersen (standing), George Johnston, and
Charmian Clift. Hydra, 1960.

In spite of his often drug-drenched state and the distance he had put between himself and his readership, Leonard's literary career continued to thrive. Brought out in May 1961 by the established Toronto publishers McClelland & Stewart, *The Spice-Box of Earth* was greeted with unexpected acclaim. Montreal tastemakers squealed with delight over their prodigal son's newest effort; one critic even proclaimed that Leonard had supplanted Irving Layton as Canada's preeminent poet. The public seemed to concur – the book became a bestseller. The object of all this swooning took his bows during a visit to Canada and made haste back to Hydra. Even the bouquets of love from his homeland paled in comparison to the sensual inducements of the Aegean.

Ira Nadel: Jack McClelland took an early gamble in publishing his work, and Leonard stuck with him, although it was not always sweetness and light, partly because Leonard always missed deadlines, sometimes by years. But McClelland was there from the start, and Leonard had some very good editors at the firm who understood him. They also understood he was an outsider, often far from the Canadian literary scene (often in Greece and later in Los Angeles), but saw his appeal to a multiple readership. *(2013)*

Sylvie Simmons: A mature, exquisite work, *The Spice-Box of Earth* was about sex and God, the sacred and the profane – concepts that have always been in Leonard Cohen's writing and likely always will. And it was published at what appeared to be a particularly crazy period, during which Leonard had begged Marianne to come to Montreal to live with him, then left her behind to go to Cuba and follow close up the Socialist Revolution, returned to celebrate the release of his new book, then got himself involved in another extraordinary adventure in which he helped rescue and house a Scottish poet who was about to go on trial in New York for giving heroin to his young American girlfriend. *(2014)*

Following some negative reviews of The Favourite Game (1963), Leonard called the reviewers "unhappy people who've failed in an art form they would have liked to excel in."

In March 1961, while he should perhaps have been concentrating on the forthcoming publication of *The Spice-Box of Earth*, Leonard took a trip to Cuba – just as a fearless Fidel Castro was kicking sand in the face of the American bully and the Bay of Pigs fiasco was about to explode. As if stepping off the pages of a Graham Greene entertainment, our man in Havana used a Canadian grant to underwrite his trip to the balmy Caribbean at the moment of maximum intrigue. Amid the glamorous desuetude of the old haciendas, the pervasive aroma of *pollo con ajo*, the *chicas* hustling for their street-corner pimps, Leonard trolled for poetic visions. He may have been modeling himself on a young George Orwell in Catalonia at the time of the Spanish Civil War. Leonard, however, soon realized that his Cuban escapade needed an exit strategy … pronto!

As if in a scene from the film *Argo*, Leonard waited anxiously to board an international flight when he was accosted by armed security and led to an interrogation area. A providential distraction allowed him to grab his bag and slip out unnoticed, find a seat on the plane and breathlessly wing his way back to the decadent West. Apparently God does look after fools, children, and the brazenly naïve.

After his brief brush with international relations, Leonard returned to the safer pursuit of writing. *The Favourite Game*, the novel Leonard had drafted in London, was published in the UK in 1963 and in the United States during 1964. It was a highly sought after import item in Canada until 1970 when McClelland & Stewart finally published it.

Dense, enigmatic, epigrammatic, the novel found a small but passionate following. Leonard's publisher had grave misgivings about its suitability for publication; he countered by withdrawing behind the sublime nature of the artistic impulse – the words chose me, he claimed, not I them.

Dr. Steven Marx: Leonard spent the summer of 1948 at Camp Wabikon on Lake Temagami in northern Ontario.

In graduate school during the sixties, I felt a kinship with his smoldering Jewish intellectual sexuality and a tremendous admiration for his ability to turn all that desire into beauty.

My wife Jan and I worked as counselors at that camp in 1970, on our way north and west as refugees from the political battles at Columbia University, where I'd been teaching and she earned her master's degree in comparative literature. We were already fans of his first album, *Songs of Leonard Cohen*, when someone at the camp showed us an inscription over one of the bunks carved with a pocket knife – as I remember it, "Lenny Cohen slept here."

That was exciting, but not as exciting as coming across *The Favourite Game*, in 1973, as I was looking for Canadian novels to teach in an Introduction to Literature course in Vancouver and discovering that the last section of the book was largely taken up by a narrative set at the camp including unmistakable descriptions of its boat dock, mess hall, and mosquitos. *(2013)*

Ira Nadel: A rewrite of a better first draft that had more power and energy, but still, *The Favourite Game* is a bildungsroman with the traditional features of the youth-to-man story. *(2013)*

Flowers for Hitler, a new collection of poems, was written in the aftermath of *The Favourite Game* and published in 1964. Leonard was fully aware that his incendiary title (originally *Opium and Hitler*) would incite readers and critics alike, possibly at the expense of a more nuanced examination of the work's merit. He was prepared to make this sacrifice; becoming a bad boy at the dawn of pop celebrity (the Beatles had just landed) would provide its own rewards. In fact, the book received largely favorable reviews, but it also dramatically raised and redefined Leonard's profile.

Sylvie Simmons: When I was writing about *Flowers for Hitler* for my biography of Cohen, the first thing that came to mind was Serge Gainsbourg and his album *Rock Around the Bunker*.

Both were shy men, but not afraid of provocation. I spoke to Arnold Steinberg, a close friend of Leonard's at McGill, who recalled that Leonard did not openly rebel. It was something much more personal and inward. But, perhaps buoyed by his celebrity in Canada as a poet, which allowed him to adopt more of a persona or a mask, Leonard openly provoked his publisher. He seemed anxious not to be defined by this role as golden boy of Canadian poetry, and wanted very much to have a wider, more universal audience. *(2014)*

Leonard's emergence at the forefront of the Canadian poetry scene was documented by filmmakers Don Owen and Donald Brittain in the 1965 work *Ladies and Gentlemen … Mr. Leonard Cohen*, commissioned by the National Film Board of Canada. Originally shot to record a tour of four universities by four leading literary lights, including Irving Layton, the film was then edited to focus on Leonard's rising profile.

With his too-hip-for-the-room pose, tousled hair, black leather jacket, and feigned detachment, Leonard came across like Bob Dylan during his electric stand at Newport '65, the high priest of a newly sanctified church dedicated to the fine art of lyrical seduction. There are priceless reaction shots of Leonard's dedicated, mostly young female listeners, who appear to hang on his every diphthong. In later years Leonard would hide behind a crippling stage fright, a reluctant star nudged time and again to face the music at center stage. But here, at the lectern, he is suave and commanding, controlling his materials and voice for optimum effect. In other words … a natural.

The 1965 documentary Ladies and Gentleman ... Mr. Leonard Cohen was reconceived and edited to put Leonard in the spotlight.

Ira Nadel: It was as much promotion as profile. Leonard has always understood the value of publicity, as long as he could manage it, not control it but manage it. The film is a surprisingly revealing document of the early Leonard Cohen, important for its cinema vérité style as well as its content, and made by a sympathetic director. *(2013)*

Sylvie Simmons: He was very entertaining. He had the timing and delivery of a stand-up comic. The film struck me as almost an infomercial for the pop musician he would soon become. He was almost practicing and rehearsing his pop-star image. He was playing games with his image and with the unseen viewers of the film. It was playful and ironic and very smart – on the bathroom mirror he had written *caveat emptor*, let it be known there was an element of the scam. He was very much playing with the idea of celebrity. But he was enjoying it. *(2014)*

Being the celebrated cynosure of Canadian letters was proving to be a mixed blessing. On the one hand, his detached posturing, topped with a sprig of mannered drollery, heightened his starry presence and by extension promoted the entire Canadian poetry community, which could certainly use a lift. On the other, however, as he reached deeper and deeper for new creative insights, his book sales languished, publicity being no substitute for a healthy royalty statement.

With the publication in spring 1966 of his Joycean historical novel *Beautiful Losers*, Leonard came face to face with this irresolute quandary. The book explores, through a rigorous absorption of Canadian historical sources, religious and philosophical texts, and a speed-induced sense of urgency, an idiomatic panorama of every windmill he'd ever tilted at. Any attempt to describe the story is to deny the reader the unique pleasure of grappling with its near impenetrability. Leonard saw it as his creative zenith, the critics responded with a barrage of barely constrained calumnies, and its publisher anguished over ever seeing it turn a profit.

Leonard's literary achievement was greeted with particular scorn from Toronto, his hometown's great rival: "This is, among other things, the most revolting book ever written in Canada," claimed Robert Fulford of the *Toronto Daily Star*. "I have just read Leonard Cohen's new novel, *Beautiful Losers*, and have to wash my mind," declared Gladys Taylor of the *Toronto Telegram*, while the *Globe and Mail* dismissed *Beautiful Losers* as "verbal masturbation." (It should be noted that the novel has since been reevaluated as one of the most significant in recent Canadian literature, and has gone on to sell several million copies.)

"Beautiful Losers knocked over Canadian literature in the sixties. It was history, confession, religion, and sex, lots of sex, all set against the rebellious life of Quebec at a volatile time. Leonard did not, and likely could not, write another work of fiction after that tour de force. It still has punch."

– Ira Nadel, 2013

What could a poor poet do 'cept sing for a rock 'n' roll band, to paraphrase another renegade presence in the popular culture.

And so Leonard, exhausted by too many drugs and too much authorial strain, turned to music – as an escape, a comfort, and a possible career strategy. He always claimed that he couldn't sing a lick, but clearly he had a voice … like Mr. Zimmerman, that wily rebel from Hibbing, Minnesota who'd captured the culture's undivided attention. Well then, two could play at that game.

Sandra Djwa: In January 1966 Frank [Scott] had this big party, which [Louis] Dudek and Cohen attended. Leonard played a Bob Dylan album at the party. And it was at this point he said he was going to become the "Canadian Bob Dylan." According to the guy who has published us both, Lenny denies this. I think that it has to be true because both Frank and Louis told it to me independently for my book. *(2014)*

In 1966, Leonard composed instrumental music for *Angel*, a short film by his Montreal friend Derek May. He would then publish his fourth poetry collection, *Parasites of Heaven*, which contained blueprints for some of his future songs, including "Suzanne" and "Avalanche." "Suzanne" was a nearly journalistic account of his brief acquaintance with a young dancer called Suzanne Verdal during the early sixties; their time walking and talking along Montreal's St. Lawrence riverfront, the very clickety-clack of their footsteps transposed into the hallowed words of Leonard's signature anthem.

That summer Leonard was courted by the Canadian Broadcasting Corporation, which wanted him to host an arts and current affairs television show, but he decided to pass on their offer.

In late September 1966, Leonard planned to travel to Nashville, Tennessee and pursue a career in country music. He borrowed some money from his old friend Robert Hershorn, so he could travel to America, focus on songwriting, and peddle his tunes in the town.

But Hershorn advised Leonard to first make a stop in New York and meet a fellow Canadian and music manager called Mary Martin …

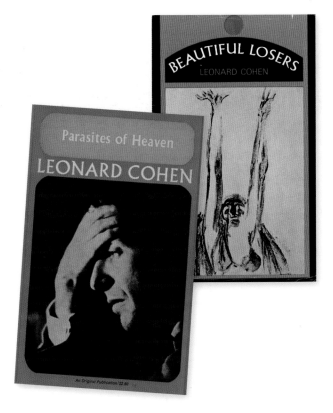

"How can I begin anything new with all of yesterday in me?" Beautiful Losers (1966).

"I've been on the outlaw scene
since I was fifteen. I had some
things in common with the Beatniks,
and even more things with the hippies.
The next thing may be even
closer to where I am."

— LC, 1968

3. A CANADIAN IN NEW YORK

"I came to New York and I was living at other hotels and I had heard about the Chelsea Hotel as being a place where I might meet people of my own kind. And I did. It was a grand, mad place. Much has been written about it."

— LC, 1986

TIMELINE

1966

Summer:
Heads to New York, intending to carry straight on to Nashville to pursue a career in country music

Caught up in the folk-rock boom of Bob Dylan, Joan Baez, Judy Collins etc., he decides to stay in New York in a succession of cheap hotels

Fall:
Meets Judy Collins through Canadian music manager Mary Martin and sings "Suzanne," "The Stranger Song," and "Dress Rehearsal Rag" for her

November:
Release of Judy Collins' album In My Life, which contains versions of "Suzanne" and "Dress Rehearsal Rag"

1967

Winter:
After a brief trip back to Montreal, he returns to New York, where he meets Lou Reed (a fan of Beautiful Losers), Nico, and Andy Warhol, and clocks in intermittently at the Factory

Falls in love with Nico, but though the two of them become close, she does not respond to his advances

Nico serves as the muse for a number of his songs from this period, including "Take This Longing" and "Joan Of Arc"

Moves in to the Chelsea Hotel, long-stay residence of musicians such as Jimi Hendrix, Janis Joplin, Bob Dylan, and Patti Smith

Plays some songs for legendary Columbia A&R man and producer John Hammond, who is impressed

February 22:
Makes his official live musical debut at a benefit concert in the Village Theatre (later the Fillmore East) in the East Village, New York – nerves and tuning problems cause him to walk off halfway through his first song, "Suzanne," but he returns to complete it with Judy Collins

April 26:
Signs his first record contract with Columbia, and his plans to return to Hydra to write another book are put on hold

May-November:
Records his first album, initially with Hammond himself acting as producer; then, from October, with John Simon

Summer:
Marianne and Axel join him in New York, staying in an apartment on the other side of Manhattan from the Chelsea Hotel

July 16:
Performs at the Newport Folk Festival, where he meets Joni Mitchell and embarks on a relationship with her that lasts into 1968

July 22:
Plays his home town for the first time, at the Youth Pavilion of Expo '67

August 13:
Performs at the Mariposa Folk Festival near Toronto

October:
Release of Judy Collins' album Wildflowers, which contains versions of "Sisters Of Mercy," "Priests," and "Hey, That's No Way To Say Goodbye"

November:
Appears, singing "The Stranger Song," in Don Owen's feature-length TV drama The Ernie Game

December 27:
Release of debut album, Songs of Leonard Cohen

"Although my books were well received, especially in Canada, and the reviews were good, I couldn't make a living. In hindsight, it seems like the height of folly to decide to solve your economic problems by becoming a singer. But I'd always played guitar, and I'd always sung."

– LC, 1986

The timing was exquisite. In late July 1966, Dylan flew off his Triumph motorbike in the backwoods of Woodstock, New York, and into a labyrinth of self-imposed solitude. The frenzy of renown had drained him to a corpse-like visage; too many planes, too many pills, and too many soul-suckers demanding entry to his private playground. It was time to bail.

Pop culture abhors a vacuum. The market for inscrutably neurotic Jewish singer-songwriters with an unconventional vocal style had now been established. The position required a unique set of talents: a disarming blend of arrogance and innocence, a keen intelligence demanding as much from the audience as from the artist, and an intoxicating "otherness" – ideally embodied in a nomad from a distant shimmering shore – that conveyed something of the exotic, the erotic, and the romantic. Ground zero for this movement was New York's Greenwich Village, the über-bohemian enclave for in-crowd cosmopolitans.

In the fall of 1966, Leonard Cohen arrived at New York's Pennsylvania Station, resplendent in his signature blue raincoat. Grubstaked by his friend Robert Hershorn to find his musical future in Nashville, for Leonard this pit stop in Gotham would prove to be a revelation, an arcadia of strange but tantalizing fruit which would waylay his country and western intentions.

Blue-eyed songbirds, Teutonic ice maidens, the Chelsea Hotel – that decrepit redoubt along Twenty-Third Street playing host to a coven of angels and devils – it was a *Walpurgisnacht* of sights and sounds. And Leonard was soon up to his comfortless eyebrows in this miasmatic underworld.

Fellow Canadian Mary Martin was a crucial guide star. Having served as assistant to the gray eminence Albert Grossman, manager of major acts including Dylan and Peter, Paul and Mary, Martin was now running her own management agency. The music business was shark-infested waters; her shrewd feminine presence signaled a sea change that threatened the suits but empowered a legion of striving young women. Martin was responsible for putting Dylan together with the Toronto-based group, the Hawks (soon to be renamed "the Band"). Leonard, attracted to strong-willed women, sought out her counsel. She directed him to the influential singer Judy Collins. It was a match made in Manhattan.

Judy Collins: I had a friend in New York who was a Canadian who kept saying to me (she was a close friend), "I grew up with this Canadian and I want you to meet him." So in 1966 he came down to my house, my apartment in New York, and he said, "I can't sing and I can't play the guitar, and I don't know if this is a song."

He had just started to write these things. Then he sang me "Suzanne." So I said, "Well, you can sing and you can play the guitar a little. And I'm recording that tomorrow." *(2010)*

Collins was true to her word. She included versions of both "Suzanne" and another Cohen

Opposite: Notebook and Gauloises ever at the ready. Portrait by Jack Robinson, 1967.

Pages 38-9: In a New York diner, c. 1968.

"The writing of 'Suzanne,' like all my songs, took a long time. I wrote most of it in Montreal - all of it in Montreal - over the space of, perhaps, four or five months. I had many, many verses to it. Sometimes the song would go off on a tangent, and you'll have perfectly respectable verses, but that have led you away from the original feel of the song. So, it's a matter of coming back. It's a very painful process because you have to throw away a lot of good stuff. To come back, and to get those three verses of 'Suzanne,' that took me quite a long time."

– <u>LC</u>, 1986

song, "Dress Rehearsal Rag," on her fall 1966 album *In My Life*, along with compositions by Bob Dylan, Lennon and McCartney, and other established songwriters. Originally written as a poem, "Suzanne" was inspired by Suzanne Verdal, a young dancer whom Leonard had known back in Montreal.

As Leonard's new manager, Mary Martin was relentless. She formed a music-publishing company for him, hiring the Hawks keyboardist, Garth Hudson, to write and arrange lead sheets for Leonard's copyright administration. She hounded John Hammond, the legendary Columbia Records A&R man and pioneering record producer, sending him Leonard's books, urging him to watch the acclaimed 1965 Don Owen and Donald Brittain documentary, *Ladies and Gentlemen ... Mr. Leonard Cohen*. She personally delivered Leonard's demo tape (recorded in her bathtub on a Uher Werke reel-to-reel!) to the bemused executive.

Duly impressed, in early 1967 Hammond telephoned Leonard to meet for lunch and then hear songs at the Chelsea Hotel, where Leonard was now living. Like Billie Holiday, Count Basie, Miles Davis, Pete Seeger, Aretha Franklin, and Bob Dylan before him, Leonard Cohen was about to join Hammond's fabled list of musical icons.

John Hammond: So, I listened to this guy, and he's got a hypnotic effect. He plays acoustic guitar, of course, and he's a real poet, and he's a very sensitive guy. I thought he was enchanting ... because that's the only word you can use! He was not like anything I've ever heard before. I just feel that I always want a true original, if I can find one, because there are not many in the world. And the young man set his own rules, and he was a really first-class poet, which is most important. *(1986)*

Dr. Steven Marx: By 1967, it seems to me that the paradoxical combination of highbrow and pop was starting to take root everywhere. So was the combination of garbage and flowers, as for instance in the work of underground cartoonists like R. Crumb, who, like Cohen, was mixing theology and porn. *(2013)*

LC: Hammond was extremely hospitable and decent. He took me out for lunch at a place called White's on Twenty-Third Street. It was a very pleasant lunch, and he said, 'Let's go back to your hotel room, and maybe you can play me some songs.' So he sat in a chair and I played him a dozen songs. He seemed happy and said that he had to consult with his colleagues but that he'd like to offer me a contract. *(1976)*

Left: Peerless Columbia A&R man and producer John Hammond was quick to recognize Leonard's talents.

Opposite and above: Judy Collins included his songs on her albums In My Life (1966) and Wildflowers (1967). Wildflowers cover portrait by Guy Webster.

"I met Leonard Cohen in 1966, when my Canadian friend Mary Martin arranged for us to meet. He came down from Canada one night, and I listened to his songs in my living room. He sang 'Suzanne' and 'Dress Rehearsal Rag' that night, sitting on the couch, holding the guitar on his knee. I was moved by his singing voice, and by the songs, and by his whole presence. There was something very ethereal and at the same time earthy about his voice. When Leonard sang, I was entranced. I became immediately devoted to him, and we soon were friends."

– Judy Collins, 1987

Top: Leonard quickly became known on New York's booming folk scene, here hanging out with Mimi Farina, Dave Van Ronk, Joan Baez, Judy Collins, and Chad Mitchell.

Left and above: He also frequented the legendary Max's Kansas City, where he met Andy Warhol (above, wearing shades) and his Factory entourage.

Warhol, again with entourage, including Nico (second from left), who left Leonard breathless with desire, and members of the Velvet Underground, 1966. Lou Reed (third from right) was an early fan of Leonard's novel Beautiful Losers.

Hammond had first to persuade Bill Gallagher, chief executive of Columbia, who was doubtful about having a thirty-two-year-old poet join the company.

The year 1967 heralded the "Summer of Love" – flower-decked hippies gamboling in Elysian Fields. In Los Angeles and London and San Francisco, it was a regal procession of wispy maidens and princely pop stars, floating to the sounds of psychedelia. New Yorkers, on the other hand, gave this whole movement a big Bronx cheer. They weren't buying into "peace and love." This was the time of the barracudas and you'd better get your game on or get run over.

Leonard was quickly subsumed by the methamphetamine riptide of the East Village, by Andy Warhol's glassy-eyed Factory, by late nights at sad cafés and afternoons recovering at the shambolic Chelsea Hotel. Riding high on the knowledge that two of his songs were on Judy Collins' new LP – that made him a professional songwriter, right? – he had earned the right to be called a true Village habitué.

One night at Max's Kansas City, he was cornered by a frisky, on-the-make Lou Reed, who trumpeted the greatness of Leonard's 1966 novel *Beautiful Losers*. (Many years later, in 2008, Reed would induct him into the Rock and Roll Hall of Fame.) Lou ushered him over to his table and the young musician's small circle of friends, among them Warhol and the gelid goddess herself Nico, the former fashion model turned pop chanteuse. It was like

meeting the Bizarro World version of Sonny and Cher, and Leonard was breathless with desire. Alas, there would be no love connection with Nico – imagine introducing this lurid Valkyrie to Masha Cohen. There would, however, be born a perfervid inspiration – for songs like "Joan Of Arc" and "Take This Longing," work of such delicate forlornness and ugly beauty – which only extended Leonard's creative horizons.

Songwriting was a private art; performing in concert, though, was a psychic journey into the heart of darkness. On February 22, still waiting for word from John Hammond, Leonard was recruited by Judy Collins to join her and other folkies like Pete Seeger and Tom Paxton at a benefit show at the Village Theatre on behalf of the listener-supported radio station WBAI-FM.

Before a hushed gathering of three thousand, gripped by fear Leonard stammered through a few verses of "Suzanne" before retreating behind the curtain. Collins, ever the earth mother, gently coaxed him back on stage. They concluded the song as a duet. Considering how comfortably and expertly he'd performed in public at countless poetry readings, it was significant that the act of singing his words brought about this paralyzing effect. Leonard's voice has always been an acquired taste. Seasoned with his mordant wit and deadpan delivery, it has become a delicacy for many, but at this early stage of his musical career he found the sound of his own undeniably flat tones hard to listen to.

47

Shortly after Leonard's initial meeting with Hammond, Clive Davis, formerly administrative vice president and general manager, became the new head of Columbia Records, replacing Gallagher. In April, Hammond received the approval from Davis to sign Leonard to a recording agreement.

Clive Davis: I was really just getting my feet wet. I was in the business side of it for a year. I was working with Andy Williams, the young Barbra Streisand, and Bob Dylan, and signed Donovan to Epic [a Columbia subsidiary] in 1966. I was observing. When you get a title of president, before you start making active moves, you sort of appraise the situation. Columbia at the time was prominent in the field of classical music and Broadway, middle-of-the-road music, coming out of the Mitch Miller era. I was seeing the business change.

There was certainly some evidence of rock 'n' roll – clearly the Beatles had arrived, Presley. The only rock that Columbia was in was more of Bob Dylan as a writer, with some of his hits being popularized by Peter, Paul and Mary, and the Byrds. I was seeing music change, but I was waiting for the A&R staff to lead into these changes that were showing evidence of becoming important in music.

In June [1967] I came to the Monterey International Pop Festival really not knowing what to expect, but seeing a revolution before my eyes. I was very aware that contemporary music was changing. The success of the artists I signed at Monterey gave me confidence that I had good ears. It gave me the confidence to trust my own instincts. *(2007)*

Columbia originally assigned staff producer Bob Johnston to oversee the recording of Leonard's debut album. Johnston was burdened by a punishing schedule: Dylan, Johnny Cash, and his recent work on Simon and Garfunkel's *Parsley, Sage, Rosemary and Thyme*. He had to pass.

So in May, work on *Songs of Leonard Cohen* began in Studio E at the CBS Studio Building on Fifty-Second Street with John Hammond himself at the helm. He brought with him the distinguished

Portrait by Jack Robinson for the "People Are Talking About" column in the November 1967 issue of <u>Vogue</u>.

jazz bassist Willie Ruff, a veteran of stints with Dizzy Gillespie, Miles Davis, and Gil Evans, to provide ballast to anchor Leonard's twitchy guitar musings.

LC: When I first went into the studio, John Hammond arranged for me to play with four or five dynamite New York studio musicians. Those takes were lively, but I kept listening to what the musicians were doing. It was the first time I had ever played with a really accomplished band, and I was somewhat intimidated by this. I didn't really know how to sing with a band. I really didn't know how to sing with really good, professional musicians that were really cooking; and I would tend to listen to the musicians, rather than concentrate on what I was doing, because they were doing it so much more proficiently than I was.

Willie Ruff kept the time, and his slides from one chord to another just kept the song moving forward; and I put down, I think, the completed vocal track and bass of "Suzanne," "The Master Song," "Hey, That's No Way To Say Goodbye," and "Sisters Of Mercy." *(1986)*

Hammond handed over responsibility for production to a specialist producer, John Simon, before recording was completed. None of the songs from the Hammond sessions made it through to the finished album, although "Store Room" and "Blessed Is The Memory" were included as bonus tracks on a 2007 reissue.

LC: My first producer was John Hammond and I didn't know the ropes at all. We recorded some numbers, and then his wife got sick and he became ill. Then I switched producers to John Simon whom John Hammond suggested. John Simon was great, and much greater than I understood at the time. I put the tracks down with guitar and voice, and used a bass sometimes. *(1976)*

In the early 1960s, Simon had apprenticed under Columbia president Goddard Lieberson. He engineered classical recordings and Broadway shows with leading songwriters such as Richard Rogers and Stephen Sondheim. More recently, Simon had produced *Of Course, Of Course* by the Charles Lloyd Quartet and the Cyrkle's 1966 hit, the Paul Simon–penned "Red Rubber Ball."

"I'm adjusting the mike, and Leonard is very quiet and then says in a hushed voice, 'See that mirror?' 'Yes.' 'I want it in front of me.' 'OK. What's the mirror for?' 'Well, let me tell you.' He leans forward and whispers, 'When I'm playing sometimes I get lost in my music. And then a line to recite will come and all I do is look up and see where I am.' I'll never forget that. I could tell by his quietness in the small conversations we had, he was a little bit not of this Earth."

— Fred Catero, 2013

John Simon: Lieberson decided to add rock to the Columbia catalogue after the Monterey Pop festival. Lieberson was a real class act. English and all. Funny, urbane, a classical composer, charming. Clive [Davis] would have liked to be him. John Hammond, also a class act, would schedule a session then cancel and reschedule a month later – which drove Leonard crazy, staying at the Chelsea Hotel. So they assigned him to me. We went to my folks' house in Connecticut (they were away) to go over material. Leonard stayed up all night going through my dad's library. I slept. He didn't.

I'm proud of the experimentation I did using wordless women's voices instead of instruments – mostly Nancy Priddy, my girlfriend at the time. About the chorus in "So Long, Marianne," I guess it was the logical step to try adding words after we'd done the wordless thing.

The engineer was Fred Catero, a wonderful guy. Columbia had a sort of "caste" system (being unionized). You were either a recording engineer like Roy Halee, who did most of the "rock" stuff, Frank Laico, or Fred Plaut. Or you were a mixing engineer, like Fred Catero, at first, and a half dozen others. I mixed my first hit with Fred, the Cyrkle's "Red Rubber Ball." Then, Fred, talented as he was, moved up to be a recording engineer. *(2013)*

Fred Catero: The Columbia studios had great echo. And you wanted that. In fact, it added to the drama. Also, I knew the rooms and where the best place was for piano or bass or the singer. Like, when you are doing an acoustic thing like Leonard I had that chair just where I wanted it in order to get the right reverb. I had to take that into account. Because there would have been a big difference if I put him against the wall or in the middle of the room. A whole different ambience. I had him in the sweet spot and knew the kind of natural reverb and leakage I was gonna get.

We did the Cohen session in Columbia's smallest studio. Maybe twenty by forty at the most. I came into the room. Incense or candles were burning. Nobody was there. Just a chair and a huge mirror in the corner of the room. A stand-up dressing-room mirror – five feet by three feet. What is this about?

We're waiting, and finally Leonard comes in with his guitar. We were introduced by Hammond. I go into the studio. Two Neumann mikes. One for the guitar, which I aimed at an angle down, so it's not picking up too much voice, and then the vocal mike, not in front of his face, but almost where the mike for the guitar is, facing upward. 'Cause they tend to look down anyway as they play.

I only spent a few days at the most with Leonard and I never really got to know the man. Now, he had a dark sense of humor. We were doing a session. A union representative came in, who had pulled the switch before on sessions I worked on. There were mandatory studio breaks every three hours. Yet another union rep that had a real negative attitude about the new rock people coming into Columbia. "You fuckin' guys. You're so crazy. Why don't you get some respect for yourself?"

So one day, on this session, Leonard came over to me, and started to speak on the loud side so the union guy could hear: "Hey. I got an idea." "Yeah. What?" "When the sessions are over one of these days let's kidnap him. Then we'll rape him …" And the union guy heard it but he didn't say anything until later. "What was that? What was that? You're crazy! You and him …" *(2013)*

Portrait by Jack Robinson from the Vogue session, 1967. Having given up smoking in 2003, Leonard told recent concert audiences that he plans to take the habit up again when he turns eighty.

"He was a man, while the other rock acts I worked with were boys. He was an established poet. Real bright and clever with words. And he had that finger-picking triplet style that was very impressive. Sort of a classical technique. Leonard said a phrase that I've never forgotten: 'There's no accounting for taste.'"

– John Simon, 2013

Sing Out!, August/September 1967

SING OUT!
THE FOLK SONG MAGAZINE
VOLUME 17, NUMBER 4   AUGUST/SEPTEMBER 1967 $1.00

TYING THE KNOTS IN THE DEVIL'S TAIL PAINTING BY GEORGE PHIPPEN

The Man by Ellen Sander

Leonard Cohen, incredibly handsome, immensely articulate, tough-tender young man of our times. Or possibly he is a man of his times, and we are just arriving.

Cohen maintains a home on the Greek isle of Hydra, but frequently returns to the States to renew his "neurotic afflictions" and brings more songs and poetry with him. Lately he has been prowling New York, Los Angeles, and Montreal folk and rock houses for a taste of the new sounds. In April he gave a reading of his poetry and Beautiful Losers at Buffalo State University, and sang some of his songs. This reading was in conjunction with their Festival of Arts program.

No comparison can be drawn between Leonard Cohen and any other phenomenon. Many will undoubtedly attempt such a comparison, but the result will be, at best, fragmentary. For Cohen is a rarity, if not a scarcity. And though he will always be rare in the true sense of the word, he will be listened to, sung, and read by an ever-increasing entourage, those of the new awareness, those seeking artists of sensitivity.

His Songs by Buffy Sainte-Marie

There's something uncomfortable about hearing a Leonard Cohen song for the first time. It seems to lack roots or direction or something. But be patient; that's you, not him. The melodies are "unguessable" but listen again. When you have gotten used to the idea of chord X following chord Y, though it has possibly never dared to do so before, the pattern becomes clear to you, and clearly unique it is.

Cohen's songs are both other worldly and incredibly "mortal" … as I find Cohen himself to be. Most of his melodies are not immediately "catchy" but are, you'll find, after hearing him, amazingly sophisticated to much more extended form than Anglo-Saxon folk and pop music employs. With the exception of "Suzanne," the musical figures inevitably take a long time to repeat themselves as they do in some kinds of Indian and American Indian music. So it is that a casual listener might miss these patterns. I'm sure that Cohen will be criticised for this. He will be called vague, aimless, cloudy. But I, for one, am grateful to him for lifting me off the familiar musical ground. It is curious to start off in one key and then find yourself in another, and to have no idea how you got there. It's like losing track of time, or realising you have outgrown your name; or getting off at Times Square and walking into the Bronx Zoo; you don't know how it happened or who is wrong, but there you are.

PAINTING BY GEORGE PHIPPEN

Left: With Judy Collins
backstage at the Newport
Folk Festival, July 1967.

Overleaf: The festival
introduced Leonard to Joni
Mitchell, with whom he would
have an intense year-long
relationship.

In July 1967, Leonard was strong-armed yet again by Judy Collins to perform onstage, this time at the world-renowned Newport Folk Festival. Quaking with anxiety, he managed to channel his *spilkes* into a powerful rendition of "Suzanne," which won the audience over. His reward was waiting for him backstage, a fellow Canadian singer-songwriter of prodigious talent and ambition named Joni Mitchell. Scarily young, blonde and beguiling, Mitchell drew Leonard into an intense year-long relationship, a mentor–acolyte dynamic which lasted until their fuel was spent. Mitchell was percolating with new music, new chord progressions, and new ideas that left Leonard clinging to her capo. This whirlwind produced the imperishable "Chelsea Morning," among many other Mitchell classics – yet another reminder that heartbreak is often the greatest inspiration.

Later that month, Leonard returned to Montreal to perform at the 1967 Expo. It was a watershed moment for him and his country, bringing the international spotlight to this most demurely dignified nation. Standing before an adoring audience at the Youth Pavilion, he blinked, his nerves getting the better of him. It was an inauspicious return to his beloved homeland.

Back in New York, work resumed on the album. His confidence, never a given, received a boost from the ever-dependable Ms. Collins, whose fall release, *Wildflowers*, featured another three of his compositions: "Sisters Of Mercy," "Priests," and "Hey, That's No Way To Say Goodbye."

With its luminous cover, shot by the famed photographer Guy Webster, *Wildflowers* confirmed Collins as the premier vocal interpreter of her generation, and glory be to any songwriter who found favor with her. Leonard's bona fides were firmly established; as for his own album, well, that would require a little serendipitous intervention.

In advance of Leonard's debut release, writer and music journalist Ellen Sander and singer-songwriter Buffy Sainte-Marie wrote a profile for folk-music magazine *Sing Out!* (opposite).

From mid-May to near the end of November, Leonard cut some twenty-five tunes with Hammond and Simon in three Columbia studio rooms. Simon withdrew from the collaboration at the mix-down stage, and then went on vacation.

LC: He [Simon] took them and worked on them, and he presented me with the finished record, but I felt there were some eccentricities in his arrangements that I objected to. *(1976)*

"My lyrics are influenced by Leonard.
After we met at Newport last year we saw a lot of
each other. Some of Leonard's religious imagery,
which comes from being a Jew in a predominantly
Catholic part of Canada, seems to have rubbed
off on me, too. Leonard didn't really
explore music. He's a word man first.
Leonard's economical, he never wastes a word.
I can go through Leonard's work and
it's like silk."

– Joni Mitchell, 1968

Ukulele-toting Tiny Tim was host at Steve Paul's the Scene on the night in October 1967 when Leonard encountered Kaleidoscope and recruited the band to play on his first album.

On October 27, near the end of his recording sessions, Leonard headed over to Steve Paul's the Scene, a gopher-hole of a nightspot frequented by heads, squares, straights, and the to-be-determined. Nico was headlining, promoting her first solo album, *Chelsea Girl*. Opening was a West Coast band called Kaleidoscope, which was making its New York debut. Kaleidoscope was a quartet of stringed-instrument wizards (Chris Darrow, Chester Crill, David Lindley, and Solomon Feldthouse), who were backed up by drummer John Vidican. Their otherworldly eclecticism drew from folk, bluegrass, psychedelia, and Middle Eastern music.

Chris Darrow: We were staying at the Albert Hotel. In our first half hour in New York we were robbed of some of our instruments – the van had been left unattended. The next morning on the street I ran into Frank Zappa, who was in town with the Mothers of Invention. I knew Frank and went to Claremont High School with his brother Bobby in Southern California. And Frank loaned us some of his amps and drum stuff so we could finish off a week-long stint at the Scene.

The host for the club was Tiny Tim, who announced all the acts and would play a song or two as well. Opening night was very crowded. Frank Zappa and members of the Mothers of Invention showed up to lend their support. There were very few West Coast groups that had played in the East yet, and we "long-haired hippies" were the antithesis of the New York vibe at the time. Andy Warhol and Edie Sedgwick were there along with the Cyrkle, the Chambers Brothers, David Clayton-Thomas pre–Blood, Sweat & Tears, and Jim Fielder – and I was thrilled to see one of my favorite guys, Sir Monti Rock III. The house band was led by Rick Derringer.

Following our first set, a man came up to me wearing a black leather suit jacket and carrying a black leather briefcase. There in the bar light, stood one of the palest human beings I could ever remember seeing. He almost glowed. He said he was recording an album for Columbia Records and that he loved our band and was curious if we might be interested in recording with him. The man was Leonard Cohen. I wasn't really aware of him at the time, so I suggested that he speak with our managers, who were at the bar.

"I hadn't seen Leonard Cohen since the recording session thirty-five years earlier. Then one day in 2002 I spotted him in downtown Claremont at a local Greek restaurant called Yiannis. I said, 'Remember me?' He graciously replied, 'Of course I do. You guys saved my album.'"

The next day David Lindley, Chester Crill, Solomon Feldthouse, and I were in his apartment trying to work out some of his songs. He had a unique, minimal guitar style and he claimed he was having a hard time getting what he wanted on his album. I later found out that he had gone through one producer, John Hammond, due to illness, and had just worked with John Simon. Leonard gave us the impression that he was having trouble finding the right sounds for a few of his compositions. He seemed happy when we were able to come up with some solutions to his musical needs. *(2013)*

Chester Crill: At Steve Paul's the Scene someone gave me a book of Leonard Cohen's poetry one night to take back to the hotel to read and told me he was going to be there that evening. I was a little perplexed by the poetry but did remember that it seemed much more focused than the immediate geek show. Leonard talked to all of us one evening about having us record with him and honestly I thought it was all just hot air.

We did a sort of short rehearsal with Leonard of some of his songs one afternoon and the material was folk-rockish and we and he could see how easily we could adapt to his tunes, some of which were sort of off-kilter in their construction. He also seemed very stressed about the overall production of the album, and wanted it to be more intimate. We couldn't really understand what he was talking about until we heard it.

We did not see the album's producer in the flesh the first time but he was sporadically on the phone to Leonard about what was transpiring. He did not seem too happy about what we were going to try. Leonard didn't seem to communicate with him very well either – he had lots he was not happy with but wasn't sure what he wanted to change or replace it with.

By the second session, the producer was in physical evidence and total charge. He slowly applied the brakes to Leonard's attempts to change things too radically. Our acoustic sound combinations were nothing like anything on the tracks, which were crammed full with everything possible.

Most of all, Leonard seemed unhappy about his lack of control overall. *(2013)*

Chris Darrow: I ended up playing my rare 1950s Premier bass and my 1921 Gibson F-4 mandolin on "So Long, Marianne" and bass on "Teachers." The slow build of "So Long, Marianne" is one of the secrets of its success and, at nearly six minutes long, it has a hypnotic, repetitive groove that carries on throughout the song. The twin acoustic guitars, playing two separate time signatures, create a smooth bed for the lyrics to lie on. The mandolin comes in at just over three minutes and knocks the song up a notch and adds a different tonality that is not expected. The memorable chorus gets slightly more powerful each time it repeats and brings the song all together at the climax. "Teachers" is a darker, minor-key song, that uses one of Solomon's Middle Eastern instruments, the caz, and Chester and David's twin fiddles, to give a very exotic, international flavor. Once again, there is a rather insistent rhythmic feel to the song, which counters perfectly the ethnic sounds. *(2013)*

Chester Crill: A few weeks later Leonard asked us up to where he was staying to hear the acetates of his album. I remember being very polite about it all, and grateful for the opportunity and the work, but thinking what a train wreck of a record it was and what a spectacular mess for someone to try and start their career with. It reminded me of the excesses of Tiny Tim's first album, which seemed a more fitting place for them to occur. I honestly think any of his other albums are superior to this one and closer to the spirit of who he is and what he has written. His first album seems more like the industry's tribute to itself. *(2013)*

Grateful for their instrumental input, Leonard recorded in his journal of the time: "The Kaleidoscope delivered me. ... May I bless them as they have blessed me." He enlisted Kaleidoscope again for the songs "Sisters Of Mercy," "Winter Lady," and "The Stranger Song," all heard on the soundtrack of Robert Altman's 1971 Western *McCabe & Mrs. Miller*.

Chris Darrow with the Premier scroll bass that he played on Songs of Leonard Cohen.

Released on December 27, 1967, *Songs of Leonard Cohen* struck just the right note between beguiling amateurism and adult sophistication. The songs lacked the craftsmanship of Leonard's celebrated contemporary Paul Simon. The melodies flitted about like Miró squiggles, shorn of any harmonic depth. But there were enough telling details, both in his idiosyncratic guitar accompaniment and his unapologetic vocalizing, to draw the wary listener in close. Evidence of his French Canadian influences can clearly be heard, suggesting an aesthetic kinship with *chansonniers* like Jacques Brel and Serge Gainsbourg.

John Hammond: So, the record came out, and it sold remarkably well. And I had a lot of fun with him [Leonard]. He was a completely weird guy, who liked to go around the streets of Montreal and play pinball. And I liked to play pinball, too, so that was a great bond that we had, in the beginning. And he was extremely well read – he lived on a little isle outside of Greece and, eventually, of course, it got him down to Nashville. And Nashville was astounded by him, because they hadn't seen anything like him, and they never will again. Well, that's the way he was. He never sold out. He never did anything, except what he wrote. He knew about three chords, and I think he still knows about three chords, and it didn't matter. The only thing I could do was to stay out of his way and give him whatever reassurance he needed, and I could do that pretty well. *(1986)*

Leonard's emotional transparency, forged by his rigorous poetic training, lent the music a gravitas that spoke more to the heavy-hearted than the hard-hearted. Needless to say, the album was a kind of litmus test for critics worldwide. *Rolling Stone* held its nose, while in England, the land of the Bard, it was received with rhapsodic praise.

In the February 17, 1968 issue of *Melody Maker*, Karl Dallas declared, "I predict that the talk about him will become deafening. His songs are pretty complex things. No one could accuse him of underestimating his audiences." In its May 1968 issue, *Playboy* magazine hailed Leonard and his album. "His melodically simple, lyrically rich ballads – including the hit 'Suzanne' – are genuine contributions to the pop-folk repertoire. More accomplished performers should latch onto these compositions."

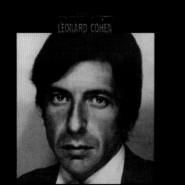

James Cushing: By the summer of 1967, some of Cohen's poetry collections had made their way to book and underground head shops in America, and hipper university professors assigned *Beautiful Losers* in modern literature classes. By early 1968, with *Songs of Leonard Cohen*, we could hear him sing some of his poems, like "Suzanne," or lyrics that were crafted for songs.

Remember, he did not make this LP until he was thirty-three years old. Like Howlin' Wolf, who first recorded at age forty-one, Leonard Cohen was not an adult offering supervision, but an adult giving us permission.

Willie Ruff's bass provides a chamber-jazz aspect to the production of the album. Ruff, as one half of the Mitchell Ruff Duo [with Dwike Mitchell], was used to the idea of creating a whole presentation with very sparse instrumentation – bass and piano. The players must listen to each other's every gesture and play together to serve the music. The first Cohen album exemplifies non-egocentric collaboration. The whole group creates a single organic sound, not a hierarchy with the singer being "backed up" by other musicians.

At the same time, this quiet and revealing record lands in the middle of the psychedelic world, in post–"Summer of Love" culture. Members of the Kaleidoscope perform on several tracks. So, we have psychedelic roots-based folk-rockers joining with a jazz master to enhance the intimate vision Cohen was seeking. Or the vision that found him. *(2013)*

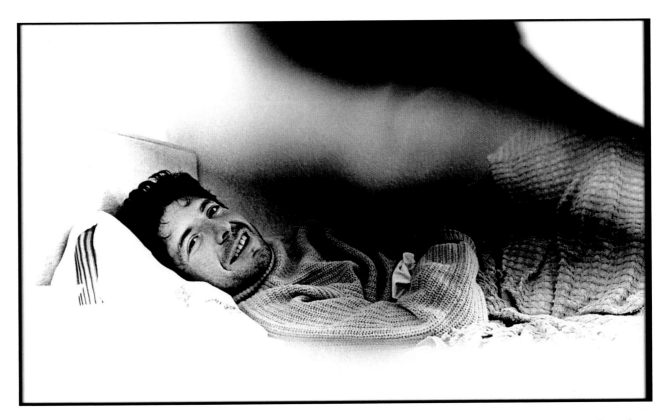

"I have to insist that the first Cohen LP is one of the absolute best, most effective boy-girl make-out records of the very late sixties, totally equivalent to Marvin Gaye's Let's Get It On from a few years later. As a radio DJ for over a third of a century, I still get lovers requesting cuts from those two albums."

– James Cushing, 2013

Robert Inchausti: Cohen was now in the record-shop bins under his own name. He also reached us through the radio for the first time. Leonard gets through the door to the FM airwaves on progressive outlets like KZAP-FM in Sacramento, KSAN-FM in San Francisco, and Pacifica stations like WBAI-FM in New York, or the affiliates in Berkeley and Los Angeles. "The good old left."

The arrival of Cohen's album also coincides with the expanding record business. The Tower Records chain was started by Russell Solomon in 1960 in Sacramento, where I lived. In 1967, a Tower branch opened in San Francisco. Record shops became record stores. Plus there was now a new breed of late-night radio DJs and music journalists eager to expose us to Cohen and other important new recording artists.

And the picture of the Anima Sola ["lonely soul"] on his back-cover sleeve was incredibly compelling for some reason that really spoke to me and many others as well. And in my conversations with my friends, Cohen seemed older than the other rock guys. Like somebody you could grow up and be like. And have women and be a mystic and hang with real hip people. Cohen was a rock guy not a folkie.

As a counterculture figure he always seemed to be somewhere near the center of the whole thing. That was kind of religious and mystical in a way that seemed more true to me than the political. He never spoke like a guru or anything. It was always with this incredible humor, irony. *(2013)*

By any measure, *Songs of Leonard Cohen* was a record in tune with its time, while not being beholden to the times themselves. For the one-time aspiring magician, this was a most impressive trick.

Above: "I was handsome I was strong, I knew the words of every song." "Teachers" from Songs of Leonard Cohen (1967).

"I know there is a craft of poetry, but if it doesn't touch you, then all the technology in the world means nothing. I always like to think of poetry as being a verdict that time gives to a man's writing. A song is something else. I think it's the language itself that draws the melodic phrasing. There are certain ways of saying a thing that make it sound natural, and there's a natural rhythmic pattern that's suggested by the language itself that you try to be faithful to. Generally, the music and lyric come together. At the same time. Whatever the forces are that guide the rising and falling of ideas that burn the mind is a mystery. And whatever I represent subjectively or objectively beyond this tiny moment, or whatever transmissions my audience has built for themselves to receive are all really beyond everybody's knowledge."

– LC, 1975

Backstage at the Newport Folk Festival, July 1967.

4. FROM MUSIC CITY TO THE ISLE OF WIGHT

"I used to be petrified with the idea of going on the road and presenting my work. I often felt that the risks of humiliation were too wide. But with the help of my last producer, Bob Johnston, I gained the self-confidence I felt was necessary. When you are again in touch with yourself and you feel a certain sense of health, you feel somehow that the prison bars are lifted, and you start hearing new possibilities in your work."

– LC, 1975

TIMELINE

1968
June:
Publication of Selected Poems 1956-1968

Summer:
Marianne and Axel return to Hydra, and Leonard spends some time with them there before traveling to London to promote his album, then returns to the Chelsea Hotel

Has a one-night stand with fellow Chelsea Hotel resident Janis Joplin, which he later sings about in "Chelsea Hotel" and "Chelsea Hotel #2"

Develops an interest in Scientology

September:
Finally makes it to Nashville and moves in to a remote cabin

September-November:
Records Songs from a Room in Nashville, with renowned Bob Dylan producer Bob Johnston

1969
Winter:
Meets Joshu Sasaki Roshi for the first time

Turns down the Canadian Governor General's Award for literature for his Selected Poems

Spring:
Meets Suzanne Elrod at the Scientology Center in New York and starts a relationship with her

April 7:
Release of Songs from a Room

June:
Travels to Italy to discuss collaborating with Leonard Bernstein on the score of a Franco Zeffirelli film, but nothing more comes of it

June-July:
Continues to Hydra where he is joined by Suzanne, who also accompanies him when he returns to Tennessee

Fall:
Distances himself from the Church of Scientology

1970
Spring:
Contracts Marty Machat as his manager, who continues in that position until his death in 1988

May:
Goes on a nine-date tour of Europe, almost causing a riot on stage in Hamburg by giving a Nazi salute, and in Amsterdam by inviting the audience back to his hotel

July:
Premiere in Paris of The Shining People of Leonard Cohen, a ballet by the Royal Winnipeg Ballet accompanied by readings of several of Leonard's poems

July 25:
Meets Bob Dylan backstage at the Forest Hills folk festival in New York

August 2:
Rides on stage on horseback at a free festival in Aix-en-Provence, France

August 31:
Memorable performance at the Isle of Wight Festival, UK

Intersperses his conventional touring with performances for patients in psychiatric hospitals

"'Bird On The Wire.' It was begun in Greece because there were no wires on the island where I was living to a certain moment. There were no telephone wires. There were no telephones. There was no electricity. So at a certain point they put in these telephone poles, and you wouldn't notice them now, but when they first went up, about all I did was stare out the window at these telephone wires and think how civilization had caught up with me and I wasn't going to be able to escape after all. I wasn't going to be able to live this eleventh-century life that I thought I had found for myself. So that was the beginning."

– LC, 1992

At the start of 1968 Leonard was feeling betwixt and between. He had turned to music in the hope of making some real money and the expectation that his songs could reach a far greater audience than his poetry ever would. Now, with a debut album earning hipster status points and fueling his rise to cult icon, the question was, what next?

In May, Joni Mitchell tried to provide an answer. Having just recorded her first album, *Song to a Seagull*, produced by her then inamorato David Crosby, she implored him to cut some tracks in Los Angeles with Leonard. It was not a constructive pairing. (Of the three songs recorded, two were eventually released as bonus material on a 2007 reissue of Leonard's eventual second album.)

Crosby, by his own admission, had no real production skills and was ill-prepared to grapple with Leonard's *sui generis* material. But this time in Los Angeles wasn't completely without value. At the airport Leonard crossed paths with Bob Johnston, a man with legitimate producer's credentials, who had originally been slated to produce his first album. This chance encounter planted the seed for a relationship that would lead to Johnston producing the follow-up.

But first, there was the siren's call from Hydra; Leonard's relationship with Marianne was ending, a casualty of his endless peregrinations. Then it was to London in July and appearances on the BBC, including DJ John Peel's *Top Gear* radio show. *Songs of Leonard Cohen* was top twenty in the UK charts. And then it was back to New York for more dabbling with the literati, the glitterati and the Warholian demi-monde. The reluctant rock star was not above engaging in some well-considered social networking.

Toward the end of the promotional cycle for his album, however, Leonard fell into a funk, experiencing a creative and emotional exhaustion which may have reflected his deep-seated ambivalence to success. His American publisher, Viking, had no qualms about exploiting his new-found "pop star" status, bringing out a new edition of his 1966 novel *Beautiful Losers* as well as an anthology, *Selected Poems 1956–1968*, shortly after.

Leonard himself was perfectly content to linger in New York, allowing chance to play the decisive role in his direction. One night at the Chelsea, it delivered to his unmade bed Janis Joplin, another orphaned soul looking for love in all the wrong places. "Chelsea Hotel #2," Leonard's famously revealing account of this episode, was later included on his 1974 album *New Skin for the Old Ceremony*.

LC: It was very indiscreet of me to let that news out. I don't know why I did. Looking back I'm surprised I did because there are some lines in it that are extremely intimate. And since I let the cat out of the bag, yes, it was written for her. *(1992)*

Opposite: "Like a bird on the wire, like a drunk in a midnight choir / I have tried in my way to be free." Hydra's newly installed telephone wires, the inspiration for the timeless song.

Pages 64-5 and 66: Isle of Wight Festival, UK, August 1970.

Overleaf: "I remember you well in the Chelsea Hotel / You were famous, your heart was a legend." Janis Joplin on an unmade bed at the Chelsea Hotel, 1969.

"In June of 1968, Joni Mitchell and Judy Collins were standing with Leonard on a Saturday afternoon at Doug Weston's Troubadour club in West Hollywood. Joni was going to debut there.

   Hedge and Donna, who worked with my friend producer Nik Venet at Capitol Records, were on the bill. I walked by the Troubadour and there was Leonard Cohen looking out the window down at the back alley where I was. He was with the two girls. Leonard didn't know who I was. He looked like a guy who was a gigolo from the south of France.

   I knew about him from the music trade magazine ads, 'Suzanne' and his new Columbia LP, 'cause my friend Chris Darrow and the Kaleidoscope guys had played on it. And Chris touted Leonard to us around our recording sessions and the LA love-ins in Elysian Park.

   And I suggested when I saw him glancing down from a window at me next to Doheny Drive, 'Leonard. Let's have a poetry duel.' And he said 'OK.' And they start giggling. Judy and Joni looked like their album covers.

   So we slung some words back and forth and I got him on cabbage. He could not come up with anything to rhyme with the word cabbage. They all laughed, tightly held on to him, shut the window. I thought I could get on the guest list that night. But I did notice his impact on women."

                                                        – Kim Fowley, 2013

As fall approached, Leonard was finally ready to commit to a new album. It was his long-cherished dream to record in Nashville, to partake of country livin', to cowboy up and sidle down to "Music City."

Bob Johnston was now running Columbia's Nashville operation. Never one for formality, he treated his artists with the wariness of a rattlesnake wrangler, giving them all the space they needed to find their creative core. Johnston let his charges make all the creative decisions … until he decided they shouldn't. It rarely came to that. Building trust, that wide-open space beneath the Smoky Mountains, was the key to the highway and Leonard responded in kind.

Bob Johnston: When Leonard first came to town he was in an old person's hotel and stayed about the first week. And then me and [songwriter] Joy [Byers], my wife, leased acres from Boudleaux Bryant and his people and it was a little house by a creek. And then Leonard looked at this house and went all through it, and saw the 1,500 acres, and he said, "One day I'll have a house like that and I'll be able to stay and write when I want to write." And I replied, "Why don't you just begin now?" And I gave him the key and he moved in.

When I first went down to Nashville I took all the fuckin' clocks out in the Columbia studio and I tore those rooms down and put the cords underneath the floor and the room was as big as a football field. And we made a ping-pong room. Had a pool table and everything.

I'll tell you something else I did recording Dylan, and Cohen. I put them in the studio booth surrounded by glass and air where it used to be wood. Now everybody else could walk around and see them and talk to them. And that's the way that it was. You can't record in a room, not see the people, and not know what the other guy is gonna play.

Everybody else was using one microphone. What I did was put a bunch of microphones all over the room and up on the ceiling. I would use all that echo as much as I wanted. I wanted it to sound better than anything else sounded ever, and I wanted it to be where everybody could hear it. I always had four or eight speakers all over the

room. The louder I played it, the better it sounded to me. As far as recording or playback, I like to blast shit loud. Damn it! If I don't feel it in my chest, I can't tell if I have it.

I put together the studio band for Leonard. I hired all those guys who were doing the demos from the South. Charlie McCoy [harmonica and guitar], Charlie Daniels [bass, fiddle, acoustic guitar] who I knew from 1959, Ron Cornelius [acoustic and electric guitar], Elkin "Bubba" Fowler [bass, banjo, acoustic guitar] – and I played keyboards. *(2007 & 2013)*

Charlie Daniels was a good ol' boy from North Carolina, a mean fiddler who could bust out a toe-tappin' bluegrass lick or break your heart with the sustain of a lonesome E minor chord. He kicked around a bunch of road-dog rock 'n' rollers, crossing paths with Bob Johnston, who invited him to Nashville. Anxious to get off the Greyhound, he settled down by the Grand Ole Opry to a steady diet of well-paying studio dates. He's there with Dylan on *Nashville Skyline*, with Marty Robbins and later, with Ringo Starr on *Beaucoups of Blues*. But nothing proved quite as challenging as squaring his sound with the assonant style of the man from Montreal.

Charlie Daniels: I actually picked up Leonard Cohen at the airport when he arrived in Nashville with his friend Henry [Zemel] from Montreal. Johnston was booked in a studio. I had long hair and a mustache. I didn't know who Leonard Cohen was. I knew he was a recording artist and comin' to town and that we were gonna do some sessions with him. I didn't know what he did. I knew he had a song called "Suzanne." You don't know what to expect when you go to meet somebody for the first time who is a totally different kind of musician than anyone you've ever been exposed to. You don't know what kind of personality they have or what they're gonna be like. But it was a very pleasant surprise that Leonard Cohen was as down to earth and nice as he could be. He spoke a different way than everybody else around there did. But he had a great sense of communicating with people.

There was skepticism about Bob coming to Nashville because he was taking the place of a legendary producer, Don Law, who was an institution. Here's this guy Johnston from New York,

Kim Fowley, a mover in the 1960s LA scene, speaking at a 1967 love-in.

"I will never forget that when Leonard came to Nashville he lived out in the country for a while. And there was a guy who lived out there, an old cowboy called Kid Marley. I mean, people who came from totally opposite ends of the spectrum. It was Leonard Cohen and Kid Marley. But they hit it off and got to be friends. Leonard was just that kind of guy."

— Charlie Daniels, 2013

who had been doing Simon and Garfunkel, Dylan, and now Leonard Cohen, who were not really thought of as being country. But the first thing Bob did was a number-one song with Marty Robbins. He had gained credibility. *(2013)*

Bob Johnston: Leonard and I walked into Columbia Studio A. It had a bench there. A little stool. He said, "I want to play my song." And I said, "We're going to get some hamburgers and beer." And he said, "I want to play my song." I said, "Go ahead and play it and turn the button on there." "No. I want you around." And I said, "I want to get some beer." So we walked over across the street to Crystal Burgers, he came, had a couple of hamburgers and beer and came back. "What do you want me to do now?" he asked. I said, "Why don't you get your guitar and tune it?" And he looked at me, so I had his guitar tuned, and he got on the stool. And I said, "Play anything you want to." OK. Roll tape. And Leonard played

the song "The Partisan." And he got through it and asked to hear it. "Yeah." Played it back to him. He looked at me and said, "God damn. Is that what I'm supposed to sound like?" And I said, "Forever." And there it was.

The only thing I told everybody was to keep playing. If you stop playing you might as well pick up your briefcase and go on out the door. Don't plan on comin' back. We did about ten studio sessions. I always ask the artist "What do you want to do?" You get better performances when you make the artist comfortable. Dylan, Cash, Cohen were just wonderful people and they should be treated as such.

What attracted me to Cohen and songs like "Bird On The Wire"? What attracts you to Leonardo da Vinci? Leonard was the best I'd ever heard. And Dylan was the best I'd ever heard. And [Paul] Simon was the best I'd ever heard. And Cash was the best I'd ever heard. And all those fuckin' people were the best I'd ever heard. *(2013)*

<u>Below:</u> Bob Johnston (left) and Charlie Daniels (right) trying to stay out of Leonard's way.

<u>Bottom:</u> Bob Johnston (left) and Ron Cornelius (right) on stage with Leonard, Royal Albert Hall, London, March 23, 1972.

<u>Opposite:</u> Charlie Daniels, 1980s.

"Now Leonard Cohen tuned his gut-string guitar down a full step and how he played it I could never figure out … That was the thing about his music, though. It was so fragile. It was so 'Stay out of the way.'"
   – <u>Charlie Daniels</u>, 2013

Charlie Daniels: Most of the Nashville sessions, the country artists they would bring a demo in, they'd play the demo. You play it like the demo, you may change a key on it, but basically it's gonna be the same thing. So you're playin' pretty much inbounds. Cohen and Dylan were singers and songwriters. They write their songs, they weren't coming in from a music-publishing company. It was a lot different because there is no hurry.

Must have done ten songs, including "The Partisan." Five or six were on *Songs from a Room,* and another on his *Songs of Love and Hate. (2013)*

LC: I liked the work Johnston did with Dylan and we became good friends. Without his support I don't think I'd ever gain the courage to go and perform. He played harmonica, guitar, and organ on tours with me. He's a great friend and a great support. We worked hard on the albums we did together, but I wasn't totally happy. Overall, I couldn't find the tone I wanted. There were some nice things, though. *(1976)*

Kenneth Kubernik: Songs from a Room may be Leonard goin' country, the echoes of George Jones and Hank Williams crowding his inner ear, with the heartache of poor white folks transformed into jubilation. But there is no escaping the emotionally fraught cast of characters who fill Leonard's blighted universe, his bloodhound delivery sagging under the weight of the forever forlorn. The songs, unlike the timeless country formulation, offer no liberating exits for his subjects, or the listener. There are no lessons learned, no redemption for the philanderer, the wastrel or the woman of constant sorrow. Leonard

remained a steadfast *haut bourgeois;* his themes of political and personal betrayal, Old Testament judgment, and the pitilessness with which we treat each other are tropes that reflect his deeply cosmopolitan world-view. Leonard's songs are daunting, and to the suggestive mind their appeal is mesmeric. *(2013)*

To many others, the charms of Leonard's songs remained a complete mystery. Released in April 1969, *Songs from a Room* did not break the top fifty of the *Billboard* album chart but rose to number two in the UK. American reviewers were parsimonious in their praise, reluctant to dismiss the album out of hand – is there a pearl at the heart of this incessant irritation? – while British and other European critics worshipped at the altar of all this *Sturm und Drang.* This reaction from *Record Mirror Review* to the opening track, "Bird On The Wire," was typical:

"The usual superb arrangement backs his mournful pained voice. It's very beautiful and I must admit I cried when I heard it."

Above: The back cover of Songs from a Room features a photo of Marianne in Leonard's house in Hydra.

Opposite: Leonard's brief dalliance with Scientology in 1968 and 1969 led to a much more significant relationship with Suzanne Elrod, who quickly became his muse.

Dressing up as Roy Rogers in the backwoods of Tennessee had its charms, but Leonard's nagging restlessness soon had him on a plane to Los Angeles. In early 1969, he served as best man at the wedding of an old friend, Steve Sanfield. The ceremony was conducted at the city's Zen Center, presided over by a Zen master of the Rinzai school, a Buddha-like presence named Joshu Sasaki Roshi. Leonard's brief encounter with this impressively jovial and deeply spiritual man touched a nerve. In time, Zen Buddhism would become the prism through which he found if not enlightenment, certainly a world of abiding quiet.

The journey to this peaceable kingdom, though, was years in the offing. For now, the Dark Knight of the Soul continued his Sherman-esque march through convention, declining, for example, Canada's prestigious Governor General's Award for literature, much to the dismay of his fellow writers.

Upon his return to New York, Leonard pursued a short-lived acquaintance with Scientology. His greatest takeaway was a propitious hook-up with a fellow explorer, the bewitching Suzanne Elrod. She quickly became his muse, his talis-woman, and the mother of his children. She joined him in sun-swept Hydra, in his ramshackle cabin in Tennessee, and most revealingly, in Montreal, to meet his mother, Masha.

Columbia Records, meanwhile, was itching to get a return on its investment – which meant touring, a fact of pop-star life that rankled with even this most inveterate of travelers. Leonard turned to Bob Johnston to arrange a band, manage the tour, and provide a comfort zone from which he could keep the terrors of stage fright at bay.

Bob Johnston: I put his 1970 band together for him and told him I'd get him the best musicians in the world. And he said, 'Bob. I don't want the best musicians in the world. I want friends of yours.' I said, 'Good enough.'" *(2013)*

The band included the players who had accompanied Leonard on the album – Ron Cornelius, Charlie Daniels, Bubba Fowler, and Bob Johnston himself – plus background singers Susan Musmanno, Corlynn Hanney, and Donna Washburn. Michelle Phillips, formerly of the Mamas and the Papas, guested at a couple of Californian dates.

In May Leonard headed to Europe with a desire to provoke. He taunted the Hamburg audience with the Nazi salute; in Amsterdam he invited everyone back to his hotel, which caused a minor riot. If it didn't reach the bacchanalian excess of the Rolling Stones, Leonard and company indulged mightily in the warm embrace of this gypsy parade. At Forest Hills in New York, Dylan barely made it past security for a terse/tense audience with Leonard who played him to a standoff in the "meet your enigmatic doppelgänger" charade.

Bob Johnston: On that tour there was a guy in Germany who was gonna shoot Leonard. And we went over the time limit and I told the guy, "If you do that what's gonna happen? You're gonna end up in jail and everything." And they said, "Call the police!" "No. Don't call the police. Bring him up here." And I brought him up on stage and put him in a chair by the curtain. And he got to watch Leonard's concert. That's a true story.

Not only that, but Leonard said, "I'd like to play a crazy house." He wanted to play shows at a mental institution. "I'd like to look at one." OK. We played the first one near south London and they can't even talk down there. OK. Let's go do it right. The whole goddamn thing was crazy. And we did that. Mental hospitals and festivals. We had been booked in a circus but the police closed it. *(2013)*

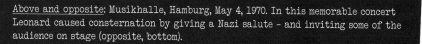

Above and opposite: Musikhalle, Hamburg, May 4, 1970. In this memorable concert Leonard caused consternation by giving a Nazi salute – and inviting some of the audience on stage (opposite, bottom).

Right: "And there was a festival in the south of France. ... We couldn't get through because the traffic was lined up to Paris. So I said, 'Get some horses.' So we took them and rode the back way." Bob Johnston recalling the Army ... at a festival in Aix-en-Provence, August 2, 1970.

PROGRESSIVE
MUSIC
FESTIVAL D'AIX EN PROVENCE

Leonard COHEN · Johnny WINTER
THE FLOCK

ALEPH
ARTHUR CONLEY
CHICO MAGNETIC BAND
COLOSSEUM
DEEP PURPLE
DINASTY CRISIS
FAMILY
IRRESISTIBLES

JULIAN'S TREATMENT
LABYRINTHE
MAGMA
MAJORITY ONE
MUNGO JERRY
PACIFIC DRIFT

PETE BROWN and the
PIBLOKTO
RAHDA KRISHNA TEMPLE
RARE BIRD
RENAISSANCE
TITANIC
TRIANGLE
WALLACE COLLECTION

Présentés par
Michel LANCELOT & Jacques BAL

1-2-3 AOUT 1970
Soirée d'animation le 31 juillet - Prix d'entrée pour les 4 jours : 55,00 F

Château de Saint-Pons, AIX-EN-PROVENCE

Billets en vente : Drugstore Champs-Elysées - Lido Musique - FNAC - Specta-Club-Olympia - Journal POP MUSIC et tous
les grands disquaires de province ● Voyage organisé par la S.N.C.F. ● Renseignements bureaux S.N.C.F. Tourisme.

"I don't think the sixties ever began. I think the whole sixties lasted maybe fifteen or twenty minutes in somebody's mind. I saw it move very, very quickly into the marketplace. I don't think there were any sixties."

– LC, 1992

On August 31, the road ended on a small island off the southern coast of England. The Isle of Wight had hosted its first pop-music festival the previous year, the highlight of which was Dylan's first full concert in three years. The promoters doubled down for their sophomore effort, scheduling such diverse and influential artists as Miles Davis, Joni Mitchell, Jimi Hendrix, the Who, and the Doors. The crowd, alas, had its own agenda, metastasizing into a heaving, barreling beast, crushing the gates and fences, rubbishing the tranquil rural community.

When Leonard finally took to the stage, it was two o'clock in the morning. The audience, restless after Hendrix's incendiary performance, was instantly tamed by this unkempt, unprepossessing gentleman, dressed in pajama bottoms (he'd been having a nap backstage and barely answered the bell to perform). As poised as Caesar before his legions, Leonard took command of his "Army" – his group's nickname – and held the half million attendees in thrall.

Bob Johnston: Leonard had to find me a keyboard for the Isle of Wight. Jimi Hendrix was on stage. And Kris Kristofferson, and the audience was throwing beer bottles at both of them, 'cause Jimi wouldn't quit playing "The Star-Spangled Banner." Leonard walked in and it was barely misty rain, just a little bit, and everybody got silent. And Leonard said, "Everywhere I go I like to see people and I can't see you tonight. Can anybody who has a match or a lighter light it up for me so I can see?" Six hundred thousand matches came alive. *(2013)*

Charlie Daniels: The Isle of Wight was a mess. Everyone was so high no one knew what the hell was going on anyway. The stage was only four feet high and the people could climb up on it. It was just nuts. We didn't have any really big trouble but the potential was there. They could not control the crowd. They had gone in and torn down the fences.

It was a period before they knew how to handle crowds that size. *(2013)*

Documentary maker Murray Lerner got it all on film. The resulting DVD, *Live at the Isle of Wight 1970*, finally released in 2009, demonstrated Leonard's gift for conjuring magic out of mayhem. The oft-derided listless baritone, the unorthodox rhythms, and the deathly pallor of the lyrics conspired to produce an all-encompassing calm. Whatever his musical idiosyncrasies, Leonard proved a formidable charismatic.

Murray Lerner: I felt hypnotized. I felt his poetry was that way. I was really into poetry and that is what excited me about him. To put music to poetry was like hypnosis to me. People were hypnotized during "The Stranger Song" performance. You can see that in the DVD. It's a beautifully written poem.

There were also moments, banter, like when he told the audience before a number how his father would take him to the circus as a child. He didn't like circuses, but he liked when a man would stand up and ask everyone to light a match so they could see each other in the darkness.

But when he sang the lyrics of the songs they took over and he had the audience in the palm of his hand. Even removing myself from being the director, how this guy could walk out and do this in front of 600,000 people? It was remarkable. It was mesmerizing. And the banter was very much in tune with the spirit of the festival. And the problems of the festival. And, more particularly, what he said, you know. "We're still a weak nation and we need land. It will be our land one day …" It was almost biblical. When he did "Suzanne" he said, "Maybe this is good music to make love to." He's very smart. He's very shrewd.

The other thing he was able to do, the talking. I think the audience was able to listen to him. They heard him and felt he was echoing something they felt. … That night, Leonard was on some sort of mission. *(2013)*

<u>Left and overleaf</u>: Leonard's 1970 festival season culminated with his hypnotic performance at the Isle of Wight Festival, captured on film by documentary maker Murray Lerner.

"Leonard was so natural on stage. Even at the Isle of Wight. If you wanted to get into Leonard you had to chill out. Jimi Hendrix was on just before us with all sorts of rock bands and then Joan Baez and Leonard Cohen. Everyone toned down the energy, sat there, and listened to Leonard Cohen sing his songs and his band play. It was a really nice evening and experience but it had the potential at any time of just blowing completely out of whack."

– Charlie Daniels, 2013

ISLE OF WIGHT FESTIVAL
AUGUST 26-30 1970

CHICAGO
FAMILY
TASTE
PROCOL HARUM
JAMES TAYLOR
ARRIVAL
MELANIE
VOICES OF
EAST HARLEM
LIGHTHOUSE

THE DOORS
THE WHO
TEN YEARS AFTER
JONI MITCHELL
SLY &
THE FAMILY STONE
CAT MOTHER
FREE
JOHN SEBASTIAN
EMERSON,
LAKE & PALMER
MUNGO JERRY
SPIRIT

JIMI HENDRIX
EXPERIENCE
JOAN BAEZ
DONOVAN
NATERNIGAL
LEONARD COHEN
STEELEYE
RICHIE HAVENS
MOODY BLUES
PENTANGLE
GOOD NEWS
RALPH McTELL

SPECIAL GUESTS
JETHRO TULL

WEEKEND £3

5. LOVE AND HATE, NEW FOR OLD, AND UNFINISHED BUSINESS

"With each record I became progressively discouraged, although I was improving as a performer."

– LC, 1976

TIMELINE

1970
September:
Travels back to Nashville to record Songs of Love and Hate

1971
January:
Release of Dynamite Chicken, a feature-length collection of countercultural sketches and clips in which Leonard reads "What Am I Doing Here" from Flowers for Hitler

March:
Awarded honorary doctorate by Dalhousie University, Halifax, Nova Scotia

March 19:
Release of Songs of Love and Hate

May-August:
Release of three movies all featuring Leonard Cohen music on their soundtrack - the German films Fata Morgana by Werner Herzog and Beware of a Holy Whore by Rainer Werner Fassbinder, and Robert Altman's McCabe and Mrs. Miller

With his back catalogue earning its keep, Leonard turns his attention back to writing - drafting a novel about his family (working title "The Woman Being Born") that would remain unpublished

September:
Travels to Switzerland to attend lectures by Immanuel Velikovsky, a Russian psychoanalyst and catastrophist

1972
January:
Publication of his fifth poetry collection, The Energy of Slaves, but it is less well received than his previous volumes

March-April:
Under pressure from Columbia, embarks on a second tour of Europe, playing in Israel for the first time; among the new recruits is backing singer Jennifer Warnes

April 19 and 21:
Sparks a near riot on stage in Tel Aviv, and breaks off the Jerusalem show two days later because he doesn't think his performance is up to standard (he is persuaded to finish the concert once he's had a calming shave)

September 18:
Birth of Suzanne and Leonard's son, Adam

Fall:
Finding it hard to adjust to parenthood, heads for the Chelsea Hotel

Winter:
Visits Joshu Sasaki Roshi at the Zen Center in Los Angeles, then spends a week at Roshi's retreat on nearby Mount Baldy, after which he returns to Montreal and his family commitments

CBC broadcasts a one-act ballet-drama based on his poem "The New Step"

1973
April 1:
Release of Live Songs, containing recordings from the 1970 and 1972 tours

Spring:
Demands the re-editing of Bird on a Wire, a behind-the-scenes feature documentary filmed by Tony Palmer during the 1972 tour

Summer:
Harboring the intention of quitting the music business, spends time with Suzanne and Adam on Hydra,

War, October 1973. Portrait by Uri Dan.

Pages 84–5: Royal Albert Hall, London, May 25, 1976.

painting and working on another draft of "The Woman
Being Born" (by now called "My Life in Art")

July 4:
Gene Lesser's Sisters of Mercy: A Musical Journey into
the Words of Leonard Cohen opens off Broadway

October:
Upon the outbreak of the Yom Kippur War, travels
from Hydra to Israel to try to enlist for the Israeli
army, but is instead recruited into the entertainment
corps, performing for small groups of soldiers up to
eight times a day

November:
Visits Ethiopia, where he works hard on new songs and
refines existing ones such as "Take This Longing" and
"Chelsea Hotel" (which becomes "Chelsea Hotel #2")

Winter:
Next to Mount Baldy, and then rejoins Suzanne
and Adam in Montreal

1974
July:
Records New Skin for the Old Ceremony with
new producer, John Lissauer

July 5:
Bird on a Wire is finally broadcast by the BBC

August 11:
Release of New Skin for the Old Ceremony

September:
Birth of Suzanne and Leonard's daughter, Lorca

Starts his biggest tour yet, which covers both Europe

December:
Tour includes a short residency at the Troubadour
in Los Angeles, during which he meets Phil Spector
for the first time

1975
March:
Goes to New York to work with John Lissauer on
songs for a new album with the working title
"Songs for Rebecca," then breaks off to spend the
summer in Hydra

Fall:
Spends time in Los Angeles with Roshi and resumes
work on "Songs for Rebecca" with Lissauer

Release of The Best of Leonard Cohen/Greatest Hits

November:
A short US tour curtails work on the new album

December:
Back home in Canada with Suzanne, Adam, and Lorca,
Leonard declines Bob Dylan's invitation to join his
Rolling Thunder Revue when it calls at Montreal

1976
April-July:
Another tour of Europe with another new lineup –
John Miller takes over from John Lissauer as musical
director, and future solo star Laura Branigan is one
of the backing singers

Summer:
Winds down on Hydra with his family and
Irving Layton

"'Famous Blue Raincoat.' That was one I thought was never finished. But I always thought that that was a song you could see the carpentry in a bit. Although there are some images in it that I am very pleased with. And the tune is real good. But I'm willing to defend it, saying it was impressionistic. It's stylistically coherent. And I can defend if I have to. But secretly I always felt that there was a certain incoherence that prevented it from being a great song."

– LC, 1992

Following the Isle of Wight, Leonard led his Army back to Nashville to record his third album, *Songs of Love and Hate*. Nothing like truth in advertising!

Charlie Daniels: I did learn from working with Johnston and Cohen that less is more. I came out of the nightclubs, thirteen years of beating my brains out playing every kind of music you could think of. You played the hits of Marty Robbins, Stonewall Jackson, and Little Richard. So I played a variety of music. Most of it was bang, slap, get it going, turn it up loud and let it rock. And to go play music with a guy like Leonard Cohen, whose music was so fragile, you just stayed out of his way. … And after I got used to the mindset it went really well. That was the approach. It was relaxed. *(2013)*

Bob Johnston: I grew up with classical music. I wanted the sound to be classical and I wanted it to be pop, too. I then went to England with Leonard and brought him to Paul Buckmaster. *(2013)*

Buckmaster had been on scholarship to the Royal Academy of Music in London, graduating in 1967. He then toured Germany as a cellist with the Bee Gees' backing orchestra. Prior to working with Cohen, Buckmaster had written the musical score and string parts for David Bowie's 1969 debut hit, "Space Oddity," and arranged Elton John's second and third albums, *Elton John* and *Tumbleweed Connection*, both released in 1970.

Paul Buckmaster: In 1970, I received a phone call from Bob Johnston that Leonard Cohen was coming to London to record, and would I like to write

arrangements? Bob was very affable and I immediately took a liking to him. He asked me to write arrangements for Leonard's album, then under production.

Of course I knew who Leonard was and had listened to his records. I was very attracted to his understated, somber, darkly romantic vocal style and accompaniments, and much liked the lack of histrionics.

Upon meeting Bob, he turned out to be an even nicer guy. Bob and Leonard came over to my place in Fulham [in southwest London]. One guy from Texas and one from Canada. I believe this was the first time working with Americans!

Leonard was a quiet guy – as I met him in 1970 – darkly handsome, with a frank, penetrating but not intimidating gaze. I felt the same kind of presence that one feels from his records; what you hear on his records is what he is in real life. We listened to and discussed the songs Bob and Leonard wanted me to write for. I got working, followed by the recording sessions. Bob gave me a quarter-inch stereo tape of the basic tracks – vocal and guitar – to which I listened while writing the arrangements directly from head to paper. I did not add any strings etc. on the tracks with rhythm section, only the vocal-guitar ones.

The tracks I arranged were "Avalanche," "Last Year's Man," "Dress Rehearsal Rag," "Love Calls You By Your Name," "Joan Of Arc," and "Famous Blue Raincoat."

My interventions as such are intermittent. I could have written more, developing the string

"It's four in the morning, the end of December."
The not-so-famous beige raincoat. Amsterdam, 1972.

orchestral compositions more extensively. Perhaps I was too "careful" to not "interfere" with the raw vocal/guitar. As I say, I can hear lots more that I could have written. Listening to Leonard's songs today, they are more powerful and deeply moving now than I perceived them at the time – and they had a powerful effect on me even then, a testimony to his skill and inspiration as an artist and song-craftsman. *(2013)*

Despite Columbia's best efforts, *Songs of Love and Hate* failed to break into the *Billboard* top 100 upon its release in March 1971. In the UK, however, it went to number four. The *New Musical Express* headline (approvingly) declared "Morbid Cohen," *Melody Maker* bannered "Leonard at his gloomiest," while another British periodical, *Sounds*, ended its review with the words "delicious masochism."

If record sales suggested a small, albeit devout following in the US, Leonard's stature among the movers and shakers in the liveliest arts was outsized. Filmmakers like Robert Altman and Germany's Rainer Werner Fassbinder and Werner Herzog integrated his music into the soundtracks of their movies, valuing the songs' capacity to help explore character.

LC: There's an interesting story regarding *McCabe and Mrs. Miller*. Director Robert Altman actually built the film around my music. The music was already written, and when he heard it he wanted to ask me to let him use it. I was in Nashville at the time and had just gone to the movies to see a film called *Brewster McCloud*.

I thought it was a fine movie. That night I was in the studio and received a call from Hollywood.

It was from Bob Altman saying he would like to use my music in a film. Quite honestly, I said, "I don't know your work, could you tell me some of the films you've done?" He said "*M*A*S*H*," and I said, "That's fine, I understand that's quite popular, but I'm really not familiar with it." Then he said there was a film I've probably never seen called *Brewster McCloud*. I told him I just came out of the movie and thought it was an extraordinary film. Use any music of mine. *(1976)*

Leonard gained valuable US midnight-movie exposure in January 1971 when he read "What Am I Doing Here" from his poetry collection *Flowers for Hitler* in the film *Dynamite Chicken*, a collage of peace-movement sketches, interviews, and narratives written, directed, and produced by Ernest Pintoff. It stars a young Richard Pryor with cameos by Allen Ginsberg, Jimi Hendrix,

Top: In 1971 Leonard's songs featured in three feature films, including Werner Herzog's Fata Morgana (above left) and Robert Altman's McCabe and Mrs. Miller (above center).

Opposite: Portrait of Nick Cave by Stephanie Chernikowski, 1980. Cave covered "Avalanche" from Songs of Love and Hate on his 1984 album From Her to Eternity.

"I grew up in a small country town in Australia and access to new music was difficult at the best of times. I was maybe fourteen and I met a girl who had a few cool records. She played me Songs of Love and Hate and all that summer, in her darkened room, we listened to it. Songs of Love and Hate corrupted me, essentially. This was the dark stuff, and it stamped a footprint so deep into my young life I could never listen to music in the same way again.

The complexity of the lyrics - that I barely understood at the time but through which I intuited all sorts of forbidden meanings - the trance-like picking of the guitar, the brutal black-and-white cover, all were foreign to me, but just drew me in. It spoke to some part of me that music had yet to touch. Play that record now, today, and it still has that power. It seethes and spits with a kind of violence unlike any other record ever made."

– Nick Cave, 2014

Joan Baez, B. B. King, and Andy Warhol, and also includes archive footage of Malcolm X; it was part-financed by John Lennon and Yoko Ono.

Leonard's fifth poetry collection, *The Energy of Slaves*, was published a year later. Unlike his earlier volumes, it received a critical drubbing. His harsh, minimalist verse pushed readers to the limit of their appetite for brutalism.

With his personal life in a state of exalted disarray – Suzanne would give birth to their first child, Adam, in September 1972 – Leonard took to the road once again, finding succor among the wandering tribes of musicians and enthusiasts along the European festival circuit.

The 1972 band, besides Leonard on acoustic guitar, organ player Bob Johnston, acoustic and electric guitarist Ron Cornelius, bassist Peter Marshall, and acoustic guitarist David O'Connor, enlisted backing singers Donna Washburn and, for the first time, Jennifer Warnes.

Bob Johnston: I must have auditioned fifty or sixty people in 1972 and Jennifer came in. "We got one more from California." She came in with her red hair lookin' ragged, no makeup on. Sang her ass off. "You're hired." That was it. *(2013)*

Jennifer Warnes: I was already singing Leonard Cohen's material when I first met him in a hotel lobby in Hartford, Connecticut when I was on tour. Years later, I was taping a television show in Nashville when I got a call if I wanted to go on tour with Leonard Cohen in Europe as a background singer. I had never sung backgrounds before – I was too much of a solo singer to be good at it. I said, "Yes, absolutely." *(1987)*

Under the shrewd direction of Marty Machat, Leonard's manager since 1970, this tour would be documented by the renowned London-based writer and filmmaker Tony Palmer, who specialized in capturing the peculiarities of the musician's life in works as diverse as a BBC documentary on composer Benjamin Britten and the Frank Zappa collaboration *200 Motels*.

And there was a bounty of memorably peculiar concerts for Palmer to work with on this trek, culminating in some wild goings-on in Israel. Leonard, dosed with Owsley Stanley's "desert dust" LSD, danced along the razor's edge.

In Tel Aviv he urged the audience to come closer to the stage, sparking a violent clash with baton-happy security staff that he managed to calm only by offering "So Long, Marianne" as a soothing benediction.

The responsibilities and rewards of command and control, however, came at a great cost for someone preoccupied with preserving his solitary self. The darkness at Leonard's core – the "black dog" of depression or simple mental exhaustion – led to a spate of rumors about his retiring from music altogether. Disillusioned with "the industry," he told journalists that he was creatively played out; but that stance lasted only until he disavowed comments attributed to him as being a media misrepresentation. Playing fast and loose with one's public persona is a perquisite of stardom and Leonard, however high-minded his credentials, was no different.

His vacillation reached a peak during the postproduction of Palmer's documentary, called *Bird on a Wire*. He loved it, then hated it, spending a small fortune to re-edit it toward some unrealizable end, an exercise in vainglory that came to nothing. The BBC were eventually able to broadcast the film in July 1974, two years after the tour it documented.

Tony Palmer: My film about Leonard Cohen's 1972 European tour has a complicated history. Let me clear up one or two complete misconceptions – I might want to say misrepresentations. I was asked to make the film by Marty Machat. It was essentially his initiative, at least in part because he feared Leonard might never tour again thereafter. Mercifully, this did not turn out to be the case, but remember that at the time Cohen had frequently asserted: a) that he did not enjoy touring, saying it exhausted him for no good purpose; b) that he hated having to repeat the same old songs night after night, claiming he was rendering them meaningless by endless repetition; c) that he was a poor performer on stage, crippled by an indifferent voice; and d) that, as his first three albums had sold indifferently, he might not have an audience.

Memories and memorabilia from the 1972 European tour, the subject of Tony Palmer's 1974 documentary (top left) – including the tour book (left) and the April 4 show at the Falkoner Teatret, Copenhagen (all three concert photos).

"Now, looking back, my admiration for Leonard as a poet, a singer and as a man remains undiminished The original film was made with love, and I hope that quality once again shines through the restored film."

— Tony Palmer, 201

All of this Leonard explained to me the first time we met, in Machat's office in New York, in October 1971. He was resigned to a film being made about the tour, however, because he hoped this might just bring him to a wider audience. I say "resigned" because he was less than enthusiastic, especially when I said a condition of my becoming involved was that I would require total access to whatever I thought was necessary for a stimulating, and I hoped positive, film. Very reluctantly he agreed, and Machat said he would finance the film himself so that Leonard would not be burdened with the expense.

Leonard kept his word, and I was given complete access and encouraged to interpret the material collected in any way I thought desirable. I also said it would be pointless recording all of the songs for every single concert, so we agreed that although I would be there for all twenty concerts, I would only record the music on four or five occasions to be agreed. And as I felt very strongly that his poetry was a key to understanding the man, I also suggested that we film him reading some of the poems. With this he readily agreed. Indeed, so pleased was he with this idea that he even composed a poem especially for me, and wrote it out by hand and signed it in the frontispiece of my copy of *The Energy of Slaves*.

Maybe what is valuable about the film today is not only that it contains seventeen of his greatest songs performed by him in his prime (and it's nonsense of him to say he has no voice), but it has a real feel for the rough and tumble and difficulties of life on the road.

I know of few other films where the backstage confusion comes so vividly to life, with Leonard apparently taking no notice whatsoever of the camera. And don't forget, this film was shot in 1972, with slow celluloid color stock, requiring a lot of light to get any decent exposure at all. With today's digital technology, we would have been virtually invisible. But I doubt if today we would be allowed such access.

Alas, Leonard told me he thought the film was "too confrontational" and worried that he often appeared "exhausted, even wasted." While the latter is undoubtedly true, about the former I believed he was wrong. *(2013)*

Leonard danced along the razor's edge throughout the 1972 tour. This intriguing 1972 photograph (by Arnaud Maggs) hints at the darkness at his core.

"I have occasionally thought about the differences in my audiences. I think that maybe my music fits into the European tradition. America has its own version of the blues. What I do is the European blues. That is, the soul music of that sensibility - white soul. Even though Europe has its own version of bubblegum."

– <u>LC</u>, 1975

<u>Above</u>: Portrait by Tom Hill, 1975.

<u>Opposite</u>: A reflective moment backstage at the Musikhalle, Hamburg, April 5, 1972.

When the Yom Kippur War broke out in October 1973, Leonard enlisted
in the Israeli Army Entertainment Corps. Portrait by Uri Dan.

"Leonard wrote songs because he had to, and because he wanted to get laid. Later he wrote songs because he wanted to get paid. That's when I decided he had something to say."
— Andrew Loog Oldham, 2013

In July 1973 *Sisters of Mercy*, a theatrical interpretation of some of Leonard's lyrics and poems, debuted at the Shaw Festival in Niagara, before heading south to New York for an off-Broadway run. It couldn't escape the long knives of Gotham's critical community. Clive Barnes of the *New York Times* wrote, "while Cohen may very well be God's final gift to women, he doesn't shape up so well as either a poet or musician."

If his detractors viewed him as nothing more than an energetic windmill-tilter, Leonard's next quixotic adventure was certain to earn their haughtiest disdain. In October, at the height of the Yom Kippur War, he decided to enlist in the Israeli Army, opening the door to a host of wildly speculative theories as to the motives behind this reckless behavior. He was talked out of this particular tree by some more sober-minded associates, assisting in the war effort instead by becoming an alt–Bob Hope, entertaining troops and sampling the sweet wine offered by many of the young female enlistees. A faux warrior never had it so good.

Also in 1973 came *Live Songs*, a compilation of tracks drawn from tour dates in 1970 and 1972, capturing some of the hypnotic power Leonard and his group exerted over his reverential flock.

LC: The album *Live Songs* represented a very confused and directionless time. The thing I like about it is that it documents this phase very clearly. I'm very interested in documentation and often feel that I want to produce a whole body of work that will cover a wide range of topics and themes. Not necessarily personal reflections, but a sort of look at the last two decades. My first book was published at twenty, and that was twenty years ago. *(1975)*

Upon renewing his contract with Columbia, Leonard began recording material for a new album. *New Skin for the Old Ceremony* was finally released in August 1974, nearly three and a half years after his previous studio album.

LC: For a while, I didn't think there was going to be another album. I pretty well felt that I was washed up as a songwriter because it wasn't coming anymore. Actually, I should have known better. It takes me a long time to compose a song.

I heard John Lissauer playing in a club in Montreal with Lewis [Furey]. John and I started talking and I played him a bunch of songs, almost half-finished. Lissauer has the deepest understanding of my music. I had finished most of the songs that previous summer, got the group together and toured the United States for the last year.

Now I've entered into another phase, which is very new for me. That is, I began to collaborate with John on songs, which is something that I never expected, or intended, to do with anyone. It wasn't a matter of improvement, it was a matter of sharing

"Roshi used to come to the sessions. He was the coolest. He would just sit there and smile. When we were doing the album Leonard introduced all of us to something called ng-ka-py, a Korean liqueur that was only sold in a store in Chinatown. Roshi introduced it to him and it was kick-ass. And I got a bottle every once in a while to bring to the studio. And you can hear it, for instance, on 'Leaving Green Sleeves.' Where Leonard was pretty far gone when we were doing that vocal. Usually we waited to the end of the night to have these little tiny things."
– John Lissauer, 2013

the conception, with another man. I work very slowly and abandoned hope for many of them. However, last summer I went to Ethiopia looking for a suntan. It rained, including in the Sinai desert, but through this whole period I had my little guitar with me, and it was then I felt the songs emerging at least, the conclusions that I had been carrying in manuscript form for the last four or five years, from hotel room to hotel room. *(1975)*

Leonard recruited Lissauer, a young, talented multi-instrumentalist, as his producer. A student of classical and jazz music with an Ivy League pedigree, Lissauer seemed unlikely producer material, especially in the eyes of Marty Machat. Machat turned to John Hammond for his input; together, they monitored Lissauer at work in the studio and decided that he could indeed do the job.

John Lissauer: I was starting to work in Montreal for a producer/engineer and studio owner, André Perry. I get a call from a guy out of the blue, Lewis Furey. "I'm a friend of Frazier Mohawk." Who I had worked with. "OK." "You're gonna work with me." Lewis was a violin player and he and I connected. We did his record and some performances at the Nelson Hotel. Lewis was really happening in the Montreal scene.

And Leonard comes up to me after the show at the Nelson Hotel, after the first set, and introduces himself. Leonard is famous and this is his hometown. Fortunately, I already knew who he was. He just said, "I really like your work. Lewis has told me about you." Lewis had been taken under Leonard's wing as a poet. And the new music Lewis and I did had an edge to it. Leonard says, "I'm gonna be in New York in a week or two. Will you be back in New York then?" "Yes. I'm returning after this." "Let's get together there." "OK." I give him my number. And he calls. I had a third-floor loft walk-up, two-thousand square foot, previously owned Mafia bar, an after-hours club.

He came up, we sat around, and we hit it off. Leonard made it clear right from the beginning that we should work together. And he played me three songs on guitar. Two of the songs were very rhythmical: "Lover Lover Lover" and "There Is A War." He had spent some time in Africa. They were strumming songs. It wasn't the finger-style European continental French poet thing. This was gonna be something different. He also played me "Chelsea Hotel." And I responded, "Man, do I have an idea for this."

So Leonard calls up Marty Machat, his lawyer. And then Leonard says, "Well, I'm gonna introduce you to John Hammond." So the three of us, Leonard, myself, and Hammond meet at the Algonquin Hotel

in New York City. I'm looking for Lillian Hellman.
We have a lovely dinner. I know every artist
Hammond signed to Columbia Records.

Then we did the three-song demo. I used a
Columbia engineer wearing a lab coat. It was
clear what I'm doing with Leonard is totally
different and it's going to give him a broader
audience. There's gonna be rhythm on his records.
Hammond was at the sessions, even though I was
gonna be the producer and he was the executive
there. "This is the best. We're doing this," and he
signed off on it immediately. And Marty, of course,
was on board.

The musicians are my buddies. We had come
up together and done a lot of creative projects.
Lewis Furey on viola, Ralph Gibson, guitar. Erin
Dickins, backup vocal, who became my first wife
in 1977, Jeff Layton, a friend of mine, who was one
of the virtuoso guitar players. The drummer was
Roy Markowitz. Bassists were Don Payne and John
Miller, who had played with everyone, including
Mose Allison and Phil Ochs. So John seemed like
a good fit. *(2013)*

John Miller: I made my living as a studio musician.
It was the first time I had ever really experienced
someone who was so committed to leaving so
much air and space in his music. It was my first
hands-on experience with the musical idea of
less is more. The music lent itself to playing as
few notes as possible and letting the air and the
space of the music happen. I think the bass and
all the instruments in the mix, the orchestrations,
were Lissauer's concept where every instrument
is like folk chamber music. *(2013)*

John Lissauer: We started at the Columbia studios.
I said, "I want to record at Sound Ideas." I had
worked there before. It was quiet, out of the way,
a block and a half from the Royalton Hotel where
Leonard was staying. And there was a cool vibe.
The gear was the best. One thing that we did use
at Columbia and Sound Ideas were Neumann 49
and 67 German broadcasting microphones from
World War II. With the depth of Leonard's voice,
we knew it was the way to go.

Leanne Ungar was the assistant engineer and
attached to the studio. She was like age eighteen.
Or younger. She had worked on Lewis Furey's
record. She became my engineer. I think I gave

her a first lead engineer credit. She has gone
on to engineer studio albums with Leonard for
decades. *(2013)*

Kenneth Kubernik: Choosing the more intimate
Sound Ideas, Lissauer swept away all the distractions,
the girlfriends, the hangers-on, the label reps and
forced Leonard to focus. The result was an album
of greater musical depth and atmosphere than
anything he'd previously recorded. Lissauer's
smart orchestrations – well served by members
of the New York Philharmonic – and the enthusiastic
accompaniment of bass, drums, and guitar gave
Leonard the confidence to finally sing out on his
own songs, to own his voice.

Lyrically, Leonard continued to explore the
brutal dynamics between men and women,
his sniper's eye targeted on naked backsides
just out of reach, desire thwarted by sentinels
lurking in the shadows. In songs like "A Singer
Must Die," "There Is A War," and the pseudonymous
"Field Commander Cohen," the carnal merges
with the political to suggest war is both an intimate
and large-scale act. Combined with the furtive
adornments of strings and brass, *New Skin for
the Old Ceremony* shines as a complete statement
and not simply a collection of itinerant songs as
in previous releases. Even the cover, a libidinous
Renaissance-era woodcut, illustrates the idea that
love and politics are simply more polite terms for
domination and submission. *(2014)*

John Lissauer: To tell you the truth, in retrospect,
I'm amazed. He just let me go. I never said, "Let me
try this." He'd just say, "What do you want to do?"
"Well, I got this idea. Let me do this. Let me try
this." Things were really working. This was very
adventurous. Leonard went with it. He lit up when
I started doing some string arrangements and
some different stark things. And the way I treated
"Chelsea Hotel," just with the different colors.
I played some funky little clarinet in some places.
And it got more illustrative. And the songs came
to life. Leonard would know if he had a line that
was commanding your attention. *(2013)*

The release of *New Skin for the Old Ceremony*
coincided with the birth of Leonard's daughter,
Lorca, named in honor of the Spanish poet
Federico García Lorca. As if to acknowledge

his good fortune, the critics reached a rare favorable consensus, noting that the sophistication of Lissauer's production allowed the shadowy songwriter a glimmer of light.

LC: I must say I'm pleased with the album. It's good. I'm not ashamed of it and am ready to stand by it. Rather than think of it as a masterpiece, I prefer to look at it as a little gem. The original cover was a sixteenth-century picture from an alchemical text depicting two angels in an embrace. Columbia felt unclothed angels were too much for the American public. A quarter of a million copies have been sold in Europe with this cover and there was not a single reference made to it. Since I designed it, I finally won the battle with Columbia, and they are reinstating the old album cover with a modesty jacket. With the exception of these minor problems, I've been very happy with the album. *(1975)*

John Lissauer: I put together a band for Leonard and we toured. It was the band from the album plus another background singer who I didn't know that Leonard recommended: Emily Bindiger.

Leonard became a mentor to me. He talked to me about philosophy. He told me all about reflexology, which I got tremendously interested in and practice to this day. He talked to me about everything because we had a lot of time on the bus. We traveled all over Europe and England a couple of times. Leonard introduced me to Japanese food. We were comrades.

On stage Leonard's songs became bigger. The audience is very devoted. The chicks bring the guys. But there were certainly more chicks and more single chicks. We'd have fifteen chicks in the dressing room. They just want to be around the scene. So I was always standing next to Leonard as music director. I had hair down to my ass and I was single. This was heaven for me. *(2013)*

Scenes from the 1974 European tour. Musical director John Lissauer manning the keyboards (opposite); Congress Centrum, Hamburg, September 26 (this page, top); and, left to right, John Lissauer, Jeff Layton, Leonard, John Miller, Emily Bindiger, and Erin Dickins during the UK leg (this page, bottom).

<u>Opposite</u>: Portrait by Laurens van Houten, 1974.

<u>Overleaf</u>: On stage with background singers Erin Dickins and Emily Bindiger and bassist John Miller. De Doelen, Rotterdam, October 1, 1974.

With four albums' worth of product to exploit, Leonard's label decided that now was the time to issue a compilation. *The Best of Leonard Cohen* came out in the fall of 1975. In an interview I conducted with Leonard for *Melody Maker*, he admitted, "I was against the idea at first. But I don't quite remember why I was convinced of it. There's a new generation of listeners who don't know a lot of the work. I picked the songs and had total artistic control. I designed the package and I insisted the lyrics be included, and there are notes on the songs."

John Lissauer: Leonard and I were on this high. Our 1974 tour was so successful and not crazed like the 1970 or '72 bands on his last tour. This was serious music for a popular audience. Leonard was the greatest poet I had ever come across and his stuff was deep. I was reading his books. So we really saw eye to eye. And then he said, "You know what we should do? We should do an album together. Write it together." And I replied, "Wow. That sounds great." Because I'm a melody guy. And Leonard never considered his melodies. *(2013)*

Los Angeles would prove to be an invaluable setting for the next stage in Leonard's endless odyssey. Roshi was based there, the recording industry was centered there with its inexhaustible supply of musical and technical talent. He'd spent most of the year on the road, snatching an open week in New York or Los Angeles to lay down tracks for his album with Lissauer, tentatively titled "Songs for Rebecca." Holed up on the Sunset Strip's jazz-aged Chateau Marmont, Leonard and Lissauer were seemingly on a creative roll; months on tour had solidified their partnership.

John Lissauer: We go to LA and stay at the Chateau Marmont for about two weeks and write a bunch of songs. And they're really good. I have an electric piano. He's writing the lyrics and gave me some poems that were lyrics. And I said, "Let me come back with some ideas. The melody and the chords." If I wrote something too melodic that he wasn't comfortable singing and it sounded like I was trying to turn him into Kenny Rogers or something, if it just wasn't working, I would know I had blown it.

Then we go on tour and we've got these songs and we'd rehearsed them and they were really good on the road. So we come back and everything is sounding pretty good. And then Leonard said, "I'm gonna go to Hydra for a month. And when I come back we'll jump in the studio and go crazy." I never hear back from him. *(2013)*

This sudden, unexplained ending left Lissauer confused. Leonard vanished into the ether. Lissauer, whose supple aesthetic elevated Leonard's work, was thrown under the proverbial bus, the "Songs for Rebecca" master session tapes going under the wheels with him.

"Leonard gave me a complete open slate. He was very judicious about who he was going to give that position to. When I suggested we go with drums, I think it was the first time he'd used drums and it wasn't anything like, 'I want you to audition drummers for me.' It was 'Whoever you think is the right guy for my music.'"
— John Miller, 2013

John Lissauer: And it turns out that Marty Machat, who also managed Phil Spector, had made a huge deal with Warner Bros. for Spector, something like a US$2 million advance, in which he got ten or fifteen percent, and Spector hadn't done an album. So Warner calls up Marty and says, "We get something from Phil Spector or you give all the money back." So he says to Leonard, "Forget the John thing. Let's, you know, do a deal with Phil."

So no one tells me this. I'm just waiting to hear from him. I'm busy. I've got other projects going. Leonard will call when he's ready. We have these songs. And everything was left on a love fest. We're happening. I call Marty and he's not really taking my calls. And Leonard doesn't call me and I don't have a private number for him. So I'm getting the feeling that, "Oh, they hate this. Something has happened. They just don't want to work with me." I just said, "It's not meant to be." Something must be going on. Maybe they really decided they didn't like me and the record. Or Leonard is doing something else. *(2013)*

Taking to the road was a productive escape for the reticent superstar. He'd come a long way from

his stammering debut at the Village Theatre; like Jim Morrison, whose earliest Doors gigs were performed with his back to the audience to cover his stage fright, Leonard had soldiered on to become a charismatic front man. Machat booked fifty-five dates from April to July 1976, crisscrossing Europe with stays in England. The road had its own peculiar appeal, a hermetically sealed world where Newton's laws were routinely violated by an excess of wine, women, and song.

John Miller, Leonard's bassist, took over from Lissauer as musical director. His recollection of the tour was of sold-out shows, consorting till dawn, Leonard's unstinting generosity to his bandmates and fans, and the blessed experience of sharing a stage with a steely-eyed alchemist masquerading as a forlorn wandering Jew.

John Miller: Leonard asked me, on my second or third tour, if I would become the music director. From the experience he had with Lissauer to the little that I know of Roscoe Beck [Leonard's future music director], clearly Leonard doesn't make these decisions without a great deal of thought and confidence about who he feels has a sort of

"A Zen monastery is a place with a great deal of movement. True, few words are spoken, but there is much activity. There is a Zen saying: "Like pebbles in a pouch, the monks polish one another." One is closely together with others when there. The life is less solitary than in the city, because you sleep, you work, you meditate with other people."

– LC, 2001

Right: A typically unconventional viewpoint backstage at De Doelen, Rotterdam, October 1, 1974. Leonard also stood on his head during the UK leg of the tour – by the side of a busy road, to attract attention when the tour bus broke down.

Opposite: John Miller took over as musical director for the fifty-five-date 1976 European tour.

inner understanding of his music. Because, certainly in my case, there was very little that I remember suggesting that we do that I had to run by Leonard.

No matter how many players there were with Leonard, it always seemed extremely open and nothing ever felt gratuitous. The challenge was to find the essence of Leonard's music and then add whatever Lissauer's touch was or my touch. It's not night and day because it's still Leonard's thing and it's so strong, it's just a slightly different hue of the same color. (2013)

Following the tour, Leonard retreated to Hydra, to Suzanne, Adam, and Lorca. It was a safe harbor, a time for rejuvenation and reflection. They were soon joined by his old friend Irving Layton and his

wife, Aviva. Never one to pull his punches, Layton was unforgiving of Leonard's latest poetic output; his critique, though, was always tempered by an unabashed enthusiasm that stilled the younger writer's crippling doubts.

Los Angeles was the last port of call in this peripatetic year. Leonard was keen on spending time at the Zen Center and its retreat high atop Mount Baldy in the nearby San Gabriel Mountains. Roshi's stalwart presence was a palpable reminder of roads to be traveled, values to be imbibed, and choices to be acted upon. Touring was an adult's playpen; in the company of Roshi, it was time to buckle down, question deeply, and behave honorably. But first Leonard recorded an album with one of the least Zen-like people he had ever encountered.

109

6. THE ODD

COUPLE

"I can really belt 'em out, you know."

— <u>LC</u>, 1977

TIMELINE

1976
<u>Fall</u>:
Rents a house in Los Angeles to spend more time
with Roshi and to work on new material; "Songs for
Rebecca" is shelved and John Lissauer is replaced
by Phil Spector as songwriting partner and producer

1977
<u>January-February</u>:
Main recording sessions for <u>Death of a Ladies' Man</u>
in Los Angeles

<u>June</u>:
Final <u>Death of a Ladies' Man</u> session

<u>November 13</u>:
Release of <u>Death of a Ladies' Man</u>

<u>Fall</u>:
Breakdown of his relationship with Suzanne

1978
<u>February</u>:
Death of mother, Masha Cohen, aged sixty-nine;
Suzanne and the children come back to Montreal
to be with Leonard

<u>Spring</u>:
Suzanne leaves for good

<u>Fall</u>:
Publication of <u>Death of a Lady's Man</u> (not to be
confused with the album of almost identical name),
a collection of poems and prose poems written over
the previous decade

<u>Right</u>: Doug Weston's Troubadour in West Hollywood, where
Leonard first encountered Phil Spector in December 1974.
The venue is still going strong forty years later.

<u>Pages 110 and 111</u>: Just once in my life. During the recording
of <u>Death of a Ladies' Man</u>, Leonard and the legendary producer
did not always see eye to eye.

doug weston's
Troubadour

presents

INDIE
GIANT
DRAG
DIRTY
LITTLE
SECRET

Tavern

Troubadour

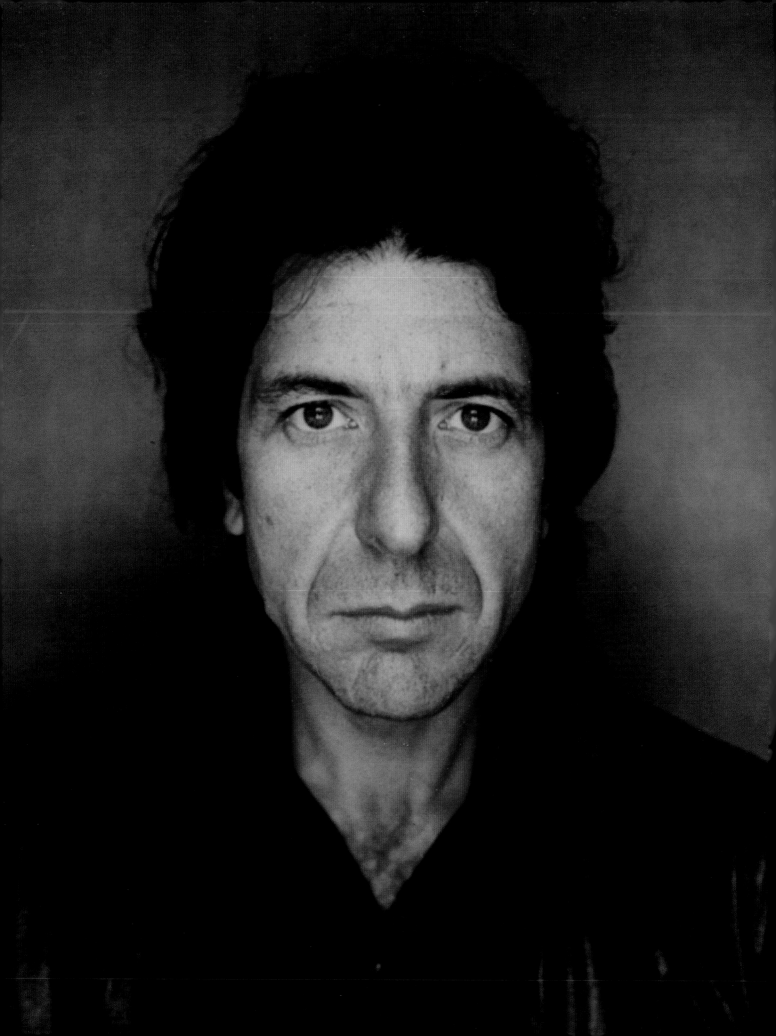

"I'm feeling more tender about the record now. It really was a Dr. Jekyll and Mr. Hyde situation. Phil turned into another person in the studio. That album keeps turning up in critics' lists. It has a certain power to it. But it's the only piece of work that I've ever put out in my whole life of twenty-five or thirty years working, that I didn't form the final product. But I'm glad I met Phil and he remains in my mind as one of the most extraordinary men I've ever met."

– LC, on Death of a Ladies' Man, 1985

The mid-to-late 1970s was a period of unlikely artist/producer combinations – Helen Reddy and Kim Fowley, Grand Funk Railroad and Frank Zappa. But perhaps the most unlikely: Phil Spector, demon genius of the rock 'n' roll production number, and Leonard Cohen, ascetic prophet of acoustic disaffectedness.

Leonard first met Spector in late 1974, when Leonard was in Los Angeles for a rare club appearance – a December 6–8 engagement at Doug Weston's Troubadour club in West Hollywood. After the last show on the third night, Spector hosted an informal reception for Leonard at his home, a Spanish-style mansion in Beverly Hills.

Leonard was brought to Spector's attention, and vice versa, by their mutual manager, Marty Machat – who took Spector to see Leonard perform. The pair got on well at the post-Troubadour gathering, and kept in loose touch thereafter. Later in 1976, when Leonard visited Los Angeles again, Spector invited him to be his houseguest.

The first night, the two worked out a new version of Patti Page's "I Went To Your Wedding"; by dawn they'd co-written two new songs, Leonard writing the lyrics, Spector picking out the music on a piano. The seed was sown for what was to become Death of a Ladies' Man.

Leonard had recently moved to Los Angeles. "I like it," he said to me in a 1977 interview. "It's so desperate here that it's really not bad at all. And besides, this is the only city in the world where I've ever written a song while sitting in a driveway in a parked car."

LC: Phil is not a great songwriter, but he's a bold one. He's bold enough to employ the most pedestrian melodies, and yet somehow make them absolutely successful. That is why his compositions are brilliant. (1977)

Leonard was especially impressed by Spector's early works – timeless classics like "To Know Him Is To Love Him" and "You've Lost That Lovin' Feelin'."

LC: In those songs, the storyline was as clear as clear could ever be. The images were very expressive – they spoke to us all. Spector's real greatness is his ability to induce those incredible little moments of poignant longing in us. (1977)

In early 1977, the Cohen and Spector songwriting team entered Gold Star recording studios in East Hollywood, a landmark facility owned by engineers Dave Gold and Stan Ross. Since opening for business in 1950, its client list had logged Eddie Cochran, Ritchie Valens, Herb Alpert and the Tijuana Brass, Bobby Darin, the Righteous Brothers, the Ronettes, Jack Nitzsche, Sonny and Cher, Buffalo Springfield, Brian Wilson and the Beach Boys, the Monkees, the Turtles, Hugh Masekela, and Iron Butterfly.

"Do not be afraid to be weak. Do not be ashamed to be tired. You look good when you're tired." "How to Speak Poetry" from Death of a Lady's Man (1978). Portrait by Arnaud Maggs, 1977.

"Working with Phil I've found that some of his musical treatments are very ... er ... foreign to me. I mean, I've rarely worked in a live room that contains twenty-five musicians – including two drummers, three bassists, and six guitarists."
– <u>LC</u>, 1977

<u>above and right</u>: Phil Spector firmly in control in the Gold Star Studios in Los Angeles, where he constructed his Wall of Sound in the 1960s and produced Leonard's <u>Death of a Ladies' Man</u> in 1977.

Stan Ross: Gold Star was built for the songwriters. They were fun, wonderful people to be around – Jimmy Van Heusen, Jimmy McHugh, Frank Loesser, Don Robertson, and Sonny Burke. The studio's echo chamber gave it the Wall of Sound feel. Dave [Gold] built the equipment and the echo chamber. Gold Star brought a feeling, an emotional feeling. Gold Star was not a dead studio, but a live studio. The room was thirty by forty feet. It was all tube microphones. We didn't use pop filters and wind screens for vocalists – we got mouth noises. Isn't that life? *(2001)*

When I interviewed Spector in 1977 for *Melody Maker*, he talked at length about his legendary production methods.

Phil Spector: When you see a Kubrick movie you tell me how many names you immediately remember in the cast. One, two? It's the same with Fellini, and that's what I wanted to do when I directed a recording. Singers are instruments. They are tools to be worked with.

There are no four-part harmonies on my records … Maybe thirty-two part harmonies … I like to have all the musicians there at once. I get everything on one track that I need. I put everything on twenty-four tracks just to see if it's plugged in.

My engineer [Larry Levine] was scared to death to work with me. When I record I put everything on tape echo, everything. My engineer said, "You're out of your mind." Do you know Ray Conniff uses more tape echo than I ever used in my life? That's a fact. I record basic tracks and then put it all on to one track or maybe two. Then I condense. I put my voices on. The finished track never ends up on more than one track. I don't wear a "Back to Mono" button for no reason at all. I believe in it.

I've used Barney Kessel all the time for the last ten years. Terry Gibbs on vibes … everybody. The better the talent is around you, the better the people you have working with you, the more concerned, the better you're gonna come off as a producer, like a teacher in a class. The musicians I have never outdo me. I'm not in competition with them. I'm in complete accord with them. You need the ability so you hire the best. I have the creativity. I know what I want. *(1977)*

Like drummers Hal Blaine and Jim Keltner, bassist Ray Pohlman, percussionist and vibes player Terry Gibbs, guitarists and vocalists Dan and David Kessel, keyboardist Don Randi was a fixture on *Death of a Ladies' Man*.

Don Randi: On the Cohen dates and every session with Phil, everybody played parts and time duplication. Like on the pianos, you would have one guy doing a thing on the high end of the piano, somebody in the middle, and Phil would want the different sounds of a concert grand, and an upright, electric or a Wurlitzer. So he liked to have the spread of the different tonality. That was Phil. He understood tonality very well. And at Gold Star it was magic because of all those harmonics rising that were part of the Wall of Sound.

You've got to remember that most of the guys that were in "Phil's band" especially were all jazz players and rock 'n' roll was a living for them. And a lot of them didn't like it as much as I did. I have to be very frank about it.

I always liked the rock 'n' roll part of it. I thought it was great fun and sometimes very musically interesting. Not all the time. Eighty per cent of the time. We got to do some things on rock 'n' roll dates we could not do in jazz and studio settings on the Ronettes, Ike and Tina Turner, the Crystals, Cher, Leonard Cohen, and later the Ramones. It's an interesting concept but those guys were very capable. They were the best musicians and still are the best musicians. There were always great songs. The songs always told a story. The songs in themselves were films. *(2008)*

Hal Blaine: We could lock in with anybody: Frank and Nancy Sinatra, the Beach Boys, Johnny Rivers, the Mamas and the Papas, the 5th Dimension, Simon and Garfunkel, and Leonard Cohen. But with Elvis on our 1968 recordings you're gonna sit up a little straighter, maybe. *(2008)*

Jim Keltner: I ended up on Leonard's *Death of a Ladies' Man* sessions by virtue of my association with Phil. He always gravitated toward the great songwriters and singers. I wasn't that familiar with Leonard at the time. But just the fact that Spector was producing was enough for me.

On the right tracks on tour in Germany, April 1976.

"One day he had a bottle of wine in one hand and a 35mm pistol in the other. He put his arm around my shoulder, pressed the muzzle into my neck and said, 'Leonard, I love you.' At which point I said, 'I hope you really do, Phil.'"

— LC, 2001

"We were preparing for the recording coming up after the break. I took out a cigarette and asked Leonard for a light, which he gave me. I felt compelled to compliment him and said, 'I've just got to tell you, man, you're great, your lyrics are just phenomenal, the poetry, I'm blown away.' He took a drag on a Gauloise cigarette, looked me in the eye, and with an ironic smile said, 'It's a living.'"

— Dan Kessel, 2013

Gold Star was one of those magical rooms. It was four doors down from the famous Drum City on Santa Monica Boulevard. Local 47 Musicians Union was just south of Gold Star on Vine Street. And Pro Drum Shop was directly across the street.

On the Cohen sessions I went into Gold Star and after a while was wondering where Leonard might be. I was looking to the front, having been set up in the middle of this huge band. Phil always liked that kind of setup. It certainly worked for him many times. As I was messing with my drums, I saw a hand come up near my hi-hat cymbal on my left side. I looked and this hand was holding a tooth pick with a smoked oyster at the end. I looked further around and it was Leonard. I had never seen him before but I instinctively knew that it was him. Dressed immaculately. He had a suit on. He was a dashing cat. A sophisticated type of dude. And that just sealed the deal when he handed me that smoked oyster. And then he handed me one of those little tiny paper cups with some Chivas Regal scotch. I thought, "This is really friggin' cool." We all got a little tipsy but not smashed.

I wish I could have played more with Leonard. I have always played to the vocal – that breaks the session-drummer rule – but that's always what I've done. I love hearing a provocative lyric in my headphones. The greatest part of that for me is that sometimes I can get real emotional and even cry. Later, I met Leonard's son, Adam, and played on one of his albums. *(2013)*

Dan Kessel: Phil and Leonard had collaborated on the songwriting, so they had that kind of rapport. Leonard had more of a reserved gentlemanly wit, with an intense sense of cool, and whether or not he may have been agonizing internally, he seemed to have no problem going along with the flow. Most of us have played with Phil long enough that we know what he wants. He wants us to play like Fats Domino's band meets the Berlin Philharmonic. He never said that per se, but that's what he wants.

There were around thirty or forty guys at each session. Leonard was a pro. He was determined. He was there to sing the songs. He enjoyed the grand spectacle of so many musicians.

On the one hand, Leonard seemed tense at first in this environment as it was a bit new and strange for him. … After a while, he became more relaxed and friendlier. He struck me as gentlemanly, sophisticated, and serious – not hyper-serious but a professional who was there to do his job. There were moments when he smiled and joked and seemed to be enjoying himself.

After Gold Star, we recorded in the largest rooms in several different studios. First, we moved over to Whitney Studios in Glendale and then over to Devonshire Studios in the Valley for a couple of sessions. *(2013)*

David Kessel: When Dan and I were working with Phil and Leonard, I really got a kick when Dylan walked into Gold Star with his arms around two broads. He was holding a bottle of scotch or Wild Turkey in his right hand and he turned up with Allen Ginsberg.

I played all kind of guitars. A Guild twelve-string acoustic and my acoustic with electric strings – 'cause there's a pickup on my guitar but I don't utilize the pickup. But on the sessions you get a more metallic and harsh sound by the electric-guitar strings. Listen to the two twelve-strings play on "Don't Go Home With Your Hard-On." I call it punk folk. Leonard was a different vocalist. More of a vocalizer. He vocalizes poetry, and sometimes addresses melody within the context of that.

I still remember Hal Blaine conducting us doing background singing with Dylan, Ginsberg, and a female singer. Allen was cool. He had the bells, finger chimes and talking peace. *(2013)*

At times it was a drag in Gold Star but Leonard stayed cool with Gauloises and whiskey. Portrait by Giuseppe Pino, 1977.

121

Dan Kessel: I sang on "Don't Go Home With Your Hard-On," "Fingerprints," and the title track. I got to share a microphone with Bob Dylan on "Hard-On." That song was the most fun to record. We were all drinking a bit and feeling good. There was a party atmosphere and we sang it in that spirit. Songwriter Doc Pomus was at Phil's house and then went with us to Gold Star when it was recorded. He sang on that, too. *(2013)*

Leonard was most impressed with the recording of "Don't Go Home With Your Hard-On," the all-out stomper on the disc, which boasted loud horns and a martial cadence that's hammered home by dueling drummers. Above it all loomed his menacing, gritty lead vocal, which held center stage in a most unexpected but effective way. "I can really belt 'em out, you know," he said as he took a swig of Jose Cuervo straight from the bottle.

David Kessel: Listen to "Fingerprints" and you will hear Jim Keltner playing sticks on the string bass. ... Stuff that they did on rockabilly records on the Sun label. ... Or they would have them play sticks on a suitcase or something that had a real marble feel to it. And you add echo on top of that.

We did some live things with Leonard singing with the guys. The one that blew my mind was "Memories." Ronee Blakley sang on it. Phil was actually doing backgrounds live with Leonard in the vocal booth. *(2013)*

Dan Kessel: That year [1977] was the year punk rock was breaking. After a play back, in the booth at Whitney, drummer Jim Keltner and I were discussing the Ramones who had just released their first album. I knew Keltner was hip but was surprised that he knew of them, as they were extremely underground at the time. Leonard was listening to our conversation and soon joined in with us, singing the lyrics to their song "Beat On The Brat" from their first album.

The title track was the most monumental session of the album. Phil called a break one night and everyone had left the recording area except Leonard and me. Leonard was standing about three feet from me, smoking and going over

Above: Hanging out with art-rockers Devo after their gig at the Starwood, West Hollywood, October 10, 1978. Martine Getty is the woman next to Leonard. At the front is 1960s folksinger David Blue, a friend from his Greenwich Village days.

his lyrics. I was still sitting in my chair with my German guitar, a Hofner acoustic/electric that John Lennon traded to me for my Everly Brothers acoustic when I played on his *Rock 'n' Roll* album. (He called it "Roger.")

Leonard had his Zen master, Roshi, with him in the studio at Whitney when we were recording the title song. Roshi was wearing proper monk's garb and was friendly and soft-spoken. Phil and I got a chance to have a nice talk with him when he and Leonard joined us for drinks inside the booth, during the album's final session. *(2013)*

Over the years, Leonard has complained about Spector's high-handed – and sometimes gun-wielding – ways. He was particularly unhappy to have been excluded from the mixing of the album and not to have been allowed to rerecord some of his vocals. On the other hand, he has on occasion expressed a kind of grudging affection for the album's uncharacteristic excesses.

Leonard came away from the project feeling battered, bruised, and perhaps educated, another casualty or possible beneficiary of Phil Spector's remorseless sonic (and psychological) assault and neural imprinting.

Dan Kessel: Leonard seemed intrigued with the whole Spector milieu and often made witty comments and observations about us but I never got the feeling he was uneasy about the guns, the liquor, the bodyguards, or anything else. On the contrary, in his own low-key way, he actually seemed to enjoy himself during the production.

Leonard may have thought he had not done his best job vocally; may have felt frustrated that he wasn't afforded the opportunity to improve on that. But any of those decisions were always going to be according to Phil's sole judgment as the producer. That's how things work.

When Leonard says he felt that he lost control, I must say with all due respect, and I do respect him very much as an artist, it wasn't a co-production. It wasn't produced by Phil Spector and Leonard Cohen. It was always going to be Phil's decision as to how things happened, how the songs were arranged musically, which performances were

keepers, how the recordings were mixed and everything else. Kim Novak wanted more say-so with Hitchcock during the filming of *Vertigo*. It just doesn't always work out that way. *(2013)*

Leonard's own images were expressive too, of course. On *Death of a Ladies' Man* they seemed particularly direct. "This is the most autobiographical album of my career," he revealed to me in a 1977 interview we did in the kitchen of his Los Angeles home after I had attended numerous sessions. "The words are in a tender, rather than a harsh setting, but there's still a lot of bitterness, negativity, and disappointment in them. I wish at times there was a little more space for the personality of the storyteller to emerge, but, in general, the tone of the album is very overt, totally open."

Leonard also acknowledged that, "I was a little off-balance this year." Songs like "Iodine," "True Love Leaves No Traces," and the album's title track mirrored his situation. All the usual Cohen concerns – lost love, personal chaos, doubt, romantic dilemma, alienation, lust – were out in force. "And don't forget humor," he added. "Everybody will now know that within this serene

Buddhist interior, there beats an adolescent heart."

Death of a Ladies' Man could easily have been titled "Two Jews' Blues." Whatever the circumstances that brought Leonard and Spector together (business before pleasure), here were the febrile imaginings of two immensely talented, immensely idiosyncratic individuals, driven by a multitude of artistic impulses. Like hothouse orchids, they thrived in extreme settings; Spector's near-pathological need for control had him setting the thermostat at freezing in all his surroundings, to the great discomfort of everyone but the tyrannical tycoon of pop.

Leonard could be excused his trepidations. Both men suffered from a piercing intelligence that made workaday reality a deathless chore. Hence, the need to push and push some more the boundaries of decorum in their personal and professional lives: the Canadian, cool to the touch, his prose and poetry cutting like ice knives; the Bronx-born Spector, brash, hectoring, obstinate to the point of infantilism.

Kenneth Kubernik: But what to make of the music? Not surprisingly, it rang of pastiche. The much-vaunted Wall of Sound came across as a viscous stew of triple percussion, double keyboards, thrumming guitars swaddled in a blanket of backing vocals which, paradoxically, rendered many of the songs both unripe and overcooked. There were some wonderful moments – on "Memories," when the chords marched in time to Leonard's swooning romanticism, the narcotic gaze of "Fingerprints," and the anthemic refrain of the album's closing title track.

Spector's production stature rested on his ruthless command of the material. In fact, Phil's greatest gift was placing the studio at the service of the singer and the song. Artists like the Ronettes and the Righteous Brothers could never be subsumed by Spector's ego, no matter how many glazes he applied to their surfaces. All the musical weight on *Death of a Ladies' Man* was more an echo of an era than the portrait of an artist operating in the here and now. *(2014)*

The reviews were all over the map, some cruelly dismissive, others enthralled by the mercurial personalities involved. The *Los Angeles Times* music critic, Robert Hilburn, was particularly enthused, calling it the album of the year.

In the UK, a consensus emerged around the music's abiding strengths; the Brits had long championed both artists and had no trouble tweezing out things to admire. Despite the radical change of style, the album still cracked the UK top forty. Sandy Robertson of *Sounds* placed *Ladies' Man*

alongside Dylan's *Desire*. "Yes, Cohen's dirge-like pessimism would hardly appear to be the perfect fodder for Spector's Wall of Sound-cum-Richard Wagner ecstatic street noise. But amazingly enough it works for some unfathomable reason. Applause to all concerned taking chances without disowning their pasts."

In the United States it failed to chart; there was a burble of critical interest and then a quick descent into the vinyl graveyard. In the decades since its initial release, a cult-like interest has surfaced around the recording, indicative of the continuing fascination pop-music aficionados feel for both men.

Death of a Ladies' Man coincided with other transformative events in Leonard's life. His beloved mother, Masha, was struggling with leukemia. Ever the dutiful son, he commuted between Montreal and Los Angeles, providing her the love and comfort of his unwavering attention. Her battle concluded in February 1978.

A different kind of ending, a final parting with Suzanne, took place during this period as well. She had weathered too many starless nights to remain committed to Leonard's wanderings. She took the children and sallied forth without him, eventually settling in the southern French village of Roussillon.

The year 1978 also saw the publication of a new book, *Death of a Lady's Man*, a collection of poems and prose-poems inspired by the ineffable Suzanne. The difference in title from the album is subtle but significant. The book explored their ten-year relationship, their endless travails, the point-to-point navigations between love and desire, submission and self-effacement, and the thrum of ambivalence which troubles us all.

Leonard included a set of commentaries on each entry, a kind of mischievous critique of his aesthetic pretensions, underscoring the unreliability of the narrator. It was a mordant touch to cast suspicion on one's own writing, but it fit Leonard's devil-may-care persona. *Death of a Lady's Man* drew scant critical attention; his own affection for the book was sufficient.

> "I have never been a good civilian. My children like me. But the truth is that I tried to be a good father and husband, but I was not very good."
>
> — LC, 2001

Spending time with son, Adam, and daughter, Lorca. Having become a songwriter and musician in his own right, Adam has talked of belonging "to a long line of people who have embraced their father's business." Lorca, too, has joined the firm, notably as photographer and videographer during

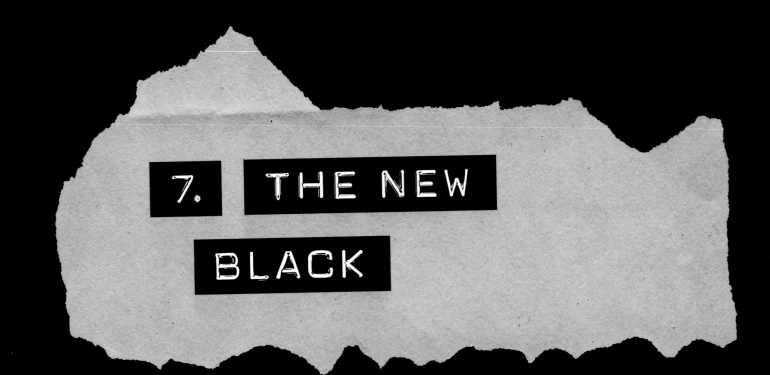

7. THE NEW BLACK

"I remember hearing I'm Your Man a handful of years after it was released. I thought, 'He's cool again.' He'd always previously worn the time he was in well but had lost that in the eighties."

– Anthony J. Reynolds, 2014

TIMELINE

1978
November:
Buys a house in Los Angeles, near the Zen Center

1979
Leonard and Suzanne make a formal "divorce" agreement (despite their never having been married); Suzanne, Adam and Lorca move to France

April–May:
Records Recent Songs in Los Angeles with Henry Lewy

September 27:
Release of Recent Songs

October–December:
Tours Europe to promote the new album, with backing singers Jennifer Warnes and, for the first time, Sharon Robinson; Roshi also joins the entourage

1980
March:
Tours Australia for the first time

October–November:
Tour of Europe, during which Leonard writes his first song with Sharon Robinson ("Summertime")

November:
The Song of Leonard Cohen, a documentary filmed by Harry Rasky during the 1979 tour, is broadcast by CBC

1981–1984
Steps out of the spotlight, dividing his time mainly between Mount Baldy, Montreal, Hydra, and France

1982
Spring:
While on Hydra, receives a visit from friend Lewis Furey, his wife, and their friend, French photographer Dominique Issermann; Leonard and Dominique embark on a long-term relationship

Starts work with Furey on writing a musical fantasy film called Night Magic

1983
Uses his late-1960s experience of long-stay hotel-living to write a short musical TV film called I Am a Hotel, which is broadcast by CBC

1984
Spring:
I Am a Hotel wins the Golden Rose award at the 1984 Montreux International Television Festival

April:
Publication of Book of Mercy, a collection of prayers, psalms, and meditations

June:
Records Various Positions in New York with John Lissauer

December 11:
Release of Various Positions in Canada

1985
January–March:
Tour of Europe to promote the new album; John Lissauer recruits backing singer Anjani Thomas

February:
Release of Various Positions in Europe; Columbia declines to release the album in the United States

April–July:
Tour of North America, Australia, and Europe

May:
Premiere of Night Magic at the Cannes Film Festival; the soundtrack double album is released in France

1986
January:
Belated US release of Various Positions by independent label Passport

February 21:
Broadcast of an episode of Miami Vice in which Leonard plays a small part

September:
Records "Take This Waltz" for compilation album Poetas en Nueva York, a tribute to Federico García Lorca

1987
January:
Release of Famous Blue Raincoat, Jennifer Warnes' album of Leonard Cohen cover versions

August-November:
Records I'm Your Man in Los Angeles with Roscoe Beck

Final stages of his relationship with Dominique

September:
Starts an initially platonic friendship with actress Rebecca De Mornay

1988
February 2:
Release of I'm Your Man in Europe

March 19:
Death of Marty Machat, Leonard's long-standing manager, aged sixty-seven; Machat's associate Kelley Lynch takes over Leonard's business affairs

April:
Release of I'm Your Man in the United States and Canada

April-July:
Tour of Europe

July:
Broadcast of BBC TV documentary Songs from the Life of Leonard Cohen

October-November:
Tour of United States and Canada

October 31:
Broadcast of a studio performance for Austin City Limits, a US music show on PBS

December:
I'm Your Man is the New York Times' album of the year

1989
February 13:
Performs "Who By Fire" with Sonny Rollins on US music show Night Music

Broadcast of the National Ballet of Canada's A Moving Picture, a dance fantasy featuring Leonard's music

1990
Around this time, Leonard's relationship with Rebecca De Mornay becomes more intimate

When his son Adam is seriously injured in a car accident, Leonard spends four months by his bedside in hospital in Toronto

1991
March 3:
Inducted into the Canadian Music Hall of Fame

October 30:
Becomes an Officer of the Order of Canada

November 26:
Release of I'm Your Fan, a tribute album featuring cover versions of Leonard Cohen songs by artists such as R.E.M., Pixies, and Nick Cave and the Bad Seeds

1992
January-June:
Records The Future in Los Angeles with a variety of co-producers

September 29:
Release of Hal Willner's Weird Nightmare: Meditations on Mingus, on which Leonard recites Mingus's poem "The Chill of Death"

November 24:
Release of The Future, including the song "Waiting For The Miracle," which contains a proposal of marriage to Rebecca

Awarded honorary doctorate by McGill University, his alma mater

1993
March:
Wins Juno Award for Male Vocalist of the Year

Publication of Stranger Music: Selected Poems and Songs, an anthology of his work

April 18:
Recording of a private performance from the rehearsal studio for syndicated radio broadcast The Columbia Records Radio Hour Presents Leonard Cohen Live!

April-May:
Tour of Europe

June:
Leonard interviews Rebecca for Interview magazine, but soon after the couple break off their engagement

June-July:
Tour of North America

July 12:
Another appearance on Austin City Limits

November:
Wins the Governor General's Award for Lifetime Artistic Achievement

November 30:
Release of Elton John's Duets album, on which he and Leonard sing Ray Charles' "Born To Lose"

"The poem is nothing but information. It is the constitution of the inner country. If you declaim it and blow it up with noble intentions then you are no better than the politicians whom you despise."
— LC, "How to Speak Poetry" from Death of a Lady's Man, 1978

Leonard spent the majority of 1978 in Montreal, but toward the end of the year he went back to Los Angeles, back to the studio, back to Joni Mitchell, his onetime muse turned icon herself, who directed him to her producer/engineer, Henry Lewy. After the enervating pomposities of Phil Spector, Lewy's European gentility provided a soothing, recuperative balm.

Born and raised in Germany, Lewy left on the eve of World War II, finding his way to America and its bounty of opportunities. A knack for electronics pointed him toward the burgeoning field of sound engineering, and a career was born. Jazz DJing in the Southern California area on KNOB-FM in the early sixties and working with the "High Priestess of the Canyon" made Lewy the perfect confederate for Cohen's own elliptical orbit.

A&M Studios on La Brea, just south of Sunset Boulevard, sits in the heart of Hollywood. It was here, in the twenties, that the "Little Tramp," Charlie Chaplin, ushered in the golden age of cinema. A series of bungalows configured into a bucolic village was transformed in the sixties by trumpeter/music industry titan Herb Alpert into a teeming complex of record-label offices and state-of-the-art recording facilities. It was the right fit for Leonard's next project.

Recording started in April 1979 for what would become Recent Songs. Lewy's long association with Mitchell made him particularly attentive to the instrumental accompaniment of a poetic lyricist, and the music reflected a subtle but significant shift in Leonard's sound. Rhythm tracks were predominantly handled by the Texas-based roots rockers Passenger, with Jennifer Warnes and Sharon Robinson – a new but significant recruit – providing the stately backing vocals. The somewhat Asiatic textures were created using violin, mandolin, and oud (an eleven-string Middle Eastern instrument), the latter two played by the Armenian master John Bilezikjian. String orchestrations were provided by the English composer and arranger Jeremy Lubbock.

As always, Leonard drew lyrical inspiration from the push/pull of his adventuresome love life, though many songs suggested a deepening interest in world religions. His reading at the time included the Persian poets Rumi and Attar; sorting out the nuances of Judaism, Zen, Quebecois Catholicism and a tincture of Islam in these songs could keep a raft of grad students in doctoral studies for years to come.

Leonard was in buoyant spirits throughout the sessions – "a joy, a consummate gentleman to be around," recalled Lubbock. Nevertheless, reviewers fixated on the glum, monotone readings, torment winding its way through yet another set of dispatches from the war between the sexes. Leonard insisted that Recent Songs was primarily about love fulfilled. If that didn't square with the vigorously mythologized image of the avatar of anguish, so be it. He would take his optimism to the people, committing to an exhaustive marketing and touring schedule.

Opposite: Time out during tour rehearsals. Portrait by Stefani Kong Uhler, 1979.

Pages 126-7: Het Muziektheater, Amsterdam, April 18, 1988.

"The 1979 tour was fantastic. As I recall, the audiences were every bit as enthusiastic as they are now. The band, Passenger, had been together for some time and was very tight. It was a smaller tour in terms of personnel, so there was a strong sense of camaraderie. My first time working with Leonard and his music, traveling so extensively, doing big concerts, it was a life-changing experience."

– Sharon Robinson, 2014

Jim Devlin: Maybe the most surprising volte-face in Leonard's musical career came with his 1979 album *Recent Songs*. Because after the raucousness of *Death of a Ladies' Man*, and all those upbeat mid-seventies shows, he then gave us a bunch of songs which returned him, and us, to basics – well, I mean, to *his* basics: personally resonating stories. The album's just a gorgeous return to the slow, soft, soulful and mournful and confessional. It's brilliant. It's sheer class. *(2014)*

Leonard's two-month Field Commander Cohen tour of Europe in late 1979 would feature *Recent Songs*. The backing singers on the album, Warnes and Robinson, would also join him on the road.

Sharon Robinson was born in San Francisco. Her family moved to Los Angeles when she was five. At age sixteen she recorded a demo; the backing group was the Jazz Crusaders. Their leader, Joe Sample, immediately recognized her ability as a songwriter and encouraged her to continue. Sharon then attended California Institute of the Arts to study music. A year later she became a session singer and then a singer and dancer for Ann-Margret's Las Vegas revue.

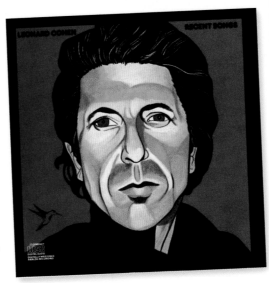

Sharon Robinson: I was singing with Ann-Margret at the time, but the recommendation actually came through my session work. Another session singer gave my name to Jennifer Warnes, who auditioned me first, then brought me in to audition for Leonard. He was warm and friendly and there was an immediate rapport. I worked closely with Jennifer on the vocal parts and by the end of the first rehearsal had the feeling it was going to work out. Before I knew it, we were off to Europe. *(2014)*

While on tour, Leonard and Sharon co-wrote "Summertime," the first collaboration in what would become an immensely fruitful partnership. The song went on to be recorded by both Diana Ross and Roberta Flack.

Opposite: Scenes from the 1979 tour. In transit, Paris (main photo); backstage with Roshi, who joined the entourage, and Roscoe Beck (inset, top); and Théâtre des Champs-Elysées, Paris, October 30 (inset, bottom).

Overleaf: *Recent Songs* sessions, A&M Studios, Los Angeles, April-May 1979.

John Lissauer knew who was calling before Leonard even spoke; there was a recognizable ruffle in his breath. Having not heard a word from him in years, Lissauer could barely stifle a smile when the Commander told him that it was time to get back to work. Yes, sir!

John Lissauer: I never hear back from him until 1984. Then, out of the blue, "Hey John. It's Leonard." "Hi. How are you doing?" "I'm gonna be in town in a couple of weeks. Let's get together." So I say, "Great."

So he comes over to my place, the same loft, and he plays me a couple of songs. And says, "I'd love to work with you." We never talk about the album that's unfinished. It's unspoken. I was just happy he wanted to do something else. He played me a couple of songs. "Wow. We're gonna have fun." And I was very enthusiastic. *(2013)*

Leonard had become enamored with a new toy, a Casio synthesizer, the kind you might give to your precocious young nephew to tinker with. It was about as professional a device as an Easy-Bake Oven. Yet it was his enthusiasm for its remedial sounds and flaccid, pre-set rhythms that gave rise to the material featured on his next album, *Various Positions.*

"I first meet him up in a little room at the Royalton Hotel. He sat down and played 'Dance Me To The End Of Love' on his little Casio."

– John Lissauer, 2013.

Lissauer patiently transcribed Leonard's cabinet of Casio curiosities and worked them up into viable songs, deftly executed by members of the group Slow Train. With few overdubs and a premium on first takes, the album developed into a resonant whole.

John Lissauer: At the time I heard "Hallelujah" it was still in the formative stage. It was early. And this whole thing about it taking four years to write. I don't think that's true. I heard it when it had four verses and he hadn't finished the song yet. In fact, I helped him with the chords and the structure of the song. It was somewhat collaborative but not officially. And I never really pushed for that.

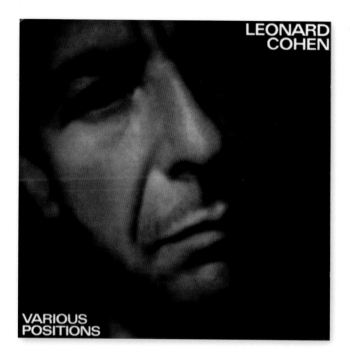

LEONARD COHEN

VARIOUS POSITIONS

"Suddenly, I knew these weren't discrete songs I was writing. I could see – I could sense – a unity; Various Positions had its own life, its own narrative. It was all laid out and all of a sudden it all made sense. It was almost painfully joyful."
— LC, 2000

And I played it on piano, and he said, "Oh. I love that feel." So I changed it from his little 6/8 way into what it became on that record.

Leonard is older and his voice is getting lower and lower. In fact, the key on "Hallelujah" was scary. If you listen to that recording of it, it's down in the depths. And it's startling.

I find him a studio. Quadrasonic in Midtown. I put the band together. And I brought in Anjani Thomas. So Leonard and I sit around the studio and he plays me the beginnings of "Hallelujah."

When we first started to record "Hallelujah," it wasn't, "Oh boy. This is gonna be this." It was really good and it was gonna be really powerful. We were building it as we went. And it wasn't until we were three-quarters through that we all said, "Holy mackerel. This is a cornerstone song."

I said to Leonard at the time, "This is the one. This is what they've been waiting for. This might be your best record, Leonard. Between "Dance Me To The End Of Love," "If It Be Your Will," and "Hallelujah." This is gonna break through and touch people in this country."

This group of songs. "A Singer Must Die." Those things were really evocative. "Dance Me To The End Of Love" had a joyousness that you didn't see with Leonard very much. It even had

a "those were the days" kind of quality. And I worked at making that an anthemic sing-along. And it worked great. I think he has done it every concert since then. *(2013)*

LC: "If It Be Your Will" really is a prayer. And "Hallelujah" has that feeling. A lot of them do. "Dance Me To The End of Love." "Suzanne." I love church music and synagogue music. Mosque music. *(1992)*

Apparently Columbia Records heard only the pain and none of the joy that Leonard and his producer identified. The imperious head of the label, Walter Yetnikoff, hated the album. Leonard, in full supplicant mode, tried kissing the king's ring, but Yetnikoff was unmoved, and dismissed his artist.

John Lissauer: We brought it up to Walter Yetnikoff. Leonard and Marty Machat went up there and played the album for him. I was there but not sitting in the room. I was waiting and expecting Yetnikoff to say this was exactly what Columbia wanted. And instead he just says, "It's terrible, it's unreleasable. I don't know what this is."

I assume that this album is dead. And I really think I've ruined this guy … *(2013)*

The album was licensed to the independent label Passport Records and sank without a trace. CBS affiliates in Europe had some success with it; it was clear to Leonard, however, that his sixties cachet was fading. LC was becoming unhip. Skinny-tied, angry pop stars and the throbbing gristle of early electronica were now the metrics of cool. Leonard countered by hitting the road yet again; playing live would be its own reward.

Leonard talked to music journalist, author, and radio broadcaster Ritchie Yorke about *Various Positions* during a promotional tour stop in Toronto:

LC: [The songs on *Various Positions*] all feel more or less the same. You pick up your guitar with a cup of coffee in the morning and start to uncover a song. That can take a long time for me. Some people come up with great songs in the back of a taxi. It's no guarantee of excellence for me but I have the commercial necessity to get behind a record by touring it.

It took me a long time to write the songs. At the same time, I worked on *Book of Mercy* and a video for it, and the script for a movie I wrote with Lewis Furey [*Night Magic*]. It's no guarantee of excellence but those songs took a long time to write. They were a culmination of five years of writing.

I was very happy with Jennifer Warnes' contributions. I think she's one of the most underestimated singers in America today. As a singer, her instincts are impeccable. We've toured together on many occasions. She was my backup singer in 1972 and on the 1979/80 tours. Even though her career is much bigger than mine, she insisted on coming out on the road with me. It is a labor of love for her. We wrote a good song recently that she's going to be recording ["First We Take Manhattan"]. All the people who worked on the *Various Positions* album were special friends and supporters. *(1985)*

Many years later, the music world would catch up with Leonard and his most devoted listeners. Hidden on side two of *Various Positions* was a minor miracle; the song "Hallelujah," would, in time, become an essential part of the cultural landscape, a new standard embraced by singers in every genre, a hymn for a post-secular world in search of deliverance.

Above: A favorite spot taking the sun in his kitchen, 1988.

Overleaf: Studying various (feminist) positions while touring *Various Positions*, Milan, March 1985.

"Jennifer helped me enormously in this country, and in many countries. In the high smoky rooms of power where these things are determined, I think maybe my career and name underwent some kind of revision."

– LC, 1988

Main photo: "I'm guided by a signal in the heavens / I'm guided by this birthmark on my skin." Portrait by Sharon Weisz, 1988.

Inset, top: With Jennifer Warnes during the video shoot for her version of "First We Take Manhattan" at the old Ford assembly plant in Wilmington, on the Los Angeles Harbor, April 1987.

JenniferWa
Famous Blue R

The Songs of LEONARD COHEN

However, in 1987, with Leonard's stock at a low, it was Jennifer Warnes' tribute album *Famous Blue Raincoat* that sowed the seeds of his revival.

Jennifer Warnes: Like a lot of people, I turned on to "Suzanne" and [other] Leonard Cohen songs in the sixties. But the advice I got from my manager and others was, "Please leave those mournful songs out of your repertoire." That was the first time I encountered the resistance Americans have to the full expression of sorrow in their music, of complex emotions rather than just sex and happiness. *(1987)*

Warnes had recorded and toured with Leonard since the early seventies, and so she knew how to interpret the cobalt tension which animated those starkly revealing songs. Jennifer sung them as a promising young talent at the Troubadour as early as 1969. She sang with Donovan and Dion DiMucci on the late-sixties television series *The Smothers Brothers Comedy Hour* and was heard with Claudia Lennear on the 1972 Chris Darrow debut LP *Artist Proof* as well as the Darrow Mosley Band album *Desert Rain*.

As a solo artist Warnes reached the top ten in the late seventies with "Right Time Of The Night," and topped the charts in 1982 with "Up Where We Belong," the Grammy- and Oscar-winning duet with Joe Cocker for the hit movie *An Officer and a Gentleman*. And yet no label would support an album of her singing Leonard compositions. Cypress Records finally threw caution, and common sense, to the wind.

Famous Blue Raincoat, co-produced by another longtime Leonard bandmate, Roscoe Beck, featured not only familiar titles rearranged by Cohen himself, but also five new songs written expressly for this album. Warnes' exuberant voice found unexpected warmth and belongingness in Leonard's doleful inventory of romance on the rocks. The record's critical and commercial success vindicated Warnes' deepest aspirations as well as liberating Leonard from a kind of perceptual jail. The man from the far north was suddenly basking in sunshine.

Jennifer Warnes: When I signed with Cypress Records, I called Leonard and said, "I'm going to sing your songs on a record." He didn't believe me. So he showed up on New Year's Eve at five minutes to midnight, completely unannounced. We started the record one month later. He stayed in town and rewrote some lyrics so that they made sense from a woman's point of view. He came to the studio every day, blessed the project, and when I had trouble, he'd help me. *(1987)*

Music-business veteran Sharon Weisz was the publicist for *Famous Blue Raincoat*.

Sharon Weisz: There was a renaissance going on. Leonard was thrilled this album came out and was showcasing his music in a really nice way. And that media were responding to it. As things started coming together Jennifer would invite him along, or he would be requested.

My first impressions were that he seemed very quiet and subdued and not very talkative. That changed, certainly. He was kind of flattered by the attention the media people were heaping on him at that point.

What happened was, periodically I would ask him to do a phone interview promoting Jennifer's record and he came down to the video shoot that Cypress did for "First We Take Manhattan." It was filmed at the old Ford Motor Company plant in Wilmington, California. An amazing location. The plant is the star of so many movie chase scenes.

I brought my camera to the shoot. I was taking some pictures, and the elevator at the far end of the room had opened, and Leonard had walked out of the elevator. It was a gigantic room, and as he was walking he was peeling a banana. And he got within a few feet of me, the banana was peeled in his hand, and I sort of pivoted and took one shot of him holding this banana. I blew up a print and sent it to him.

Two or three weeks later I got a phone call from him and he said, "Sharon. I got that photo. And I've been looking at it a lot." And I said, "I'm glad you like it." And he said, "I'm thinking of putting it on the cover of my new album." And I had no idea he was actually recording an album. "You wanna put it on the sleeve or something?" "No. I want to put it on the front." "OK." I was like startled. And asked him, "What are you calling your album?" "*I'm Your Man.*" It was used as a promo photo. *(2014)*

LEONARD COHEN

Los Angeles, California

Good Morning:

I don't quite know how this is done so please bear with me. I have a new record, I'M YOUR MAN, coming out next week. It is already a hit in Europe, and I'm on my way there now for a major concert tour.

I know I can count on your support for this new record in the United States, and if you can make a couple of phone calls on my behalf, I would really appreciate it. I've enclosed a couple of bucks to cover the calls.

Thank you in advance for your help.

Regards,

Leonard Cohen

April 1, 1988

"We concocted a letter that went out to the Columbia field radio-promotion staff. I gave Leonard the gist of what it needed to say and he wrote it. I went to the bank and got some dollar bills and then we got the story printed in Radio and Records. And then Billboard."
— Sharon Weisz, 2014

During the late summer and fall of 1987 Leonard worked on *I'm Your Man*, with Roscoe Beck producing.

Kenneth Kubernik: February 1988 saw the release of Leonard's latest musical manifesto, *I'm Your Man*. Like David Bowie in "Thin White Duke" mode a decade earlier, Leonard produced a suave union of sound and style. The onetime bohemian slacker was now sporting Armani suits and designer shades. The flamenco sketches of old were supplanted by a burbling Eurocentric electronica, the product of his increasing preoccupation with entry-level synthesizers and drum machines. The sounds were as *au courant* as the chart-topping digital glaze accompanying those MTV cops on *Miami Vice*. Opening with "First We Take Manhattan," a call to arms by the smoothest of operators, the album wore the gleaming pastel chic of the pop zeitgeist. *(2014)*

Columbia atoned for its chronic mistreatment of Leonard's career, pushing *I'm Your Man* hard. It broke the UK top fifty; and spent seventeen weeks at number one in Norway. America remained indifferent, but that in no way diminished the album's international success.

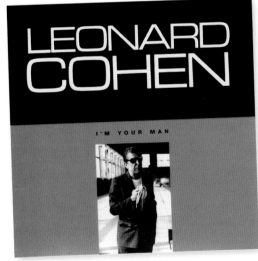

Leonard had struggled during the recording of *I'm Your Man*, bedeviled by depression, apathy, and indiscipline. The once comforting cocktail of drugs, travel, and heartache would no longer suffice. He doubled down on pure craftsmanship, arduously working and shaping the material as a sculptor would a rough-hewn slab of quarried marble.

Anthony J. Reynolds: Leonard's stance, his aesthetic, had always been timeless, but I think in the eighties the production failed him. It was neither here nor there.

But *I'm Your Man* was a perfect marriage. He's spoilt in a way because his lyrics and voice have such an integrity that you could put them with anything and get away with it. It sounded like he was working with people here who raised their game. *I'm Your Man* was a poor poet who had money, wading through the clubs and the financial district. A dude on coke holding on to a rosary. *(2014)*

I'm Your Man publicist Sharon Weisz helped Leonard come up with this droll ploy to get unenthused Columbia sales reps and radio-promotion staff on side (top), and also inadvertently shot the front cover (opposite and above).

Portrait with Suzanne Vega by Deborah Feingold, 1989.
Vega was one of a number of younger musicians who started
to sing Leonard's praises (and his songs) during this period.

"I felt for some time that the motivating energy, or the captivating energy, or the engrossing energy available to us today is the energy coming from the extremes. That's why we have Malcolm X. And somehow it's only these extremist positions that can compel our attention. And I find in my own mind that I have to resist these extremist positions when I find myself drifting into a mystical fascism in regards to myself. So this song, 'First We Take Manhattan,' what is it? Is he serious? And who is we? And what is this constituency that he's addressing? Well, it's that constituency that shares this sense of titillation with extremist positions. I'd rather do that with an appetite for extremism than blow up a bus full of schoolchildren."

– LC, 1992

Anthony J. Reynolds: When I saw him as Zolan [a 1986 cameo as the French head of Interpol] in *Miami Vice* I thought, this is a Zolan record, he's singing in that character. The songs were some of his best, especially the title track and "First We Take Manhattan." He'd cut out the ponderous and sounded indignant, angry, righteous, and the synths and drum machines kinda shuffled a wolf into Wall Street. *(2014)*

Another release meant another world tour. At fifty-three, Leonard was at his dapper best, energized by the album's reception and the excitement of having an audience no longer defined as sixties leftovers. A younger cohort of fans, including up-and-coming musicians such as Suzanne Vega, Nick Cave, and the Pixies, were now waiting for their man. Singers Julie Christensen and Perla Batalla were his band's newest recruits. Warned by Leonard of the tour's daunting itinerary – ten weeks in Europe, then Canada and both coasts – Julie was approached first and jumped at it: Join the Commander's army and see the world.

Julie Christensen: My audition was in LA with some of the members of the band, but with James Cruce playing drums. Leonard wasn't there, but Henry Lewy was, and evidently I passed muster, singing "The Window." But Roscoe [Beck] told me that to get hired it was important to meet Leonard, because the singers were so integral to the performance and were anchors for Leonard. He was given carte blanche, otherwise, to hire the other musicians.

So I went to Leonard's house one day not long after. He and Roscoe were lowering all the keys to the songs, so Roscoe had a guitar in hand. Making conversation, I announced that "Suzanne" was one of the first things I learned on guitar. Roscoe handed me the guitar and I knew that was the wrong move. I began to play, and Leonard said, "Well, that's not right, darling, but let's go have lunch." I just knew that would be the end of that. But we went to Mel's Diner and had grilled cheese, and he spoke of how difficult and grueling the tour would be, "four to five shows a week all over Europe …," and I informed him that I'd just gotten off the road with a punk rock band, changing in places like CBGB's bathroom and peeing by the side of the road. So how bad could it be? And we said, "Let's go." *(2014)*

Perla Batalla: In 1988 Leonard was auditioning for the I'm Your Man tour, I think they had already seen half the singers in LA when I got a call to come in and audition. I arrived at the studio and met this elegant man dressed head to toe in black. He looked me up and down and we laughed that I was in all white. It was love at first sight. I liked him immediately and felt a connection. *(2014)*

Julie Christensen: There was magic in the blend between Perla and me by itself, I think. And that angelic quality rubbing up against Leonard's smoky bass-baritone was a thrill to participate in daily and nightly. Because I'd been rehearsing on my own for a few weeks before Perla arrived, we were both jumping around the higher and lower harmonies. Since both of us have wide ranges, we would fit the right voice to the right part.

The experience of being on stage with him is like a prolonged meditation. If I'm not telling the truth up there, I have to pull myself back into the now. And Leonard has the most endurance in the room. *(2014)*

"I just fell in love with his first album and felt that he was my personal friend. I was listening to him in my room, I felt he was a small quiet voice that belonged to me. So back then in order to get to know somebody you'd say, 'Do you like Leonard Cohen?' and if they said, 'Who?' then you knew you wouldn't be friends."

– Suzanne Vega, 2009

"A poem takes place in a completely different landscape [from a song lyric]. There are similarities - it's language, it's rhymed, it's rhythmical - but a poem can be stopped at any moment. You can review it, read the line you've read, ponder it, taste it, go back to the line before. It takes place in silence. A lyric has to have space around the words. It's designed to move swiftly from the singer to the listener. It can't be arrested, and although the mind should be delighted, it can't be invited to stay too long with the phrase. It has to lead to the next one in an effortless way. You generally don't take the arm off the record and put it back."

— <u>LC</u>, 1988

With a penchant for handtooled boots "so lovely you want to cry with envy," as journalist Burr Snider wrote about Leonard. Portrait by Roy Tee, 1988.

Perla Batalla: First European tour … Any musician who has been on the road knows what they are in for. Of course this was my first major tour … I didn't even have a passport. When I applied for one I was shocked to learn that I had never been given a legal name – I guess my mom was kind of busy with three other babies and a musician husband who often acted like one, and just never got around to it. My birth certificate said, "Baby Girl Batalla" (which, come to think of it would have been a pretty good name if I were a hip-hop artist). In a roundabout way, maybe I have to give Leonard credit for finally becoming "Perla."

My father, who was proud and very formal and spoke mostly Spanish, saw his "baby girl" off at LAX. He took Leonard's hand and looked him in the eye and asked him to please take care of his daughter. Leonard took this vow quite seriously. When I fell ill in Madrid, there was a doctor; when I was desperately lonely, we walked the streets together and talked about anything and everything. *(2014)*

Sharon Weisz: Leonard and the band came pretty much straight from Europe to New York. I got to New York and the Columbia Records people were completely freaked out by the number of requests for his two events at the Ritz and Carnegie Hall. And Leonard delivered. As he always did. Absolutely.

I know this guy with a real droll and dry sense of humor. Leonard would leave me funny messages on my answering machine and bring me smoked meat from Montreal. I remember he had been telling me all about the smoked meat and bagels in Montreal, and he had just been there. I came home one night from work and it was Leonard on the phone. And he says, "I just got home. I brought you something." I went over and he had a vacuum-packed package of smoked meat and a bag of Montreal bagels. And I had to agree that the bagels are different and better than any bagel

that I had had before. And the Montreal smoked meat was heaven. We were two Jews noshing.

Subsequently, when we did the tour in 1988, it ended in Canada; Leonard gave me, as a gift, a plane ticket to Montreal to see him perform in his hometown. I was there for the Toronto show, which was packed to the rafters. Massey Hall. And I brought my entire family because my father's side was in Toronto.

Leonard was kind and funny and they were blown away by the whole experience. And then he played in Montreal. And he had drilled into me the whole thing about the smoked meat, "You gotta have a sandwich at the Main Deli." And it's in his neighborhood. OK. I took a cab over to the Main Deli. And I get there and Perla is sitting there. He had obviously told her the same thing. So we each had a Montreal smoked meat sandwich.

And the show was that night. I got there and the road manager was having a panic attack because of all these guests of Leonard's. Irving Layton was there at the show, and other local poets.

I remember going backstage during the intermission just to tell him all his friends were seated and would probably come back to say hello afterwards. And the door to the dressing room was open and Leonard was sitting on the makeup table, kind of in the doorway. And I'm talking to him and not even in the room and telling him what's going on. And he moves the door and says, "Sharon. Do you know my friend Pierre?" And Leonard introduces me to Pierre Trudeau. He had just been the prime minister. I told my Canadian cousins about that.

It was a different scene from seeing him in the United States. There was a different kind of crowd and a different kind of reverence. Leonard was given the kind of respect I think he deserved when he played in Canada that he didn't get in the United States at the time. "Come see me in my real element." That was his parting gift. *(2014)*

After a comparatively prolific start to his recording career, Leonard had settled into a routine in which he delivered an album once every four years or so. This Olympian schedule came to an end in 1992 with *The Future*, which was to be the only album he released in the nineties. (His next record would be *Ten New Songs* in 2001.) *The Future* expanded on many of the sonic and lyrical themes that helped make *I'm Your Man* such a sensation.

It also marked the culmination of Leonard's Rebecca De Mornay period. Ms. De Mornay, an American actress raised in England and Australia but irrepressibly Californian in her appeal, all strawberry blonde and cat-eyed, rocketed to success in 1983 as Tom Cruise's luscious tormentor in *Risky Business*. Her career had the inevitable ups and downs of an "it" girl, a onetime ingénue fighting for quality roles.

Rebecca and Leonard met at various celebrity events during the mid-eighties, including a Robert Altman party, and the filming of Roy Orbison's *Black and White Night* TV special in September 1987. They struck up a warm friendship, which evolved into a more intimate relationship around the turn of the decade. Leonard was smitten, the gulf between their ages (twenty-five years) and experiences be damned. The ageless libertine, with a roué's gleam, told *Entertainment Weekly*, "Solid-gold artists would *kill* for this kind of anguish."

Recorded in Los Angeles at some of the town's premier studios with a variety of co-producers, including Rebecca herself, *The Future* showcased Leonard's increasing infatuation with electronics, both as a tool for composing and as a means to realize unfinished tracks. The synthesizer replaced the guitar as his signature instrument. Weaving "real" strings, bass and drums, nifty guitar fills, and dexterous keyboard filigrees, the music provided a wry sophistication that burnished the lyrical litany of despair that listeners had long come to expect.

The album's centerpiece was "Democracy," a multi-versed (Leonard claimed to have originally written eighty stanzas) anthem to an alternative universe, where cynicism and political dread are vanquished by an appeal to our better selves … or not. Unleashing his most stentorian croak, Leonard ascended the pulpit and announced that democracy was coming to the USA. Was Leonard being willfully naïve, indulging in vicious irony, or just enjoying a good laugh at the expense of his liberal-hearted audience? The song's louche undercurrent was mitigated by a Stevie Wonder–esque synth figure which added a fillip of melodic grace. "Democracy," like Leonard himself, was a study in fiendish contrasts, a baleful delight.

Many of the songs on *The Future*, like "Democracy" and the title track, with its apocalyptic images of torture, crack, and anal sex, were loaded with political and social comment. However, another standout song, "Waiting For The Miracle," could not have been more personal. With a breezy "Ah baby, let's get married," Leonard proposed to Rebecca. She accepted, but the couple broke off their engagement the following year, and Leonard's closest brush with marriage came to nothing.

Anthony J. Reynolds: The Future was the first ever Leonard Cohen album I bought as it came out. He made a wonderful appearance on the UK TV show *Later with Jools Holland*. It was pure class. He looked like royalty compared to the rest of the guests, like some king in exile. He had an authenticity that was just glaring. I remember him being on the radio, too, being interviewed. It was afternoon and I was at my parents' house. When he came on, the cat's ears pricked up, you know? He filled the room, even though my parents barely knew who he was. There was an undeniable presence. He brought the mountain to Mohammed whenever he deigned to do some kind of promo.

stranger music
LEONARD COHEN
selected poems and songs

You just thought, "Thank God, it's not all shit out there." A kind of holy class. Unfortunately, I felt he could be a little too tasteful at times and I thought this album patchy compared to the previous. I felt his cover versions [Frederick Knight's "Be For Real" and Irving Berlin's "Always"] were a little indulgent. It wasn't what I wanted to hear, especially when you had "Be For Real" next to "Waiting For The Miracle," which for me was a mountain of a song. Such a spooky beast. I loved "Tacoma Trailer," too … I wish he'd done more instrumentals. *(2014)*

As stimulating as the write/record/tour roundelay appears to the outsider, inside this velvet cocoon the pressures can become intolerable. Leonard promoted *The Future* with a soldier's call to duty, engaging with the press and his increasingly wide fan base with apparent relish. Upon receiving Canada's prestigious Juno Award as Male Vocalist of the Year in 1993, he told the warmly appreciative audience, "Only in a country like this with a voice like mine could I receive such an award."

Later that year he was the recipient of the Governor General's Award for Lifetime Artistic Achievement. An omnibus collection of lyrics and poems – *Stranger Music* – along with the republication of long-out-of-print titles brought Leonard a deserved sense of accomplishment. His touring schedule demanded Springsteen-like levels of endurance. Nearing sixty, he found himself in a time of exhilaration, summation, and finally, inescapably, debilitation.

Below: "I've seen the future, brother: It is murder." Portrait by Terry O'Neill, 1990.

"This last album I think is very, very sturdy. If it has any fault it's that it's a little too well armored. It seems to have a kind of resilience like a little Sherman tank, that it can go over any landscape. I don't know whether that's something you want parking in our garage, but it seems to have a kind of armored energy. I've tried to make the songs sturdy over the years."

– LC, 1992

8. TEN NEW SONGS AND ONE OLD ONE

"'Hallelujah' lay dormant for ten, fifteen years or more, before it started to get that kind of momentum. How does that happen? What gave this song an afterlife so unlike any other?"

— <u>Alan Light</u>, 2013

TIMELINE

1994
Winter:
Leonard goes to live in the Zen Center monastery on Mount Baldy

March:
Wins a Juno Award for Songwriter of the Year

June 28:
Release of <u>Cohen Live: Leonard Cohen in Concert</u>

August:
Oliver Stone's <u>Natural Born Killers</u> features three songs from <u>The Future</u> on its soundtrack

1995
September 26:
Release of the <u>Tower of Song: The Songs of Leonard Cohen</u> tribute album

1996
August 9:
Leonard is ordained as a Zen Buddhist monk and is given the name Jikan ("silent one")

1997
March 15:
Broadcast of Armelle Brusq's documentary <u>Leonard Cohen: Portrait, Spring 1996</u> on Norwegian TV

September:
Broadcast of another European documentary that visits Leonard on Mount Baldy - Agreta Wirberg's <u>Stina Möter Leonard Cohen</u>

October 7:
Release of an updated compilation, <u>More Best of Leonard Cohen</u>

1998
March 28:
Inaugural Leonard Cohen Fan "Event," in Lincoln, UK

1999
January:
Leonard leaves Mount Baldy and travels to Mumbai to study with Advaita Hindu teacher Ramesh S. Balsekar

May:
Returns to Los Angeles and records "Villanelle For Our Time," a song tribute to Montreal poet F. R. Scott

Fall:
Starts work on <u>Ten New Songs</u> with Sharon Robinson; he also starts a relationship with singer Anjani Thomas

2000
October 3:
Serves as a pall-bearer at the state funeral of former Canadian prime minister Pierre Trudeau, a friend dating back to 1950s Montreal

2001
February 20:
Release of <u>Field Commander Cohen: Tour of 1979</u>

October 9:
Release of <u>Ten New Songs</u>

2002
October 22:
Release of another compilation, <u>The Essential Leonard Cohen</u>

Spends the next two years making <u>Dear Heather</u> with Sharon Robinson, Leanne Unger, Anjani Thomas, and Henry Lewy

2003

February 28:
Release of a Canadian film adaptation of
The Favourite Game, directed by Bernar Hébert

June 28:
Hal Willner stages a tribute concert called Came So
Far for Beauty: An Evening of Songs by Leonard Cohen
under the Stars in Prospect Park, Brooklyn

October 24:
Appointed a Companion of the Order of Canada

2004

May 22 and 23:
The Came So Far for Beauty show is restaged at
the Brighton Festival, UK (and again at the Sydney
Festival in Australia the following January)

September:
Release of Democracy: Judy Collins Sings Leonard
Cohen, a compilation of all Judy Collins' versions
of Leonard's songs

October 26:
Release of Dear Heather

Fall:
Fires his manager, Kelley Lynch, after discovering
that she has been selling off the rights to his music
and taking most of the proceeds out of his account

2005

August:
Starts legal proceedings against Lynch

September 11:
First screening of the Lian Lunson documentary
Leonard Cohen: I'm Your Man

Fall:
Appoints Sam Feldman as his new manager

2006

January 4:
Death of Irving Layton, aged ninety-three; at his
funeral Leonard delivers the eulogy to his great
friend and is one of the pall-bearers

February 5:
Inducted into the Canadian Songwriters Hall of Fame

May 9:
Publication of Book of Longing, a collection
of poetry, prose, and artworks

May 13:
Sings in public for the first time for thirteen years
at a book signing in Toronto

May 19:
Release of Anjani's Blue Alert - Leonard produced
the album and provided the lyrics

May:
A Californian court orders Lynch to pay Leonard
US$7.3 million, but he receives only $150,000

July 25:
Release of the Leonard Cohen: I'm Your Man
soundtrack, including performances from one of
the Came So Far for Beauty concerts

October 4 and 5:
Final performances of Came So Far for Beauty,
at the Dublin Theatre Festival

2007

February 10:
Birth of Adam's son Cassius Lyon Cohen, Leonard's
first grandchild

March-April:
Accompanies Anjani on her tour to promote a reissue
of Blue Alert, and occasionally duets on "Whither
Thou Goest"

June 1:
Premiere in Toronto of Philip Glass's Book of
Longing: A Song Cycle Based on the Poetry and Images
of Leonard Cohen

June 3:
Opening, also in Toronto, of Leonard Cohen: Drawn
to Words, an exhibition of Leonard's artworks

September 25:
Release of Herbie Hancock's album River: The Joni
Letters, a tribute to Joni Mitchell on which Leonard
recites the lyrics to "The Jungle Line"

Fall:
Appoints Robert Kory as his new manager

December 11:
Release of the album of Philip Glass's Book
of Longing

"I am not a Buddhist, but a pseudo-Buddhist. I began my studies with my old teacher not to find a new religion. He was not looking to convert me to Buddhism. I am happy with my religion, it is the religion of my parents and grandparents. My work with him was not centered on my beliefs. It had more to do with the mechanics of living with a religious dogma or a certain vision of God. It was a study of friendship."

– LC, 2001

Returning to Los Angeles in early 1994 at the end of an epic stretch of promotion, touring, and plaudits, Cohen took the deepest of breaths, pushed pause, and donned the robes of a Zen monk. He headed for Mount Baldy, to Roshi, to a soundless, contemplative life; the lone remnants of his "other" life, a modest synthesizer and a portable radio, adorned the threadbare cabin he now called home. His path was taking an interior direction, the journey to wellness bounded by the beauty of small things.

While Leonard rose before dawn each day of his self-imposed exile, resolute in his menial tasks, his fans were basking in a whirl of activities dedicated to their blithely indifferent god: more Juno awards; a live DVD; and the September 1995 launch of the Leonard Cohen Files, a website out of Finland, run by father and son Jarkko and Rauli Arjatsalo, which has received numerous contributions of artworks and writings from Leonard himself.

Jarkko Arjatsalo: I had been listening to Leonard Cohen since the early seventies. After the Helsinki concerts of 1988 and 1993, I began collecting rare recordings of his music and, subsequently, came across the Cohen Newsletter, which was published in England by Jim Devlin. When the newsletter was discontinued in 1994, we had just gotten an Internet connection in our home and were excited about the possibilities it presented.

Together with my then teenage son we searched for a topic on which to create a website, and my interest in Cohen made him a natural choice. The website was designed for an international audience from the start, and we opened the site

in September 1995. I supplied the content for the pages while Rauli took care of all technical issues.

We did not intend to make the pages quite as extensive as they turned out, but we soon realized that Cohen's art had a global fan base that had lacked a channel for communication.

In 1997 Leonard emailed me from the Zen Center at Mount Baldy in California, and suggested that he could provide some items from his notebooks for the Files: "I want to send, among other things, the first manuscript scratchings for 'Suzanne' and other early songs. I'd like to make the process clear, or at least throw some light on the mysterious activity of writing."

After that first contact, we started emailing each other on a regular basis and became friends. The Zen Center at Mount Baldy had a slow dial-up modem for Internet connection, through the only telephone line they had in use. Today, we take the Internet and its services for granted, but in the mid-nineties all of us were barely on the threshold of the new international era we live in today.

It soon became clear that Leonard had closely followed the growth of network communication, and was one of those who very early on understood the prospects for this new channel of communication. He found the Internet a useful tool for staying in touch with his fans, and for keeping his work alive during his "silent" years at the Zen Center. *(2014)*

"While making <u>Ten New Songs</u>, I saw Leonard almost daily. On days we worked at my home studio, he would always arrive, not on time, but early - sometimes half an hour early! We'd have coffee and discuss a wide range of topics from friends and family to religion to music. Then we'd head out to the studio. Leonard brings such quality and grace and generosity of spirit, I never took a moment of it for granted."
- <u>Sharon Robinson</u>, 2014

Opposite: Sharon Robinson and Leonard have co-written some of Leonard's best-loved songs, including "Everybody Knows," "Waiting For The Miracle," and "A Thousand Kisses Deep."

In late September 1995 a tribute album, *Tower of Song: The Songs of Leonard Cohen*, hit the bins, featuring Sting, Bono, Elton John, and Suzanne Vega among its many starry voices. There were still more documentaries exploring the sublime trajectory of Leonard's inimitable career. Like some mordant mad hatter, the object of all this unordinary love couldn't resist the opportunity to tweak his celestial status; he admitted that his time in spiritual seclusion had convinced him that he had no religious inclinations whatsoever, a kind of karmic blowback that wasn't lost on a master of the droll riposte.

For five years Leonard lived in seclusion atop Mount Baldy before he came to an inescapable conclusion – he was a "failed monk." Like a venturesome mountaineer traipsing down from the thin air, he slowly re-acclimated himself to life in the balmy basin of Los Angeles, daughter Lorca joining him at his Miracle Mile duplex. Leonard had, for the most part, succeeded in putting the black dog of depression down; the rival strategies of self-medication (licit and illicit) and self-actualization had reached an accommodation. He made a brief hejira to Hydra, where inspiration remained as reliable as his old Olivetti typewriter, and spent time in Mumbai studying with a new spiritual teacher, the Advaita Hindu adept Ramesh S. Balsekar. But in the fall of 1999, he felt the lure of the recording studio, this time in collaboration with his longtime background singer and occasional songwriting partner Sharon Robinson. Together, they produced *Ten New Songs*, as much an exercise in DIY technology as it was a status report on love, life, and longing at the dawn of the twenty-first century.

Eventually released in October 2001, *Ten New Songs* was steeped in soft, soulful reveries, shorn of any enhancements that would occlude the music's intensely intimate vision. Engineer Leanne Ungar held her steady hand at the recording console, burnishing any rough edges. Outside of a guitar overdub, Leonard and Sharon wrote, programmed, and performed all the parts – the beats unhurried, the arrangements drawing long, luxuriant breaths. Leonard's first album in nearly ten years brought him someplace close to home.

Sharon Robinson: "Summertime" started with my music, but as is more often the case, "Alexandra Leaving" started with Leonard's words. Every song has its own way of coming into the world. I played the music of "Summertime" for Leonard in a hotel lobby. That song began very spontaneously. "Alexandra," as with the other songs on *Ten New Songs*, was a lyric Leonard had been working on for some time at the monastery. After we wrote the song, it got shelved for a while until we listened to it later on in the making of the record and realized it was a good song.

At the time the technology allowed us to do record-quality recordings in our home studios, so we built identical studios and worked equally at both. *(2014)*

From 2002 to 2004 Leonard and his creative team of Sharon Robinson, Anjani Thomas, Leanne Unger, and Henry Lewy collaborated on the album *Dear Heather*.

159

"[Anjani] seems to be able to channel some kind of spirit of place. Generally, people want to be generous, but they go over the top or they give too much. But to be able to be generous in this manner of real generosity, which is not to overwhelm, but to merely satisfy and nourish: That is something very rare. She has this capacity - melody after melody - to hit the mark. Not go beyond it and not fall short ... just perfect."

— LC, 2006

Kenneth Kubernik: Dear Heather, Leonard's 2004 follow-up to *Ten New Songs*, landed with a disconcerting thud. More a collection of odds and sods than a fully conceptualized album, Leonard raided his own back catalogue for tracks, some dating from 1979, which some critics derided as a deadbeat valedictory statement.

Death sounded throughout the project like a ghostly reverb; there were dedications to a gravely ill Irving Layton (who died in early 2006), the deceased poet A. M. Klein, the recently passed singer Carl Anderson, and Leonard's dear friend and publisher Jack McClelland. The album also includes Leonard's 1999 musical setting of "Villanelle for Our Time," a poem by the late F. R. Scott.

Interestingly, the CD booklet was far and away the most florid of any album packaging he'd been involved with; it featured not simply lyrics and credits but a gallery of vividly expressionistic black-and-white drawings done by Leonard himself. The record might be funereal in tone, but the presentation was artfully alive. *(2014)*

Perhaps suspecting that Leonard was considering retirement, musicians, publishers, filmmakers, and custodians of various halls of fame queued up to pay tribute to what was already at this stage a remarkable career.

The first significant event in this latest wave of appreciation had taken place in June 2003 when music producer Hal Willner staged the first *Came So Far for Beauty* tribute concert. A stellar cast of artists, including Nick Cave, Laurie Anderson, and Martha and Rufus Wainwright, interpreted

Leonard's songbook "under the stars" in Prospect Park, Brooklyn. The concert was a success and several follow-up events took place around the world over the next three years.

Lian Lunson's 2005 documentary *Leonard Cohen: I'm Your Man* featured footage from one of the *Came So Far for Beauty* shows. Leonard himself also appeared in the film, teaming up with U2 for a rendition of "Tower Of Song."

The following February Leonard was inducted into the Canadian Songwriters Hall of Fame. Two years later he would be ushered into the Rock and Roll Hall of Fame, with an induction speech given by Lou Reed.

HarperCollins published a fiftieth-anniversary edition of Leonard's first book of poetry, *Let Us Compare Mythologies*, originally published in 1956.

However, Leonard was still working hard on new projects. May 2006 saw two notable releases. First, HarperCollins published *Book of Longing*, a collection of prose, poetry, and artworks.

This was swiftly followed by *Blue Alert*, an album from Anjani Thomas. Anjani had entered Leonard's orbit in 1985 when John Lissauer recruited her as a backing singer on the Various Positions tour of Europe. Around the turn of the millennium, they had become more than just colleagues. Anjani was also part of the *Dear Heather* team, and now Leonard returned the favor, providing all the lyrics for *Blue Alert* as well as producing the album.

Made to measure: Leonard's lyrics perfectly fitted Anjani's sultry jazz melodies on their 2006 collaboration Blue Alert.

PRODUCED BY
LEONARD
COHEN

ANJANI
BLUE ALERT

In December 2008, three versions of Leonard's 1984 composition "Hallelujah" occupied the UK singles charts simultaneously: Jeff Buckley and Alexandra Burke in the top two spots, and Mr. Leonard Cohen himself at number thirty-six.

Kenneth Kubernik: It began innocently enough, in a room at the regal Royalton Hotel on Forty-Fourth Street in Manhattan. Leonard strummed some unprepossessing chords in 6/8 time – another vaguely rain-swept stroll along the Left Bank – that tweaked the ear of producer John Lissauer. He recognized its ecclesiastical undercurrent that begged for development; soon Lissauer had transformed it into an agnostic *cri de cœur* which has catalyzed generations and genders. "Hallelujah" by the early 2000s had become *the* alt-anthem, covered by hundreds of artists, most memorably k.d. lang and Jeff Buckley.

For all his nods and winks at self-deprecation, Leonard had written a signature statement as bold, beguiling, timeless as any lonesome daydream penned by his early hero Hank Williams. *(2014)*

John Lissauer: The song has a life of its own. A lot of time it's in the other artists' performances of it. That's just magic stuff. You can't plan it. Buckley's is great, k.d. lang's, too. I've heard some that are silly by a couple of tenors. I've heard some gospel versions that didn't do it for me. R&B-tinged. How much soul can we put in this? But you know, there's a lot of loveliness to it. Someone sent me some simple folkie versions, which are beautiful.

When Leonard was doing his first Madison Square Garden thing in New York about five or six years ago, I went along with some friends and my new wife Lillian. On the speaker system of Grand Central and Madison Square Garden, they're playing my recording of "Hallelujah" on a loop. It's the loudest thing you've ever heard. So we're standing there and everyone is transfixed. Looking up at the speakers and crying and applauding. And I'm just standing there. Just a guy hearing this achievement that was unknown forever. And it was really quite something. That was almost worth the price of admission. *(2013)*

"There's a blaze of light / In every word / It doesn't matter which you heard / The holy or the broken Hallelujah." More than five hundred singers have left their imprint on the song "Hallelujah" since its release in 1984. Portrait by Marcel Hartmann, 1997.

"I couldn't feel, so I tried to touch I've told the truth, I didn't come to fool you" – <u>LC</u>, "Hallelujah," 1984

"Hallelujah is a Hebrew word which means 'Glory to the Lord.' The song explains that many kinds of Hallelujahs do exist. I say: 'All the perfect and broken Hallelujahs have an equal value.' It's, as I say, a desire to affirm my faith in life, not in some formal religious way but with enthusiasm, with emotion."

– LC, 1985

Alan Light: When you think about "Bridge Over Troubled Water," "Imagine," or "A Change Is Gonna Come," these are songs that people responded to immediately.

What is so different about "Hallelujah" is that there wasn't a definitive recording. It was never a hit. And by the time it became known, this person heard one version and that person heard another version. There's not one fixed entity that defined it. It was something much more fluid than that.

When it was recorded, we're talking about 1984, and possibly the biggest moment the record business had ever had. This was the summer of "Born In The U.S.A.," "Purple Rain," "Like A Virgin," the Jacksons' Victory tour. *(2013)*

"Everything in 1984 was huge scale, and as easy as it is to vilify Columbia Records, who rejected the album, you have to remember that this was when the MTV universe was kicking into fifth gear. And they look at Leonard and say, 'Each of the last few records has done less than the one before. Why do we need to be the guys bothering with this?' It's not entirely the act of Philistines."

– Alan Light, 2013

Alan Light: I think in the journey of "Hallelujah," the original Leonard recording has been lost or at least pushed to the side. John Lissauer gave Leonard the space and the framework and the support and the confidence and the things that a good producer can do to get the recording done. One thing that John said, and Leanne [Unger] confirmed, was, for all the talk about all the different verses and all of the years and years of struggle to get this song written, that by the time he came in the studio, Leonard had the edit that he wanted. And that he didn't actually cut other verses or reshape or so much of anything.

The other thing that gets overlooked or discounted is, in the end, it's the melody of this song that people respond to first, as they always do. And for all the time we can spend on the poetry, and not in any way to undersell what the writing is, if it was with Lissauer where they were really able to get the simplicity and the clarity of that melody nailed, that's where it gets discovered. Not to reduce it to a pop song, but without that chorus, that hook, and that melody, hundreds of people do not record this song.

What is so striking is Leonard's own detachment from the phenomenon of this song. "It's this thing that happened over there." And it's why Leonard put up no objections to all of these different edits and people who drop verses. It became clear that he was gonna be OK with that and it became a very important part of this story and part of why this song could travel in all of these directions. That says a lot about Leonard as a writer but also, obviously, as a Zen practitioner. You put this stuff out there and you don't know what's going to happen. *(2013)*

But while "Hallelujah" entered its unexpected afterlife, Leonard found out something else he didn't know was going to happen.

Soon after *Dear Heather* came out in October 2004, Leonard realized that his manager, Kelley Lynch, who had been handling his affairs since the death in 1988 of Marty Machat, had been selling off rights to his music and using proceeds from his accounts and investments. He fired her, but the damage had been done.

The following year, assisted by Robert Kory, a music-industry attorney who also happened to be Anjani's former husband, and by Kory's associate, Michelle Rice, Leonard began legal actions against Lynch. Kory would later become Leonard's manager.

In May 2006, a Californian court ordered Lynch to pay Leonard US$7.3 million (some press reports put the figure higher), but he was able to recover only $150,000. Lynch then began persistently harassing Leonard by email and phone messages, which led, in April 2012, to an eighteen-month jail sentence for violating an order forbidding her from contacting him. During the trial, Leonard read out a prepared statement, including the following: "It gives me no pleasure to see my onetime friend shackled to a chair in a court of law, her considerable gifts bent to the service of darkness, deceit and revenge."

With his finances now in a parlous state, any thoughts of retirement he may have entertained would have to be put on hold. Leonard displayed a typically Zen state of acceptance, put on his man pants and went back to work.

Opposite: Jeff Buckley's landmark cover of "Hallelujah" was released with Leonard's original on a limited-edition single for Record Store Day, November 23, 2012.

Below: Propelled back on the road by the delicate state of his finances, Leonard would spend more of his late seventies on a stage than on a couch.

9. LEONARD COHEN AND THE ADULTS

To attend a Leonard Cohen concert after listening to his recordings is **to dive into the ocean after rowing a boat across it.**
Same content – entirely different experiences."

– <u>Allan Showalter</u>, 2014

TIMELINE

2008

<u>January 13:</u>
Leonard announces his first tour for fifteen years

<u>March 10:</u>
Inducted into the Rock and Roll Hall of Fame
by Lou Reed

<u>May 11:</u>
The "pre-tour" of small Canadian theater venues
kicks off in Fredericton, New Brunswick

<u>June-July:</u>
First leg of the official tour, which includes
a show-stealing appearance at the Glastonbury
festival, UK (June 29)

<u>September-November:</u>
Second leg of the world tour includes dates
throughout Europe

<u>December:</u>
Three versions of "Hallelujah" occupy the UK
singles charts at the same time – by Jeff Buckley
(#1), Alexandra Burke (#2), and Leonard Cohen
himself (#36)

2009

<u>January-February:</u>
The tour moves on to Australia and New Zealand

<u>February 19:</u>
Plays a special date at the Beacon Theatre,
New York, which is broadcast on radio and made
available as a podcast

<u>March 31:</u>
Release of <u>Live in London</u>, recorded at the 02 Arena
in July 2008

<u>April-June:</u>
The North American leg of the tour includes
a memorable performance at the Coachella Festival
(April 17)

<u>July-September:</u>
Another mammoth European tour

<u>September 19 and 21:</u>
Faints on stage in Valencia with food poisoning,
but recovers to celebrate his seventy-fifth birthday
by performing in Barcelona two days later

<u>September 24:</u>
The final show of the 2009 European tour in
Tel Aviv is his first performance in Israel since
1980; Leonard donates the US$2 million proceeds
to Israeli and Palestinian charities

<u>September 27:</u>
Death of Ramesh S. Balsekar, aged ninety-two

<u>October-November:</u>
Back across the Atlantic for fifteen more US dates

<u>October 19:</u>
Release of <u>Live at the Isle of Wight 1970</u>

2010

<u>January 30:</u>
Receives a Grammy for Lifetime Achievement

<u>Winter:</u>
A back injury forces Leonard to postpone the 2010
tour for a couple of months

<u>June 17:</u>
Inducted into the Songwriters Hall of Fame
in New York

Awards season: Induction by Lou Reed into the Rock and Roll Hall of Fame, 2008 (le
a Grammy for Lifetime Achievement, 2010 (above left); with Judy Collins who induct
him into the Songwriters Hall of Fame, 2010 (above right); and accepting the Prince
of Asturias Award for Letters, 2011 (pages 166-7).

July–December:
Tours almost nonstop across Europe, then Australia
and New Zealand, then North America

September 14:
Release of Songs from the Road, recorded at various
concerts in 2008 and 2009

December 16:
New Skin for the Old Ceremony is reinterpreted
through eleven commissioned art videos shown
at the Hammer Museum in Los Angeles; the project
is co-curated by Lorca Cohen

2011
January–August:
Records Old Ideas with former Madonna songwriter
Patrick Leonard

February 2:
Birth of Viva Katherine Wainwright Cohen,
a daughter to Lorca and her good friend singer-
songwriter Rufus Wainwright

October 21:
Gives a speech called "How I Got My Song" when
accepting the Prince of Asturias Award for Letters,
Spain's highest literary honor, at a ceremony in
Oviedo, northern Spain

2012
January 31:
Release of Old Ideas

inaugural PEN New England Award for Song Lyrics
of Literary Excellence

April 18:
Kelley Lynch is sentenced to eighteen months in
prison for violating exclusion orders forbidding
her from contacting Leonard

May 14:
Leonard receives the prestigious 2011 Glenn Gould
Prize at a gala concert in his honor

August–December:
Tour of Europe, then two weeks' break before resumi
in North America at the end of October

2013
March–April:
Tour of North America

April:
Wins Juno Awards for Artist of the Year and
Songwriter of the Year

June–September:
Tour of Europe

November–December:
Tour of Australia and New Zealand

2014
Fall:
Planned release of the Live in Ireland DVD,
filmed at the 02 in Dublin in September 2013

"It's a rigorous process. I especially don't like the beginning of tours. Because of the rehearsing, the logistics. Once I'm out on the road, I tend to get into it. We have a nice bunch of musicians and we travel well together. I thought of calling them Leonard Cohen and the Adults!"

— <u>LC</u>, 1985

In 2008 Leonard recruited another "nice bunch" of adult musicians and returned to a life on the road after a fifteen-year hiatus. A less psychically sound mind might have been driven to crippling despair or worse by the sordid turn of events in his career; the cost of the personal and financial betrayal by someone he had trusted so deeply seemed unrecoupable.

Touring, that crucible for every jobbing musician, had long been a means of escape for him; now it was to be a genuine salvation. What could have been a fatal blow rebounded into the most astutely successful stage of his long voyage. Leonard emerged triumphant, enjoying an improbable third act in an industry where most are fortunate to experience one.

Now joining Leonard's tour team were singers the Webb Sisters. Born into a family of musicians in Kent, England, Charley and Hattie Webb are performers with expressive voices and plangent harmonies. The duo are multi-instrumentalists and songwriters. Their singing and playing (harp, guitar, mandolin, piano, and drums) draw from the folk and pop traditions of Britain and the United States.

Charley Webb: We two and Sharon had the chance to get to know one another in 2007 when we did some songwriting together. Then at the beginning of 2008 Hattie and I were in Los Angeles again recording some songs for a new album with Peter Asher, and Sharon called us. Sharon said that Leonard was looking for musicians to go on tour with.

We met Sharon at the studio where the rest of the band were already rehearsing songs. In theory we intended to sing together in three-part harmony (as we had done when writing together the year before). Except this time Sharon was suffering from an extremely sore throat and

had nearly lost her voice. So Roscoe [Beck, the musical director] chose some songs such as "Dance Me To The End Of Love," "Take This Waltz," and "Closing Time," and we two sang along with the band.

It was quite relaxed, actually. We had no particular expectations of what would happen that day and we didn't know that Leonard and Roscoe had already been searching for the right singers for some time. Our approach was very much enjoy the day and see what happens … We played some of our own songs to Roscoe and he asked us to come back and sing with Leonard on a different day. We returned, with instruments again, and sang some of the same songs with Leonard and band and then Roscoe suggested a few more. Then we played Leonard some of our songs live with our guitar and harp. *(2014)*

Hattie Webb: The first tour was exciting. For me there was a sense of anticipation, an unwrapping of each song, an unveiling. We were being personally acquainted with Leonard's incredible body of work and also each other. Sometimes we would sit in a round of sofas and listen to the original recording. The songs would be coming out of the rehearsal room mixing desk speakers while we absorbed the previous incantation, allowing the space for what we could bring to the song in this present time. *(2014)*

The Webb Sisters have played more than three hundred concerts to date with Leonard's live band during its recent record-breaking tours. Charley and Hattie are spotlighted nightly during their moving performances of "If It Be Your Will."

Fedora adorer. Portrait by Ethan Hill, 2000.

Charley Webb: Toward the end of rehearsals, Leonard asked us to listen to "If It Be Your Will" [from his *Various Positions* album] and work up a version of the song. We came up with our arrangement between rehearsals and then first played it to Leonard back stage in Hamilton and he asked if we would play it during the concert. I think it went into the set list two nights later, and it rarely strayed from its position near the end of the concert.

Our approach was to consider the song as a prayer or hymn and the vocal and instrumental arrangement that we made came together very naturally. *(2014)*

Sharon Robinson: I've really enjoyed singing with Charley and Hattie on tour. There have been many magical moments musically. I think their ethereal quality with Leonard's earthy baritone, and with me in the middle, adds up to a range of texture and tone that is very complementary. It's been a challenging gig in all the right ways, causing

us to stretch and become better at what we do. And it's been a lot of fun. *(2014)*

There are musicians, friends, pals, record-business survivors, poets, and experts along with the tearful witnesses who can testify about a performance artist named Leonard Cohen.

Kim Fowley: One of the elements in the sound of Leonard Cohen began just after he completed his second or third album in 1970 with a band that implemented female backing singers onstage with him. This continues from Donna Washburn to Jennifer Warnes in 1972 to the Webb Sisters in 2013. It's Svengali and Trilby. The idea of the older crazy man having control over these young women. And the closest thing to God is an older man who has an ego and a control mechanism that they worship. Hugh Hefner has it. Sean Connery has it. Paul Newman had it. All these older men carry this authority. And a lot of these guys came of age in very traditional male eras and decades.

Another reason John Hammond and Clive Davis signed Leonard to Columbia in 1967 was that you had guilt in those days. "Let's get this Leonard Cohen in there to offset the sales of Gary Puckett and the Union Gap." Because that was white-bread goy stuff, even though Gary was a great singer and Jerry Fuller wrote great songs. But Puckett didn't have stink, poetry, doomsday, and lesbian girlfriends in turtlenecks in his demographic.

In the early nineties I'm in Vancouver. I was a speaker at a music conference. It was a Juno Awards function. I saw Leonard again. Myself and a date were whisked in to see Leonard Cohen perform. Who, by the way, is a great live performer. It was Jim Morrison meets Shakespeare. He had that Shakespearean presence and that gothic thing, and the darkness and the poetry. *(2013)*

John Lissauer: One of the reasons for his popularity and worldwide audience that continues to expand, Leonard is the most committed performer and artist. I mean, he's the most serious and sincere. He never loses concentration. He takes responsibility for his stuff. And he's only gotten more generous and more complete. And now, he's letting the full Cohen out. Before it used to be a bit of the dark side only. Now, as he says, he's letting the light shine through. And the humor, and the humanity and the twinkle is there. It is much more complete.

And it is less planned and more spontaneous than ever before. His body of work is ridiculous, you know. It really is. Leonard is one of those artists everyone knew was brilliant but just didn't catch on in a big way. *(2013)*

On April 17, 2009, Leonard and his touring company delivered a galvanizing set at the Coachella Festival in Indio, Southern California.

James Cushing: I first saw Leonard Cohen perform at Coachella, the same night that Paul McCartney headlined. "Hallelujah" functioned for the Cohen crowd the way "Hey Jude" functioned for the larger crowd gathered for the former Beatle.

Right: Waldbühne, Berlin, August 18, 2010.

Opposite: The "sublime" Webb Sisters (Charley, left, and Hattie, center) and Sharon Robinson (right) at the Coachella Festival, Indio, California, April 17, 2009.

Both songs were anthems, serious sing-alongs that allowed every one of us to put our hands over our hearts and be grateful idealists. Millennials for whom Cohen had until that moment been a name in a reference book were openly weeping.

I had grown up with the music of Leonard Cohen and Paul McCartney, but had never seen either of them live. Two master songwriters, two genius performers: the extraverted Liverpool charmer, the introverted Canadian refugee. Cohen played as the sunset drenched the polo grounds in orange and pink. McCartney played against the deep desert night, and thousands la-la-la-la-la-la-la'd with him lustily on "Hey Jude." But as Cohen sang, I stood next to a young woman for whom Cohen was mostly a name in a book. When he came to "Hallelujah," she was in tears, and the crowd was quietly, respectfully singing along. Cohen's song had become "Hey Jude" for introverts. *(2014)*

Hattie Webb: Coachella was a very different experience. When in a theater there is a tighter experience of space, a sense of security within the walls. Music has reverberated in the stone and fabric for many years. You feel free to create in such a welcoming environment. When in a larger arena or at an outdoor festival there is a wider expanse and not such a defined space for one to exist. The acoustics can be a technical challenge because sound travels out and there is a sense of it traveling away from you. There is beauty in finding your voice within that space, too – recognizing the expanse and being able to sing from a place you can find within yourself. Finding some sense of security within the walls of oneself and feeling the risk of being in that space and working with it anyway. Sometimes in the larger venues, audiences seem to be freer; there's more room to dance and people sing along. So being on stage in the larger spaces can also mean more crowd excitement and participation, which we love! *(2014)*

Above: Portrait by Ann Johansson, 2001.

Opposite: On stage at Coachella, April 17, 2009.

Overleaf: Passing through. Leeds Arena, Leeds, UK, September 7, 2013 (main photo); Beacon Theatre, New York, February 19, 2009 (inset, left); Glastonbury Festival, UK, June 29, 2008 (inset, right).

"When I was last on this stage, I was sixty years old - just a kid with a crazy dream. Since then I've taken a lot of Prozac, Paxil, Wellbutrin, Ritalin ... I've also studied the religions and philosophies, but cheerfulness kept breaking through."

– LC, on stage, 2008/2009

Allan Showalter, founder and "operator" of 1HeckOfaGuy.com (the "other Leonard Cohen website"), analyzes the components that make a twenty-first-century Leonard Cohen concert such an unforgettable experience.

Allan Showalter: The fedora and suit that have become Leonard Cohen's trademark (and the model for the costuming of his band, backup singers, and many of the tour staff) since the 2008 tour are emblematic of the effort and care he has taken in constructing the most recent iteration of his performance artist persona. He may have told his biographer Sylvie Simmons, "Darling, I was born in a suit," but he assuredly didn't always wear it on stage. As Susan Musmanno, backup singer on the 1970 tour, put it, "I never knew the dapper Leonard Cohen. That was a later incarnation."

Nor did the Canadian singer-songwriter always run onto the stage to begin a concert and depart from that same stage three to four hours later via a unique combination of skipping and dancing that would make any other entertainer look ridiculous but seems elegance embodied when executed by Cohen at every show for the past six years. Not a bad look for a guy who was forced to begin touring again at age seventy-four.

The distinctive clothing and the stage entry and exit methodologies are, in fact, components of an extensively planned, carefully enacted strategy for Leonard Cohen's presentation of himself and his music. Cohen's professionalism and his frequently articulated long-held fear of the "risks of humiliation" inherent in concerts have driven him to create a finely tuned music program with elements that are as carefully and consciously designed as, albeit less spectacular than, Lady Gaga's costume changes, Pink Floyd's Flying Pig, or the Flaming Lips' Hamster Ball. Both factors were especially pronounced in 2008, when he was seriously concerned that few would be interested in his return to the stage.

Of course, there is more to it than a hat and skipping. Cohen himself undergoes a transformation from civilian to professional performer when he ascends the stage.

A crucial but often overlooked element that enhances Cohen's live shows, making them special in a way his albums can't match, comprises those instances in which he is interacting with the audience without offering a song. He, for example, routinely thanks the audience for their attention and hospitality and, at least lately, promises to "give you everything we got." He often conjures up a city- or venue-specific anecdote, he typically introduces band members once each set, and he tells crowds who sing along with "So Long, Marianne," "Ah, you sing so pretty." Most memorable are the blessings that end most of his shows. The final benediction at the Philadelphia show on May 12, 2009 is representative: "We don't know when we'll be back again this way, so, until then, take care, friends. The weather's kinda tricky, so don't catch a cold. If you've got to fall, try to fall on the side of luck. And may you be surrounded by friends and family. And if this is not your lot, may the blessings find you in your solitude."

And finally, the concerts, especially those of the past few years, are rich in comic content that rarely if ever appears on an album.

In 2010, Cohen's stage introduction of drummer Rafael Gayol grew ever longer and more elaborate over the course of several concerts until it became a saga:

```
"On the drums, like any great drummer,
a sculptor of silence, laying it down,
bringing it home, putting it to bed,
clipping its toenails,
tucking it in, kissing it goodnight,
smothering it with a pillow,
arrested and sent to prison,
recruited by the Aryan Brotherhood,
disillusioned by the uneven quality
of their tattoos,
converting to Judaism,
disillusioned once again,
spending his final days in a halfway house
for broken vegetarians,
the prince, the priest, the poet of precision,
Rafael Bernardo Gayol."
```

Attending a Leonard Cohen concert is transformative – by design. *(2014)*

Opposite, top: Serenading guitarist Javier Mas, Fox Theatre, Detroit, November 26, 2012.

Opposite, bottom: Backed by "the poet of precision," drummer Rafael Gayol, Sint-Pietersplein, Gent, Belgium, August 12, 2012.

For those who have not attended "the Leonard Cohen Experience," there is no small ecstasy to be found in a number of live DVDs that capture him at various times and places in his musical journey.

Beginning with *Live at the Isle of Wight 1970* and on through the recent performances captured in *Live in London* and *Songs from the Road*, Leonard has been exhaustively documented, the shambolic troubadour of the early seventies evolving into a fashionista stepping out of the pages of *GQ*.

Spring 2014 saw the publication of *Leonard Cohen on Leonard Cohen: Interviews and Encounters*, edited by Jeff Burger. I asked Burger if he had any theories about the constantly expanding Leonard demographic and the fairly recent increase in foot traffic at his shows.

Jeff Burger: There is some discussion in the book about what led to Cohen's late-period success. His own answer is that "beyond a general sense of gratitude I don't really analyze the mechanism. I'm just happy that it's going well."

Partly, it may be just that once a media phenomenon gains traction, it tends to build momentum. But while Cohen has been an important artist for decades, starting with his debut album, he really is better now – his voice is better, his band is better.

Lately, I've been watching *Songs from the Road* and *Live in London*, two recent DVDs that I think contain some of his best performances ever. "Tower Of Song" and "Hallelujah" are just two of the great songs that receive fine readings on these videos. *(2014)*

Kathi Flood: Live in London brought me the comfort of campfire songs cured for half a century and served up sweet and fresh. We early-end Baby Boomers memorized "Suzanne" in 1967 and still hold those lyrics complete. Through all the traveling, career building and memorization of PIN numbers in half a century of living our lives, the intensity of these lullabies still lives within us.

Leonard Cohen's work is a unique flavor of entertainment and enlightenment that lies in the twilight zone between poetry and music, between sentimentality and blunt truth, between 1967 and 2014. He rejects the dominant cynical chill of today's word masters with their gimmicks and branding. Leonard Cohen's music is skip-a-rock graceful, allowing us the blessed vulnerability and communalism that we must suppress in this techno-cursed world. *(2014)*

Music historian Warren Zanes explains Leonard's unique part in the birth of the Oscar-winning 2013 film *20 Feet from Stardom*, a documentary about backing singers.

Warren Zanes: While working as consulting producer on *20 Feet from Stardom*, I had many long conversations with the producer Gil Friesen. The film was Gil's idea, his mission. … His starting point was Leonard Cohen and the backup singers that have often played a special role in his sound and in the internal dramatics of his material.

More specifically, the film was actually born during a Leonard Cohen performance. Gil had smoked some pot before the show. As the evening's music got under way, Gil found himself focused on those singers, Cohen's Greek chorus, used as only a poet would use them. Gil drifted into their world, and stayed there. Soon enough he was on the phone with *Rolling Stone* publisher Jann Wenner, describing an idea for a film. Later, to Morgan Neville [the film's director], he said, "It was the most expensive joint I'd ever smoked."

At the end of the day, however, with the film a breakout success, I think Cohen's inspiration cannot be underestimated. Countless are the examples of artists who have used backup singers to thicken their sound or sweeten a chorus. And, of course, many have used singers for call-and-response within a song. But Cohen has consistently used his singers to maximum effect. The recent release of his 1970 Isle of Wight performance, directed by Murray Lerner, provides solid evidence. Those singers are characters, commentators, at times watching him in his human folly, wryly noting details that might have slipped his notice. It is all done with subtlety, but it is orchestrated by a man and musician who isn't content to leave the poet's tools at the door as he goes to work on the musician's stage. He shows us all we need to know about how much those voices can mean. *(2013)*

Royal Albert Hall, London, November 17, 2008. The Live in London DVD was filmed at the 02 Arena four months earlier.

LEONARD COHEN
LIVE IN LONDON

LEONARD COHEN
SONGS FROM THE ROAD

"I was looking at life-expectancy tables, and I could probably do another seven or eight years. I don't know, friends, if we'll ever meet again - no one can know that - but tonight we'll give you everything we've got."
— LC, on stage, 2012/2013

In 2011 Leonard took an extended break from touring to record a new studio album with songwriter and producer Patrick Leonard. *Old Ideas* was released in January 2012.

Allan Showalter: Old Ideas is Leonard Cohen's most successful realization (thus far) of his goal to create art with universal application and impact by telling his personal story with absolute authenticity. He accomplishes this by presenting his experiences stripped of boasts, apologies, sentimentality, musical ornamentation, or any other potential distractions. Throughout his career, Cohen has submitted himself "to the anvil of rhythm and rhyme," creating, revising, and polishing lines and motifs only to ruthlessly eliminate them – not because the results weren't clever or pleasing but because they were not absolutely essential. *(2014)*

Jim Devlin: There's such an emotional rollercoaster of a thread running through *Old Ideas*, like a backbone connecting the very tissue and DNA of each song's textures and timbres. The honesty of the words can be breathtaking at times – just read the lyric of "Show Me The Place" or "Different Sides" out loud, well sotto voce perhaps, and tell me you can't but be holding back a sigh or even perhaps a sob.

Leonard has spoken about not wanting to write a song that wouldn't be popular. I think "Crazy To Love You" is a great song and should be more popular than it may be right now. He sings it solo backed by his own acoustic guitar, grippingly, heart-stoppingly so, and so evocative of "If It Be Your Will." Followed by "Come Healing" and the Webb Sisters' angelic harmonies, it reminds me of that perfect two-song sequence that starts side two of *Songs of Love and Hate*: "Love Calls You By Your Name" and "Famous Blue Raincoat."

An important part of a musician's craft is the art of timing. Thus, with "Different Sides," the closing track, Leonard brings his ideas on the album to a satisfactory conclusion – that slow fade-out helping us to draw a line under all those various contradictions and arguments and denials, and the rest, of the previous forty-odd minutes. And that change up from the minor, in the verse, to the major, in the chorus – "Both of us say ..." – gives us an exit strategy out of that emotional maelstrom. Like a sigh of relief. Yeah, a big sigh. *(2014)*

Above: Promoting Old Ideas, Paris, January 2012.

Opposite: "I love to speak with Leonard / He's a sportsman and a shepherd / He's a lazy bastard / Living in a suit." "Going Home" from Old Ideas (2012). Royal Hospital, Kilmainham, Dublin, September 14, 2012.

Anthony J. Reynolds: I didn't like *Old Ideas*. I felt it lacked focus, conviction, and the production was poor. It had some wonderful songs but they were much better served live. "Darkness," for instance. I thought this sounded magisterial live but the recorded version was so ... limp. The record lacked cohesion, too, I thought. I suppose the title was misleading in a way. I took it to mean "old ideas" as in "eternal ideas." But it actually sounded more like a scrapbook to me. *(2014)*

Fans may have had differing views of the album, but the reviews were almost unanimously positive. Writing for the *Telegraph* in the UK, Neil McCormick singled out "Going Home," the opening track, for special attention.

Neil McCormick: Writing in the third person about his struggles with his muse, Cohen slyly describes himself as "a lazy bastard living in a suit" but his legendarily slow working methods have less to do with sloth than depth, precision, and judgment, the exacting standards of poetic genius. The song that emerges from this particular struggle is "Going Home," an elegiac act of surrender, in which there is little doubt about the final destination.

With producer Patrick Leonard and other trusted collaborators, he has (thankfully) expanded on the keyboard plods which have been his favored backdrop since 1988's *I'm Your Man*. *(2012)*

Although the first song and the cover of *Old Ideas* (showing him relaxing in his backyard) might suggest otherwise, Leonard did not entirely suppress his wanderlust during this hiatus between tours. In October 2011 he traveled to Oviedo in northern Spain to receive the Prince of Asturias Award for Letters, the country's highest literary honor. He gave a typically gracious acceptance speech entitled "How I Got My Song," in which he explained the twin Spanish influences on his career – of Federico García Lorca and the unnamed Flamenco player who taught him the guitar when he was a teenager.

Leonard and "the world's quietest band" (as musical director Roscoe Beck described it) hit the road again in August 2012. The Old Ideas tour bounced between Europe and North America, with a final leg in Australia and New Zealand in late 2013.

Prince of Asturias Award ceremony, Oviedo, Spain, October 21, 2011.

"Everything that you have found favorable in my work comes from this place. Everything, everything that you have found favorable in my songs and my poetry is inspired by this soil."

— LC, from "How I Got My Song," 2011

Anthony J. Reynolds: When I first saw Cohen live, in Valencia [in September 2009], it was a disaster. I was in a raw emotional state and Cohen himself fell ill a few songs in. I then arranged to see him in France, but again he was taken ill and the concert canceled. Finally, Cohen played my hometown, Cardiff, in 2013, and thanks to the kindness of Sharon Robinson I was able to attend the concert in ideal circumstances.

I'd been disappointed by *Old Ideas* and my expectations were low. I felt Cohen had become a public commodity almost and I was fretful at the length of the show. I was wrong; my fears were groundless. It was the most transcendental performance I've ever experienced. It seemed to happen outside of regular time. It could have been five minutes long or forever. Cohen's commitment to every moment was unflinching and staggering. He sang beautifully, too. I was elevated and entranced. The group truly served the songs in a way I'd never known. I didn't want it to end. *(2014)*

Charley Webb: The band transitioned between the first tour (2008–2010) and the second tour, also known as the Old Ideas world tour. The first time around we had Dino Soldo in the band, who brought his zesty, energetic performance to the stage, along with his saxophone, clarinet, and electronic instruments (keyboards, EWI, Eigenharp). The rest of the band was the same apart from Bob Metzger, one of Leonard's trusty side men from many years before. Bob's bluesy, gutsy solos soared during songs like "Bird On The Wire" and his memory for details was relied upon by us all. Bob's wife at the time, Leanne Ungar (who also has a long history of working with Leonard as a recording engineer), was the band's lovely and stoic live monitor engineer, side of stage.

For the Old Ideas tour, we met Mitch Watkins for the first time, fresh from the hospital after a big surgery. We all arrived in Los Angeles earlier than scheduled because Leonard had brought forward the rehearsals, wanting to make sure we and he were all fully prepared on old and new songs. Mitch brought his incredible groove guitar, which drove the band in a whole new way on the rhythmic songs and also flowed so gracefully on the sensitive songs, not forgetting his beautiful inspired solos, also. Then, while we lost Dino for this tour, we gained the incredible violin tones and great humor of Alex Bublitchi (whom we had got to know at the Asturias awards the year before). In my mind, Alex awoke a part of Leonard's early music that we had not been able to touch upon live previously without the violin. Alex and guitarist Javier Mas's harmonic partnership of supportive arrangements also created a new musical bed on which Leonard's vocals could glide. *(2014)*

Jim Devlin: As a performance artist, Leonard takes his audience in, draws them in close. He has an unerring knack of connecting one to one with his audience. He transmits on such a personal level. Even to the back rows. A big screen helps, of course, but you can close your eyes and Leonard can be right there. Thanks to Leanne Ungar, the sound systems in the 2008–2013 concerts were uniquely excellent in rendering even the biggest arena an intimate space. *(2014)*

The Old Ideas tour ended on December 21, 2013 at the Vector Arena in Auckland, New Zealand, bringing to a close a five-year cycle of concerts. During this golden period Leonard and his band "gave everything they'd got" more than 370 times, and a burgeoning community of fans new and old received it gratefully.

10. HOW WE GOT HIS SONGS

"There are always meaningful songs for somebody. People are doing their courting, people are finding their wives, people are making babies, people are washing their dishes, people are getting through the day, with songs that we may find insignificant. But their significance is affirmed by others. There's always someone affirming the significance of a song by taking a woman into his arms or by getting through the night. That's what dignifies the song. Songs don't dignify human activity. Human activity dignifies the song."

– LC, 1992

Notwithstanding the rapturously received concerts of recent years, it is the songs themselves that lie at the heart of the Leonard Cohen experience.

Alan Light: As far as his catalogue, Leonard Cohen has crossed over into this legendary mythic sort of status. He is especially revered by so many other writers and songwriters who talk about him with such a sense of awe and worship that I think it became, as these things do, an event. That there was a meaning to going to see Leonard, or listening to a Leonard song, or using it in a movie.

There was the rediscovery around the alt-rock movement and Kurt Cobain shouting him out and Trent Reznor using him on the Oliver Stone soundtrack [to *Natural Born Killers* in 1994] and this sense of: Here was this cool, dark old guy that did have a relationship to where those guys were creatively. That was an audience that picked up on that stuff. And he's held the coolness. That's the main thing. In his own strange, skipping-onto-stage way, I think that now people look at him as such a badass in a way you never would have anticipated. I don't think there was any way to see it coming. *(2013)*

Allan Showalter: Today's music world is full of butterflies. Many artists are in the spotlight for only a moment, with just one throwaway hit, and then we never hear of them again. Leonard has released records over six decades. His long, productive career has given us a unique chance to examine his lyrics from his teenage years right through to the wisdom of a man who at eighty is still full of life.

I often find it very touching to listen to his recent live versions of songs that he wrote and first performed more than four decades ago. The lyrics may be the same, but the time that has passed is reflected, not just in his voice and his interpretation, but in the essential nature of the songs. He makes us all, his elder fans, look back in our lives. And I don't think many of us survive his reciting of "A Thousand Kisses Deep" without tears.

In my opinion, Leonard Cohen is an artist whose material carries over centuries; his listeners and readers can return to him at various points in their lives and always find something new in his work. His texts have several layers and offer possibilities for various interpretations.

Cohen said as much in an interview at the beginning of his singing career: "The words [in my songs] are completely empty and any emotion can be poured into them. Almost all my songs can be sung any way. They can be sung as tough songs or as gentle songs or as contemplative songs or as courting songs."

Opposite: "I'm turning tricks, I'm getting fixed, I'm back on Boogie Street." "A Thousand Kisses Deep" from Ten New Songs (2001). Portrait by Gered Mankowitz, 1994.

Pages 186-7: "I tried jeans, but I never felt comfortable ... So I just finally surrendered to the fact I felt most comfortable in a suit." Portrait in his backyard by Henry Diltz, 1993.

"Leonard Cohen creates songs that are mannequins. He may dress them himself one way or another, draping them with concepts that range from spiritual convictions to sexual desire to apocalyptic visions, but he is always clear that the listener is allowed, or, more accurately, required to make his or her own choices about how to receive the song. The result of this interaction is a perfect fit – a musical work that resonates with each member of the audience because each individual has intuitively tailored Cohen's song for that person."
— Allan Showalter, 2014

"As far as songwriting - I think we all borrow from each other.
I don't know. I listen to songs very critically, and I find
for me it's so often a line or a phrase or an attitude or a moment in
someone's work that really touches me. I'm interested less in
the whole work and more in just one clear, simple statement of
somebody's interior situation. Mostly, you find yourself thinking
about the urgency of expression of an emotion, and you have your
tools at hand that you've sharpened over the years - all the
skills and talents and tricks.
    The mind burns with ideas. It's never given us to know
exactly how these ideas arise or fall - they seem to rise and fall
involuntarily. We all burn in different ways, and we all clutter
the thing up in a special way. I have no idea of the larger patterns."
                                                                    - LC, 1975

And grasping his songs is not an intellectual task. Instead, Cohen says, "it's like understanding an embrace." Going on, he explains: "It's like that Jesus verse in 'Suzanne,' everyone knows what that means, but nobody can say what it means. And it's that kind of event that I'm interested in."

The first Leonard Cohen song that won me over was one of his songs that appeared on a movie soundtrack – and I didn't even see the movie until a year or two later.

"Waiting For The Miracle" was released on Leonard Cohen's 1992 *The Future* album and appeared on the *Wonder Boys* soundtrack eight years later. It is still one of my favorite Cohen songs, but the reason it proved so pivotal in my music life had as much to do with the context in which I heard it as the quality of the music. Here's the back story: Julie and I met, fell in love, and – nine years, two husbands, one wife, and two careers later – got together to spend an outrageously wonderful twenty years together before I lost her to breast cancer diagnosed the week of our wedding.

I first heard "Waiting For The Miracle" two years after Julie died; it was on the *Wonder Boys* soundtrack album playing on a CD player in a car belonging to one of the first women I dated.

The woman was a memory within a month; "Waiting For The Miracle" was the beginning of my affection for Leonard Cohen's music that endures today. Why? Well, there was that voice – it was so deep that I could feel its vibrations, and most importantly, it was an adult voice singing an adult song. I didn't grasp all the lyrics the first time, but I certainly got some of them.

It was a dignified song presented in a dignified way. It spoke to the value of going on even though – or perhaps because – life is a difficult journey through a vale of tears that inevitably ends badly. And, God, it was sexy. *(2014)*

Curtis Hanson: I've been a fan since Leonard's debut album. *L.A. Confidential* and *Wonder Boys* are the most personal movies I've ever made. I look on the music and song selection as part of telling the story. I'd rather let the words of Leonard Cohen take me where they take me. "Waiting For The Miracle" expresses where Grady's character is heading during the party scene in which it plays. It's the turnaround. Grady is not going to

be waiting any more, he's gonna do something. The miracle is gonna happen. *(2000)*

Jarkko Arjatsalo: Leonard Cohen's music is popular worldwide, in all age, economic, and social groups. He is also highly esteemed among the artist community, and one of the most covered artists in the world.

After launching the Files, we wanted to make a complete list of cover versions. In the late 1990s, we estimated that there could be as many as two to three hundred cover songs; and this was also Leonard's impression. How little we knew! As of the beginning of the year 2014, we have found and listed no fewer than 2,760 covers (and there may still be many more not yet identified). More are being released at a brisk pace – several hundred every year. The updated list is at *www. leonardcohenfiles.com/coverlist.php*.

Artists have recorded Cohen's songs on all continents, in such countries as China, Taiwan, Korea, India, Japan, Iran, and Madagascar. The songs are in every style one can imagine: punk, heavy metal, reggae, rock, blues, jazz, country …

The most covered song is now "Hallelujah," with 550 officially released versions, followed by "Suzanne" (280), which for forty years used to be at the top. *(2014)*

LC: I think Noel Harrison's version of "Suzanne" was the first. That came out before Judy Collins. I was knocked out that anybody would want to do one of my songs at all. Usually when I hear somebody doing one of my songs, my whole critical faculties are suspended. I never judge them – I'm just tickled that somebody's doing it. I didn't hear Brian Hyland's "So Long, Marianne." I love Tim Hardin's version of "Bird On The Wire." And I love Joe Cocker's version. *(1985)*

Jarkko Arjatsalo: We also know of eighty tribute albums, which is an amazing mark of respect. The complete list is at *www.leonardcohenfiles.com/ covers.html*. All or almost all tracks on those albums are Cohen songs, performed by one or more artists or bands, often translated into languages other than English. For example, Maciej Zembaty covered more than sixty Cohen songs on his ten albums, and brought Leonard's work into general notice in Poland. *(2014)*

"The hardest thing about touring with Leonard was that he spoiled me for everyone else. He treats everyone in his universe with the same degree of respect and kindness. It's normal for people in the music industry to accept dealing with assholes as a necessary evil. Leonard blows that theory out of the water. After working with him I simply made a conscious pact not to work with assholes. I've turned down a fair amount of work because of it."

– Perla Batalla, 2014

Leonard's "staying power" has been the subject of countless theories; is it sexual, intellectual, philosophical? Those who have worked closest to him have their own takes on his enduring resonance.

Sharon Robinson: Leonard's music and the way he performs it inspire a wide range of emotions in people, from unbridled excitement to profound reflection. I think there are many things that contribute to that. A lot of work goes into it, needless to say the writing, and then the performing of the music. Leonard is an extremely generous performer, giving everything in every concert, as does the band, a group of dedicated musicians at the top of their game. Leonard is meticulous in the casting and the design of the show, just as he is in the writing. We've been privileged to receive some incredibly moving reactions and stories from people around the world about the effect the concerts have had on them. *(2014)*

Perla Batalla: After hundreds of shows I could still get swept away by his storytelling. There is a little held belief (probably because it's mine) that the real attribute that makes a woman fall in love with a man is his stories and how they are told … it helps explain the droves of women dedicated to a humble poet.

When it comes to poetry and art, there are two approaches to interpretation. One approach – a common one when it comes to Cohen – is the attempt to tunnel into the poet's muse and discover exactly what he was referring to in a line or a lyric. I don't really care why Leonard wrote a line … it might not even be relevant to him today in the way it once was. For me the richness lies in letting

the work cause me to examine what it means to me and me alone. This personal authenticity can make a song – or any work of art – change meaning as one's life evolves and matures. Art resonates when it is allowed to be personal. *(2014)*

Hattie Webb: I believe Leonard sees the feminine through the eyes of the divine. And when we hear his music, we feel a connection with how we know ourselves in our deepest knowing. Leonard has an eye for elegance and when women feel he is singing for them, I don't think anyone could help but glow with gratitude and admiration!

People have said to me that they felt they went on an emotional journey with Leonard in the presence of his concert. That his songs and choice of flow and order gave them space and time, the chance to feel, to grieve, to rejoice, to hope. And they went home feeling that they had had a cathartic experience. And felt grateful for Leonard's gift and also for the gift of being with their own experience. *(2014)*

Charley Webb: It certainly feels like a spiritual evening each night on stage. The energy from the audience and from the room in many ways informs the performance. At the beginning of the LC tours it took a while for us on stage to adjust to experiencing the outpouring of emotion from the audience during the performance. It's not an easy thing to be devoid of reaction when you witness intense human emotion! *(2014)*

"If it be your will / That I speak no more / And my voice be still / As it was before / I will speak no more." "If It Be Your Will" from Various Positions (1984). Mount Baldy, 1995.

Other passionate "Cohen heads," devoted chroniclers, and industry insiders have additional theories as to how Leonard has managed to grow and nurture a fan base over the forty-seven years since the release of *Songs of Leonard Cohen.*

Kim Fowley: When we look at the last twenty years of Leonard Cohen, what has happened is father-figure rock idolatry. It started with Jerry Garcia, who became the father that all the kids of divorced families wished they had. And that was his appeal, that they all wanted a dad like Jerry. And Jerry played the father that nobody had. And that's what happens when they see Leonard Cohen. He's the father that nobody had. *(2013)*

Allan Showalter: Since the late sixties Leonard Cohen's music has been attracting fans, most of whom, from my highly unscientific observation, have continued to be fans. (I'd wager Cohen has lost more fans to death than to dissatisfaction with his music.) Folks who began following Cohen in the seventies and eighties were joined by those who first heard his work in the nineties and the true delinquents like me who didn't have our come-to-Lenny moment until the twenty-first century. From that sum, subtract the fatalities and the few musically disillusioned or burnt-out souls, then add the family members and friends coerced into attending a concert by a proselytizing true

believer, and you've got yourself a decent-sized target population. Factor in the pent-up demand (Cohen hadn't toured in fifteen years when he opened his 2008 concert series), and all those sellout shows don't seem so surprising.

In 1993 (the last year Cohen toured prior to 2008), the Internet was barely noticeable to Cohen fans unless they were the sort that could operate in hypertext. By 2008, however, the Internet was ubiquitous, and even fans who were Leonard's age were comfortable enough online to follow his tours, read reviews of the concerts, and watch good- to excellent-quality videos of his performances, often within hours of a concert's completion. *(2014)*

Jarkko Arjatsalo: Today, there are more than a thousand pages at *www.leonardcohenfiles.com.* In 2002 we also set up the Leonard Cohen Forum (*www.leonardcohenforum.com*). Still growing, the Forum now has 28,000 registered members who have posted more than 300,000 messages. Total number of hits to the front pages of these sites is over 15 million. With the worldwide, very active Forum network and excellent cooperation with Leonard and his management, we are often the first to announce the news.

My Files is not the only website dedicated to Leonard Cohen, far from it. Carter Page was the pioneer in the early nineties, and today there are several other noteworthy international websites hosted by Marie Mazur, Allan Showalter (DrHGuy), Patrice Clos, Tom Sakic, and many others. *(2014)*

However, Leonard Cohen fans come together in person as well as online.

Jarkko Arjatsalo: We have organized Leonard Cohen "Events" every two years since 1998 (in Lincoln in the UK, Montreal, Hydra, New York, Berlin, Edmonton, Krakow, Madison/Chicago, and Dublin); and a number of other meet-ups (including biennial gatherings on the island of Hydra). A recent invention is the Leonard Cohen Walking Weekend, held each year somewhere different in Europe, which was initiated by an active group of members.

The Event days are fully programed – Leonard Cohen songs performed by professional and amateur artists, poetry, films, sightseeing tours – but it is also important just to spend time together. The mix of different nationalities, generations, languages, and backgrounds of the participants offers endless chances to have fun in a most positive way. These gatherings have resulted in many lifelong friendships – and even a dozen marriages. *(2014)*

The smokey life: Filming Jennifer Warnes' "First We Take Manhattan" video, April 1987 (above); and in London before the premiere of the Bird on a Wire documentary, June 1974 (opposite).

"There's a kind of family that is gathered around my work. It's not fixed at my work, but merely uses it as a reference to their own lives and to their own very amusing and touching flirtations, communications, confessions, exchanges."
– LC, 1998

195

"I always had the sense of being in this for keeps, if your health lasts you. And you're fortunate enough to have the days at your disposal so you can keep on doing this. I never had the sense that there was an end. That there was a retirement or that there was a jackpot."

– LC, 1992

Scheduled for release in late 2014, a *Live in Ireland* DVD, featuring a pair of Dublin concerts from September 2013, provides further evidence that Leonard is still "in this for keeps." In January 2014 Roscoe Beck alluded to work he was doing on a new Leonard Cohen studio album and "maybe a little more touring with Leonard at the end of the year."

And so, thankfully, the trek of long-distance runner Leonard Cohen continues, with more people than ever helping him to carry the flame.

Left: Ice cool and carrying the flame. Portrait by Darcy Hemley, 2002.

Overleaf: On the streets of Los Angeles. Portrait by Paul Zollo, 2007.

ENVOI

During the last few decades, I ran into Leonard a handful of times around Los Angeles and Hollywood. I sat with him at a 1999 Tom Waits show at the Wiltern Theatre, and on occasion, we waved at each other at Canter's Delicatessen in the Fairfax district.

Our paths also crossed around a Sharon Robinson set at the Hotel Café in Hollywood, shortly before the last tour of Australia and New Zealand. There was a brief encounter with Leonard and son, Adam, at a café on Wilshire Boulevard.

During 2013 I gladly left him alone one afternoon when he was sitting at a nearby table with a very pretty woman at a local Greek restaurant I frequent in Larchmont Village. Not long after, I was walking around Larchmont one Sunday. I went into the Chan Dara Thai restaurant instead of picking up some fresh produce from the street vendors at the farmers' market.

As I departed, I was immediately greeted by heavy metal music scholar and environmental author/activist Lonn Friend. We were both extremely concerned about our hometown air. There was a whole different and sinister type of smog above us that has really tainted the inspirational Los Angeles skyline.

"Did you see Leonard Cohen?" Lonn asked me. "He was walking the farmers' market. I was standing next to my friend Krista's exotic cheese stand. I noticed him instantly. For the past two hours I'd been walking the market, directing strangers' eyes toward the white line festival taking place in the sky. It was a heavy day for chemtrails. I walked right up to Leonard Cohen and said, 'Hello, sir. It's an honor to meet you.' Then I looked up and said, 'So, what do you think of that?' Following my gaze, he looked up, paused, and said, 'Well, at least they're not dropping bombs.'"

Toward the end of 1974, I was present at an interview Leonard gave to poet Michael C Ford inside the Continental Hyatt House on Sunset Boulevard in West Hollywood. (The interview was published in an issue of the *Los Angeles Free Press* in January 1975.)

I was slated along with Justin Pierce of the *Hollywood Press* to interview Leonard next for *Melody Maker* and was struck by a memorable comment heard in their closing conversation.

Leonard revealed to Ford, "I don't really have any idea what the genesis for a song might be, or the emotion which causes it. It has something more to do with the appetite; it's like that moment when you suddenly realize you're hungry. I guess I'm hungry for something not yet created, so I go about making it."

At the conclusion of our interview with Leonard, he generously invited us to join him on a limo ride to the Canadian consulate in downtown Los Angeles. Leonard had some passport issues to sort out.

Besides some discussion about the Beatles, Allen Ginsberg, Ezra Pound, and someone named Lorca, I asked Leonard a question about girls and going steady with them. I figured this explorer and wordsmith just might have some answers for me.

Leonard fell silent for a while, and then slowly replied, "Relationships are complicated."

CONTRIBUTORS

Jarkko Arjatsalo is the founder and administrator of the Leonard Cohen Files website (www.leonardcohenfiles.com) and the Leonard Cohen Forum (www.leonardcohenforum.com). He also organizes the international Leonard Cohen Events held every two years since 1998.

Perla Batalla is a vocalist and composer. She first worked with Leonard Cohen as a backing singer in 1988. In 1993 Batalla issued a self-titled solo debut album and in 2005 she released *Bird on the Wire*, a tribute album to Leonard Cohen.

Hal Blaine is a drummer/percussionist and a member of the Rock and Roll Hall of Fame. He has played on countless iconic hit records by Elvis Presley, the Crystals, and the Byrds.

Paul Buckmaster is an arranger, composer, and record producer whose credits include David Bowie's "Space Oddity" and numerous Elton John albums. He has also supplied arrangements for Harry Nilsson's "Without You," Carly Simon's "You're So Vain," and the Rolling Stones' album *Sticky Fingers*, along with Leonard Cohen's *Songs of Love and Hate*.

Jeff Burger, a longtime magazine editor, edited *Springsteen on Springsteen: Interviews, Speeches, and Encounters* (2013), as well as *Leonard Cohen on Leonard Cohen: Interviews and Encounters* (2014).

Nick Cave started making music in the 1970s with the Birthday Party and has released more than twenty studio albums, including *Let Love In* (1994), *The Boatman's Call* (1997), and *Push the Sky Away* (2013). His published work includes the 1989 novel *And the Ass Saw the Angel*, and he also wrote the screenplay for the 2005 film *The Proposition*.

Fred Catero was a CBS/Columbia Records studio engineer from 1962 to 1972 and worked on the debut Leonard Cohen album. During his stint at the label's studios, Catero was on seminal sessions by Mel Tormé, Aretha Franklin, Barbra Streisand, and Santana. In the 1980s he formed Catero Records to focus on jazz artists including Herbie Hancock.

Julie Christensen became a Leonard Cohen backup vocalist in 1988 and toured with him for the next half decade. She is also seen in the documentary film *Leonard Cohen: I'm Your Man*. Christensen's debut solo album, *Love Is Driving*, came out in 1996. Other albums have followed, most notably *Soul Driver* (2000).

Chester Crill was a member of the band Kaleidoscope from 1966 to 1970.

Judy Collins has released more than thirty-five live and studio albums over the course of five decades. Collins gave Leonard Cohen's musical career an early boost by recording "Suzanne" and "Dress Rehearsal Rag" for her 1966 album *In My Life*.

James Cushing is a poet and has taught literature and creative writing at Cal Poly, San Luis Obispo, since 1989. He also hosts a weekly jazz and rock program on the college's radio station, KCPR-FM. He was Poet Laureate of San Luis Obispo from 2008 to 2010.

Charlie Daniels is a musician and songwriter. He played on the Johnston-produced Bob Dylan album *Nashville Skyline* and recorded and toured with Leonard Cohen from 1968 to 1970. Daniels cut his first solo album, *Charlie Daniels*, in 1971, and he has released thirty studio albums in total, the most recent being *Hits of the South* (2013).

Chris Darrow is a multi-instrumentalist and veteran recording artist and producer/music publisher. As a member of Kaleidoscope, he played on the debut Leonard Cohen album. In 1972 he released a debut solo album, *Artist Proof*, and in 2013 Darrow released *Island Girl* in collaboration with Max Buda.

Clive Davis was president of Columbia Records from 1967 to 1973, during which time he signed Leonard Cohen to the label. After Columbia he went on to found two new labels, Arista Records (in 1975) and J Records (in 2000). In 2000 he was inducted into the Rock and Roll Hall of Fame in the non-performer category. Since 2008 he has been Chief Creative Officer for Sony Music Entertainment.

Jim Devlin was editor of the Leonard Cohen Information Service Newsletter during the 1980s and early 1990s. He has since written three books on Leonard Cohen: *In Every Style of Passion* (1996), *Is This What You Wanted* (1997), and *Leonard Cohen: In His Own Words* (1998). After a career of more than thirty years teaching music, he retired in 2013.

Sandra Djwa is a cultural critic and biographer and is Professor Emerita at Simon Fraser University in British Columbia, Canada. Her books include *Professing English: A Life of Roy Daniells* (2002), which received the Royal Society Gold Medal for Literature (2002). Her latest publication, *Journey with No Maps: A Life of P. K. Page* (2012), received the Governor General's Award for Non-Fiction in 2013.

Kathi Flood is a visual artist and spoken-word performer in Los Angeles whose guerrilla sociology describes and categorizes contemporary urban life. She has been included in more than 250 exhibitions in the United States and Europe.

Kim Fowley has been an influential force in rock 'n' roll music since 1960, garnering well over a hundred gold and platinum records for his songwriting, music publishing, and record production skills. He can be heard as a DJ on Little Steven's Underground Garage via the SiriusXM satellite radio network.

John Hammond was a distinguished figure in twentieth-century popular music. In the 1950s he became a talent scout for Columbia Records and was responsible for discovering and nurturing, among others, Benny Goodman, Pete Seeger, Bob Dylan, Aretha Franklin, and Leonard Cohen. He became one of the inaugural inductees into the Rock and Roll Hall of Fame in 1986, a year before his death, aged seventy-six, in July 1987.

Curtis Hanson is a movie director and screenwriter. His films include *The Hand That Rocks the Cradle* (1992), *L.A. Confidential* (1997), for which he won an Oscar for Best Adapted Screenplay, and *Wonder Boys* (2000), which included the Leonard Cohen song "Waiting For The Miracle."

Robert Inchausti is a professor of English at Cal Poly, San Luis Obispo, and the author of five books, including *The Ignorant Perfection of Ordinary People* (1991), *Spitwad Sutras* (1993), and *Subversive Orthodoxy* (2005).

Bob Johnston is a record producer. Having started his production career in 1964 with Kapp Records, he joined Columbia the following year as a staff producer. He produced some of the milestone albums of the late 1960s and early 1970s, including Bob Dylan's *Highway 61 Revisited* (1965), *Blonde on Blonde* (1966), and *Nashville Skyline* (1969), Simon and Garfunkel's *Sounds of Silence* (1966), and Leonard Cohen's *Songs from a Room* (1969) and *Songs of Love and Hate* (1971).

Jim Keltner is an American drummer primarily known for his session work and touring with Bob Dylan, Neil Young, Crosby, Stills, Nash and Young, and Simon and Garfunkel. He has also recorded with artists as varied as Delaney & Bonnie and Friends, B. B. King, Booker T. Jones, the Ramones, the Rolling Stones, and Leonard Cohen.

Dan Kessel is a record producer, songwriter, publisher, vocalist, and multi-instrumentalist, who has recorded with a plethora of artists including John Lennon, Phil Spector, Dion, Leonard Cohen, Brian Wilson, Cher, Blondie, and the Ramones. Dan was on the leading edge of the original Los Angeles punk rock scene and later became co-owner of the Backstage Café in Beverly Hills.

David Kessel is a multi-instrumentalist, record producer, and an early pioneer in new media. He worked with Phil Spector for more than thirty years. David is the owner of the pop-culture website www.cavehollywood.com.

Kenneth Kubernik is the co-author, with his brother Harvey, of *A Perfect Haze: The Illustrated History of the Monterey International Pop Festival* (2011) and *Behind Closed Doors: The Music and Film Scene of Hollywood in the Sixties* (2014), and served as editorial consultant on Harvey's *Canyon of Dreams: The Magic and Music of Laurel Canyon* (2009). His writing has been featured in the *Los Angeles Times*, *Variety*, and *Hollywood Reporter*. He is currently writing a history of Weather Report.

Murray Lerner is a documentary film director and producer. His trend-setting musical documentaries include pivotal examinations of Isaac Stern, Miles Davis, the Newport Folk Festival (for which he received an Oscar nomination), Jimi Hendrix, the Doors, Jethro Tull, and the Who. Lerner directed and produced *Leonard Cohen Live at the Isle of Wight 1970*, released on DVD in 2009.

Alan Light is the author of *The Holy or the Broken: Leonard Cohen, Jeff Buckley and the Unlikely Ascent of "Hallelujah"* (2012). He is a former editor-in-chief of *Vibe* and *Spin* magazines, and a frequent contributor to *Rolling Stone* and the *New York Times*. Alan is the co-author of Gregg Allman's best-selling memoir, *My Cross to Bear*, and is a two-time winner of the ASCAP Deems Taylor Award for excellence in music writing.

John Lissauer is a musician and record producer. Originally a symphony clarinetist and jazz saxophonist, he had a short stint in the rock band Rhinoceros when they toured with Leon Russell. He produced Leonard Cohen's *New Skin for the Old Ceremony* and *Various Positions*, and was the musical director of his tours from 1974 to 1976.

Steven Marx is a retired professor of English at Cal Poly, San Luis Obispo. He has written three books: *Youth Against Age: Generational Strife in Renaissance Poetry* (1984), *Shakespeare and the Bible* (2000), and *Cal Poly Land: A Field Guide* (2002).

Neil McCormick is music critic for the *Telegraph* newspaper in the UK.

John Miller is a bassist and musical coordinator primarily known for his work on Broadway. From 1968 to 1979 he recorded with Al Kooper, Tim Buckley, Bette Midler, Lewis Furey, and Leonard Cohen. He also toured Europe and America with Cohen. He later became musical director and music coordinator for nearly one hundred Broadway musicals, including *Jersey Boys* and *Hairspray*.

Joni Mitchell is a musician, singer, songwriter, and artist. She released the first of her nineteen studio albums, *Song to a Seagull*, in 1968. Later albums such as the platinum-selling *Blue* (1971) and *Court and Spark* (1974) are often cited as being among the greatest ever made.

Ira Nadel is a professor of English at the University of British Columbia, Vancouver, and a Fellow of the Royal Society of Canada. His biography of Leonard Cohen, *Various Positions*, was published in 1996 (updated in 2006). He is currently completing a life of Philip Roth.

Andrew Loog Oldham is a record producer, music manager, and author. In 1963, he discovered the Rolling Stones, whom he managed and produced from 1963 to 1967. He is the author of acclaimed memoirs and in 2014 he was inducted into the Rock and Roll Hall of Fame as a non-performer.

Tony Palmer is an award-winning film, theater, and opera director and author. His many music documentaries include *200 Motels* (1971), about Frank Zappa, and *Bird on a Wire* (1974), about Leonard Cohen's 1972 tour.

Don Randi is a keyboardist/arranger and longtime member of the famed Wrecking Crew studio band. He is also the leader of fusion/jazz band Quest and proprietor of the Baked Potato jazz club in Studio City, California. His keyboard work has graced numerous recordings by producer Phil Spector and arranger Jack Nitzsche, among many others.

Anthony J. Reynolds is a musician and writer. From 1992 to 2002 he was a member of the British band Jack, and also released the solo albums *Neu York* (2004) and *British Ballads* (2007) and premiered the musical *A Small Spit of Land* in 2013. His books include *Leonard Cohen: A Remarkable Life* (2011).

Sharon Robinson first worked with Leonard Cohen as a background vocalist on the 1979 Field Commander Cohen tour and has since worked closely with Leonard on the albums *Ten New Songs* (2001) and *Dear Heather* (2004), as well as being a member of his 2008–2013 touring band. Robinson's 2008 debut solo album, was *Everybody Knows*, and her original compositions have also been featured in the movies *Wonder Boys*, *Natural Born Killers*, *Pump Up the Volume*, *Stakeout*, and *Land of Plenty*.

Stan Ross was the co-founder, with David S. Gold, of the legendary Gold Star Studios in Los Angeles, which operated from 1950 until 1984. He died in March 2011.

Allan Showalter, psychiatrist by training, hard-core dilettante by nature, and devotedly irreverent admirer of Leonard Cohen by cosmic serendipity, is responsible for 1HeckOfAGuy.com and DrHGuy.com – the preeminent Cohen-centered websites for enlightenment, allure, laughs, and alliterations.

Sylvie Simmons is an award-winning author and rock journalist who was born in London and currently lives in San Francisco. Her books include biographies of Neil Young and Serge Gainsbourg. Her latest book is *I'm Your Man: The Life of Leonard Cohen* (2012), which NPR named best biography of the year. When she's not writing about music, Sylvie writes songs and performs with a ukulele.

John Simon is a music producer, songwriter, composer, and instrumentalist. As a Columbia record producer, Simon worked on the debut Leonard Cohen album, *Cheap Thrills* by Big Brother and the Holding Company featuring Janis Joplin (1968), Simon and Garfunkel's *Bookends* (1968), and Blood, Sweat and Tears' *Child Is Father to the Man* (1968). Simon also produced the Band's *Music from Big Pink* (1968) and *The Band* (1969).

Phil Spector is a record producer and songwriter, primarily associated with his Wall of Sound production technique. He achieved worldwide fame in the 1960s, producing (and co-writing) iconic hits for acts such as the Crystals, the Ronettes, the Righteous Brothers, and Ike and Tina Turner. He also produced the Beatles' final album, *Let It Be*, in 1970. In 1977, he produced Leonard Cohen's *Death of a Ladies' Man*.

Suzanne Vega is a singer and songwriter. She has released eight studio albums, from *Suzanne Vega* in 1985 to *Tales from the Realm of the Queen of Pentacles* in 2014. Her best known songs include "Tom's Diner" and "Luka," both from her 1987 album *Solitude Standing*.

Jennifer Warnes is a Grammy- and Oscar-winning singer, songwriter, arranger, and record producer. She first toured with Leonard Cohen in 1972, before achieving prominence in her own right with hit singles including "Right Time Of The Night" (1977), "Up Where We Belong" (1982), a duet with Joe Cocker for *An Officer and a Gentleman*, and "(I've Had) The Time Of My Life" (1987), a duet with Bill Medley for *Dirty Dancing*. Her eight studio albums include the influential Leonard Cohen tribute *Famous Blue Raincoat* (1987).

The Webb Sisters are the vocalists, instrumentalists, and songwriters Charley and Hattie Webb. They were members of Leonard Cohen's 2008–2013 touring band, notable in particular for their stunning renditions of "If It Be Your Will." They have released three albums of their own: *Piece of Mind* (2000), *Daylight Crossing* (2006), and *Savages* (2011), and are working on a fourth album scheduled for release in 2014.

Sharon Weisz is a public relations professional in the music industry and has been the owner of W3 Public Relations in Los Angeles for more than thirty years. She served as publicist for Leonard Cohen during his 1988 tour in support of the album *I'm Your Man*, for which she also (inadvertently) shot the cover photo.

Ruth R. Wisse is the Martin Peretz Professor of Yiddish Literature and Professor of Comparative Literature at Harvard University.

Warren Zanes is a multi-tasking rock 'n' roll musician. Having made three records with 1980s band the Del Fuegos, he studied for a Ph.D. in Visual and Cultural Arts and took up professorships at several American universities, and he serves as vice president of education at the Rock and Roll Hall of Fame. He is the executive director of Steven Van Zandt's Rock and Roll Forever Foundation.

DISCOGRAPHY

By Jim Devlin with assistance from Jarkko Arjatsalo, Andy Jones, Maarten Massa, and Tom Sakic

STUDIO ALBUMS

Songs of Leonard Cohen, 1967

Recorded at Columbia Studios B, C, and E, New York

Produced by John Simon

Personnel
- Leonard Cohen: vocals, acoustic guitar
- Jimmy Lovelace: drums ("So Long, Marianne")
- Nancy Priddy: vocals ("Suzanne," "So Long, Marianne," "Hey, That's No Way To Say Goodbye")
- Willy Ruff: bass ("So Long, Marianne," "Stories Of The Street")

Additional musicians
- Members of Kaleidoscope: Chester Crill, Chris Darrow, Solomon Feldthouse, David Lindley:
- flute, mandolin, Jew's harp, violin, and a variety of Middle Eastern instruments ("Master Song," "Winter Lady," "Sisters Of Mercy," "So Long, Marianne," "Hey, That's No Way To Say Goodbye," "Stories Of The Street," "Teachers")

Cover art
- Machine: cover photo

Side one
"Suzanne"
"Master Song"
"Winter Lady"
"The Stranger Song"
"Sisters Of Mercy"

Side two
"So Long, Marianne"
"Hey, That's No Way To Say Goodbye"
"Stories Of The Street"
"Teachers"
"One Of Us Cannot Be Wrong"

Release date
December 27, 1967 (US/Canada);
February 1968 (UK/Europe)

Label and catalogue numbers
US/Canada Columbia CS 9533 (stereo),
CL 2733 (mono)
UK CBS SBPG 63241 (stereo),
CBS BPG 63241 (mono)

Highest chart position on release
US 83, Canada did not chart (DNC), UK 13

Notes
All songs written by Leonard Cohen.

John Hammond produced the initial recording sessions, but fell ill and was replaced by John Simon who also added string arrangements. The "Anima Sola" (a Mexican religious image) on the US/ Canada back cover is often mistaken for Joan of Arc. The UK vinyl edition instead featured liner notes by William David Sherman and the lyrics of "Suzanne" and "The Stranger Song."

Reissued on CD in 1990 (US CK 9533, Canada WCK 9533); and in 2001 (Europe SMM 505136 2).

Remastered and reissued on CD in 2007 with two bonus tracks (US/Canada/ Europe Columbia/Legacy 88697 04742 2), and liner notes by Anthony DeCurtis. The two extra songs, "Store Room" and "Blessed Is The Memory," were previously unreleased outtakes from the early, John Hammond–produced sessions for the album. Leonard performed these two songs in his 1976 tour of Europe.

Remastered US/Canada vinyl reissued in 2009 (Sundazed Music LP 5282); and in Europe in 2011 (Music on Vinyl MOVLP 326).

Songs from a Room, 1969

Recorded at Columbia Studio A, Nashville, Tennessee
Additional recording in a Paris studio ("The Partisan": girls' vocals, accordion)

Produced by Bob Johnston

Personnel
- Leonard Cohen: vocals, acoustic guitar
- Ron Cornelius: acoustic and electric guitars
- Charlie Daniels: acoustic guitar, bass, fiddle
- Elkin "Bubba" Fowler: acoustic guitar, bass, banjo
- Bob Johnston: keyboards
- Henry Zemel: Jew's harp

Additional musicians
- Accordion player, in Paris
- Three girl singers, in Paris

Cover art
- John Berg: cover photo
- Ira Friedlander: cover design

Side one
"Bird On The Wire"
"Story Of Isaac"
"A Bunch Of Lonesome Heroes"
"The Partisan"
"Seems So Long Ago, Nancy"

Side two
"The Old Revolution"
"The Butcher"
"You Know Who I Am"
"Lady Midnight"
"Tonight Will Be Fine"

Release date
April 7, 1969

Label and catalogue numbers
US/Canada Columbia 9767 (stereo)
UK CBS M 63587 (mono), S 63587 (stereo)

Highest chart position on release
US 63, Canada 7, UK 2

Notes
All songs written by Leonard Cohen except "The Partisan" (French lyrics by Emmanuel d'Astier de la Vigerie and music by Anna Marly, and Hy Zaret (English translation), which he sings in both English and French.

Reissued on CD in 1990 (US/Canada CK 9767); and in 1997 (Europe COL CD 63587).

Remastered and reissued on CD in 2007 with two bonus tracks (US/Canada Columbia/Legacy 88697 04740 2; UK 88697 09388 2), and liner notes by Anthony DeCurtis. The extra songs "Like A Bird" (= "Bird On The Wire") and "Nothing To One" (= "You Know Who I Am") were previously unreleased outtakes from May 1968 sessions, produced by David Crosby (of Crosby, Stills, Nash and Young fame).

Remastered US/Canada vinyl reissued in 2009 (Sundazed Music LP 5283); and in Europe in 2011 (Music on Vinyl MOVLP 325).

Songs of Love and Hate, 1971

Recorded at Columbia Studio A, Nashville, Tennessee
Additional recording at Trident Studios, London

Produced by Bob Johnston

Personnel
- Leonard Cohen: vocals, acoustic guitar
- Ron Cornelius: acoustic and electric guitars
- Charlie Daniels: acoustic guitar, bass, fiddle
- Elkin "Bubba" Fowler: acoustic guitar, bass, banjo
- Corlynn Hanney: vocals
- Bob Johnston: piano ("Sing Another Song, Boys")
- Susan Mussmano: vocals

Additional musicians
- Children of the Corona Academy, London: children's voices ("Last Year's Man" and "Dress Rehearsal Rag")
- Paul Buckmaster: string and horn arrangements, conductor
- Michael Sahl: strings ("Last Year's Man")

Cover art
- John Berg: cover design
- Jacotte Chollet: cover photo

Side one
"Avalanche"
"Last Year's Man"
"Dress Rehearsal Rag"
"Diamonds In The Mine"

Side two
"Love Calls You By Your Name"
"Famous Blue Raincoat"
"Sing Another Song, Boys" (Live, 1970)
"Joan Of Arc"

Release date
March 19, 1971

Label and catalogue numbers
US/Canada Columbia COL C 30103,
UK CBS SBP 473863

Highest chart position on release
US 145, Canada DNC, UK 4

Notes
All songs written by Leonard Cohen.
    The live take of "Sing Another Song, Boys" was recorded at the Isle of Wight Festival, August 31, 1970.
    The initial vinyl release in the US, and later releases in Europe, included a small booklet containing the credits.
    Reissued on CD in 1988 (Europe CDCBS 32219).
    Remastered and reissued on CD in 2007 (US/Canada/Europe Columbia/ Legacy 88697 04741 2) with liner notes by Anthony DeCurtis. A bonus track was included: a previously unreleased outtake of "Dress Rehearsal Rag" from the *Songs from a Room* sessions in late 1968.

Remastered US/Canada vinyl reissued in 2009 (Sundazed Music LP 5284); and in Europe (Music on Vinyl MOVLP 036).

New Skin for the Old Ceremony, 1974

Recorded at Sound Ideas Studio, New York

Produced by Leonard Cohen and John Lissauer

Personnel
- Leonard Cohen: vocals, acoustic guitar, Jew's harp
- Emily Bindiger: vocals
- Gerald Chamberlain: trombones
- Erin Dickins: vocals
- Lewis Furey: viola
- Ralph Gibson: guitar
- Armen Halburian: percussion
- Janis Ian: vocals
- Gail Kantor: vocals
- Jeff Layton: banjo, mandolin, guitar, trumpet
- Barry Lazarowitz: drums and percussion
- John Lissauer: woodwind, keyboards, vocals
- Roy Markowitz: drums
- John Miller: bass
- Don Payne: bass

Cover art
- Teresa Alfieri: cover design

Side one
"Is This What You Wanted"
"Chelsea Hotel #2"
"Lover Lover Lover"
"Field Commander Cohen"
"Why Don't You Try"

Side two
"There Is A War"
"A Singer Must Die"
"I Tried To Leave You"
"Who By Fire"
"Take This Longing"
"Leaving Green Sleeves"

Release date
August 11, 1974

Label and catalogue numbers
US Columbia C 33167, Canada KC 33167, UK CBS 69087

Highest chart position on release
US/Canada DNC, UK 24

Notes
All songs written by Leonard Cohen.

The artwork on the original US/ Canadian LP featured an image from the alchemical text *Rosarium philosophorum*, explained as "the spiritual union of the male and female principle," dating from 1550. So much naked flesh caused a lot of offence and controversy, so the front and back covers were replaced by two different black-and-white photographs of Leonard. In the UK, an alternative version of the artwork (with an extra wing added to cover the "offending female flesh") replaced the initial release's front cover, leaving a smaller version of the original on the back sleeve! The European release retained the original artwork.
    "Chelsea Hotel #2" appears as such on the back cover but as "Chelsea Hotel" on the CD and inner booklet. Over the years, the title "Chelsea Hotel #2" has been inconsistently applied; sometimes it is given as "Chelsea Hotel" and sometimes as "Chelsea Hotel No.2." The first "Chelsea Hotel" was performed on the 1972 tour in Europe.
    An earlier version of "Take This Longing" was called "The Bells." Buffy Sainte-Marie covered it on her 1971 album *She Used to Wanna Be a Ballerina*.
    Reissued on CD in 1994 (Canada CK 80207); and in 1996 (Europe COL CD32660).
    Remastered US vinyl reissued in 2009 (Sundazed Music LP 5286); and in Europe in 2011 (Music on Vinyl MOVLP 460).

Death of a Ladies' Man, 1977

Recorded at Gold Star Recording Studios, Los Angeles
Whitney Recording Studios, Los Angeles
Devonshire Sound Studios, Los Angeles

Produced by Phil Spector

Personnel
- Leonard Cohen: vocals
- Hal Blaine: drums
- Bobby Bruce: fiddle
- Conte Candoli: trumpet
- Jesse Ed Davis: guitar
- Steve Douglas: flute, saxophone, saxophone solos
- Gene Estes: percussion
- Terry Gibbs: percussion, vibes
- Barry Goldberg: keyboard
- Tom Hensley: keyboard
- David Isaac: guitar
- Pete Jolly: keyboard
- Jim Keltner: drums
- Dan Kessel: guitar, keyboard, synthesizer, organ
- David Kessel: guitar
- "Sneaky" Pete Kleinow: slide pedal guitar

– Mike Lang: keyboard
– Charles Loper: trombone
– Bill Mays: keyboard
– Don Menza: flute, saxophone
  (and all horn arrangements)
– Jay Migliori: saxophone
– Art Munson: guitar
– Ray Neapolitan: upright and
  electric bass
– Albert Perkins:
  slide pedal guitar
– Ray Pohlman: guitar, bass
– Emil Radocchia: percussion
– Don Randi: keyboard
– Jack Redmond: trombone
– Bob Robitaille: synthesizer
  programming
– Devra Robitaille: synthesizer and
  "coordinating the musicians"
– Phil Spector: guitar, keyboard,
  all rhythm arrangements except
  "I Left A Woman Waiting" and "Iodine"
– Bob Zimmitti: percussion

Background vocalists
– Ronee Blakley (and featured vocals on
  "True Love Leaves No Traces," "Iodine,"
  and "Memories"), Brenda Bryant, Bill
  Diez ("Don't Go Home With Your Hard-
  On"), Oma Drake, Bob Dylan ("Don't
  Go Home With Your Hard-On"), Venetta
  Fields, Gerry Garrett, Allen Ginsberg
  ("Don't Go Home With Your Hard-On"),
  Dan Kessel, David Kessel, Clydie King,
  Sherlie Matthews, Phil Spector (and
  all the vocal arrangements), Bill
  Thedford, Julia Tillman, Oren Waters,
  Lorna Willard

Additional musicians
– Nino Tempo: rhythm arrangements
  ("I Left A Woman Waiting" and "Iodine")
– Jane Tutor and her Little Children's
  University

Cover art
– "Anonymous roving photographer
  at a forgotten Polynesian restaurant":
  cover photograph
– John Cabalka: art direction
– Ron Coro: design
– Martin Machat: photograph of
  Phil Spector
– Bill Naegels/Gribbitt!: design

Side one
"True Love Leaves No Traces"
"Iodine"
"Paper Thin Hotel"
"Memories"

Side two
"I Left A Woman Waiting"
"Don't Go Home With Your Hard-On"
"Fingerprints"
"Death Of A Ladies' Man"

Release date
November 13, 1977

Label and catalogue numbers
US Warner Bros BS 3125, Canada
Columbia PES 90436, UK S CBS 86042

Highest chart position on release
US/Canada DNC, UK 35

Notes
All lyrics written by Leonard Cohen;
all music composed by Phil Spector.
  Gatefold cover-sleeve featuring "Eva
La Pierre, L.C., Suzanne," with all lyrics
and musician credits. Some releases had
black-and-white sleeves instead of the
usual sepia. The album was released on
Warner Bros. in the US, because this was
Phil Spector's home label.
  "Iodine" and "Don't Go Home With
Your Hard-On" were new rewrites by
Leonard of earlier versions he had
performed during a brief tour of the
US in November 1975.
  Reissued on CD in 1985 (UK COL 86042);
and in 1988 (US Columbia CK 44286).
  Reissued on vinyl in US in 2011 (4 Men
With Beards 4M 813); and in Europe in
2012 (Music on Vinyl MOVLP 476).

Recent Songs, 1979

Recorded at A&M Studios, Hollywood,
California

Produced by Leonard Cohen and
Henry Lewy

Personnel
– Leonard Cohen: acoustic guitar,
  vocals
– Charles Roscoe Beck: bass ("Humbled
  In Love," "Our Lady Of Solitude," "The
  Gypsy's Wife," and "The Smokey Life")
– John Bilezikjian: oud ("The Guests,"
  "The Window," "The Traitor," and
  "The Gypsy's Wife")
– Earle Dumler: oboe ("Our Lady
  Of Solitude"), English horn ("The
  Smokey Life")
– James Gilstrap: background vocals
  ("Humbled In Love")
– Bill Ginn: electric piano ("Humbled
  In Love," "Our Lady Of Solitude," and
  "The Smokey Life")
– Raffi Hakopian: violin ("The Guests,"
  "The Window," "The Traitor," and
  "The Gypsy's Wife")
– Garth Hudson: Yamaha keyboard
  ("Our Lady Of Solitude") and accordion
  ("The Gypsy's Wife")
– Abraham Laboriel: bass
  ("The Guests," "The Window," and
  "The Traitor")

– John Lissauer: piano
  ("Came So Far For Beauty")
– Jeremy Lubbock: string arrangements,
  conductor ("The Traitor" and "The
  Smokey Life")
– Ed Lustgarden: cello ("The Window")
– Steve Meador: drums ("Humbled In
  Love," "Our Lady Of Solitude,"
  and "The Smokey Life")
– John Miller: bass
  ("Came So Far For Beauty")
– Paul Ostermayer: saxophone
  ("Humbled In Love")
– Stephanie Spruill: background vocals
  ("Humbled In Love")
– Roger St. Kenerly: background vocals
  ("Humbled In Love")
– Julia Tillman: background vocals
  ("Humbled In Love")
– Randy Waldman: organ ("The Guests,"
  "The Window," and "The Traitor")
– Jennifer Warnes: vocal arrangement
  and background vocals ("The Guests"),
  background vocals ("The Window"),
  vocal duet with LC ("The Smokey Life")
– Mitch Watkins: electric guitar
  ("Humbled In Love" and "Our Lady
  Of Solitude")
– Maxine Willard: background vocals
  ("Humbled In Love")

Additional musicians
– Mariachi band under the direction
  of Luiz Briseño ("The Lost Canadian
  [Un Canadien Errant]" and "Ballad
  Of The Absent Mare"):
  – Luiz Briseño, Agostin Cervantes,
    Armando Quintero, Miguel Sandoval:
    violins
  – Jose Perez, Pablo Sandoval: trumpets
  – Ricardo Gonzalez: guitar
  – Felipe Perez: biguela
  – Everado Sandoval: guitarrón

Cover art
– Glen Christensen: art director
– Dianne Lawrence: cover portrait
  and illustration

Side one
"The Guests"
"Humbled In Love"
"The Window"
"Came So Far For Beauty"
"The Lost Canadian
  (Un Canadien Errant)"

Side two
"The Traitor"
"Our Lady Of Solitude"
"The Gypsy's Wife"
"The Smokey Life"
"Ballad Of The Absent Mare"

Release date
September 27, 1979

Label and catalogue numbers
US Columbia PC 36264,
Canada JC 36264, UK S CBS 86097

Highest chart position on release
US/Canada DNC, UK 53

Notes
All songs written and arranged by
Leonard Cohen except "Came So Far
For Beauty" (by Leonard Cohen and John
Lissauer, who also arranged and co-
produced the track with LC); and "The
Lost Canadian (Un Canadien Errant)"
(by Antoine Gérin-Lajoie, a nineteenth-
century Québécois poet and novelist).
On this latter song, Leonard sings
throughout in French.

Some vinyl issues have a printed
inner sleeve with lyrics and credits.
Charles Roscoe Beck was C. Roscoe
Beck by the time he produced Jennifer
Warnes' Leonard Cohen tribute album
Famous Blue Raincoat in 1987; and plain
Roscoe Beck when he produced on
Leonard's 1988 *I'm Your Man* album.
And has been so ever since.

Reissued on CD in 1990 (US Columbia
CK 36264, Canada Columbia WCK 36264,
and Europe CDCBS 86097). Booklet
containing all lyrics and credits.

Vinyl reissued in Europe in 2012
(Music on Vinyl MOVLP 311).

Dedication: "to my friend IRVING
LAYTON, incomparable master of the
inner language."

Various Positions, 1984

Recorded at Quadrasonic Sound,
New York

Produced by John Lissauer

Personnel
– Leonard Cohen: vocals, guitars
– Richard Crooks: drums
– John Crowder: bass,
   background vocals
– Ron Getman: harmonica,
   background vocals
– Kenneth Kosek: fiddle
– John Lissauer: piano and
   keyboard orchestrations,
   background vocals
– Sid McGinnis: guitars
– Jennifer Warnes: vocals

Background vocalists
– Erin Dickins, Crissie Faith, Lani
   Groves, Yvonne Lewis, Merle Miller,
   Anjani Thomas

Cover art
– Leonard Cohen: polaroid photo

Side one
"Dance Me To The End Of Love"
"Coming Back To You"
"The Law"
"Night Comes On"

Side two
"Hallelujah"
"The Captain"
"Hunter's Lullaby"
"Heart With No Companion"
"If It Be Your Will"

Release date
December 11, 1984 (Canada),
February 1985 (US/Europe)

Label and catalogue numbers
Vinyl: US Passport PB 6045,
Canada COL PCC 90728, UK CBS 26222
CD: US Columbia CK 66950,
Canada WCK 90728, UK CDCBS 26222

Highest chart position on release
US/Canada DNC, UK 52

Notes
All songs written by Leonard Cohen.

Columbia initially turned down the
opportunity to issue the album in the
US, hence its original release by minor
distributor Passport Records on their
Jem label.

A black-and-white promo video of
"Dance Me To The End Of Love," directed
by Dominique Issermann, came out in
January 1985. And for the first time on
a Leonard Cohen album, all song lyrics
are printed on the vinyl back cover and
in the CD booklet.

Vinyl reissued in Europe in 2012
(Music on Vinyl MOVLP 504).

I'm Your Man, 1988

Recorded at Studio Temporal, Montreal
DMS Studios, Montreal
Studio Montmartre, Paris
Rock Steady, Los Angeles
Additional recording at Soundworks,
New York and Stagg Street Studio,
Los Angeles

Produced by Leonard Cohen (all tracks),
Roscoe Beck ("I Can't Forget" and co-
producer "Ain't No Cure For Love" and
"Take This Waltz"), Michel Robidoux
(co-producer "Everybody Knows"
and "I'm Your Man"), and Jean-Michel
Reusser (co-producer "Take This Waltz")

Personnel
– Leonard Cohen: vocals, keyboard
   ("Everybody Knows" and "I'm Your
   Man"), piano ("I Can't Forget")

– Mayel Assouly: vocals
   ("Take This Waltz")
– Richard Beaudet: saxophone
   ("Ain't No Cure For Love")
– John Bilezikjian: oud
   ("Everybody Knows")
– Tom Brechtlein: drums ("I'm Your Man")
– Lenny Castro: percussion
   ("I Can't Forget")
– Larry Cohen: keyboards
   ("I Can't Forget")
– Vinnie Colaiuta: drums ("Ain't No
   Cure For Love," "Jazz Police," and
   "I Can't Forget")
– Jeff Fisher: keyboards
   ("Ain't No Cure For Love")
– Raffi Hakopian: violin
   ("Take This Waltz")
– Evelyine Hebey: vocals
   ("Take This Waltz")
– Jude Johnstone: vocals ("I Can't Forget")
– Peter Kisilenko: bass
   ("Ain't No Cure For Love")
– "Sneaky" Pete Kleinow: steel guitar
   ("I Can't Forget")
– Michel Robidoux: keyboard
   ("Everybody Knows") and drum-fill
   ("I'm Your Man")
– Bob Stanley: guitar
   ("Ain't No Cure For Love")
– Anjani Thomas: vocals ("First We Take
   Manhattan," "Ain't No Cure For Love,"
   "I'm Your Man," and "Jazz Police")
– Elisabeth Valletti: vocals
   ("Take This Waltz")
– Jennifer Warnes: ad lib vocals
   ("Ain't No Cure For Love") and vocals
   ("Everybody Knows," "Take This Waltz,"
   "I Can't Forget," and "Tower Of Song")

Cover art
– Dominique Issermann: inside photos (CD)
– Orchestra Paris: jacket design
– Sharon Weisz: cover photo

Side one
"First We Take Manhattan"
"Ain't No Cure For Love"
"Everybody Knows"
"I'm Your Man"

Side two
"Take This Waltz"
"Jazz Police"
"I Can't Forget"
"Tower Of Song"

Release date
February 2, 1988

Label and catalogue numbers
Vinyl: US/Canada Columbia FC 44191,
UK CBS 460642 1
CD: US/Canada Columbia CK 44191,
UK CBS 460642 2
MiniDisc: Columbia COL 460642 8

Highest chart position on release
US/Canada DNC, UK 48

Notes

All songs written by Leonard Cohen except "Everybody Knows" (by Leonard Cohen and Sharon Robinson); "Jazz Police" (by Leonard Cohen and Jeff Fisher); and "Take This Waltz" (lyrics by Leonard Cohen, which he translated from the original Spanish poem "Pequeño vals vienés" by Federico García Lorca).

"Take This Waltz" was originally recorded in 1986 for *Poetas en Nueva York*, a Lorca tribute album. The *I'm Your Man* version is a remix of the original.

All lyrics and credits printed on the vinyl back cover and in the CD booklet.

A black-and-white promo video of "First We Take Manhattan," directed by Dominique Issermann, came out in early January 1988.

Vinyl reissued in Europe in 2012 (Music on Vinyl MOVLP 424).

Around the small circular icon of a couple dancing at the top of the back cover: "ALL THESE SONGS ARE FOR YOU, D.I."

The Future, 1992

Recorded at various Los Angeles studios: Image Recording Studio, Cherokee Recording Studio, Capitol Recording Studio, The Complex, House of Soul, Village Recorder, Ocean Way Recording Studio, Studio 56, and Sunset Sound; and at Studio 11 in Athens, Greece and Studio Tempo in Montreal.

Produced by Leonard Cohen (all tracks except "Be For Real," "Always," and "Tacoma Trailer"), Yoav Goren (co-producer "Waiting For The Miracle"), Steve Lindsey ("Be For Real" and "Always" and additional production "Democracy"), Leanne Ungar (co-producer "Closing Time"), Rebecca De Mornay (co-producer "Anthem"), Bill Ginn ("Tacoma Trailer" and co-producer "Light As The Breeze")

Personnel
– Leonard Cohen: vocals, saxophone ("Light As The Breeze")
– John Barnes: synth bass ("Democracy")
– Perla Batalla: background vocals ("Closing Time")
– Peggy Blue: background vocals ("Always")
– David Campbell: string arrangements ("Waiting For The Miracle," "Be For Real," and "Anthem") and background vocal arrangements ("The Future" and "Anthem")
– Lenny Castro: percussion ("Waiting For The Miracle," "Be For Real," and "Anthem") and tambourine ("The Future" and "Always")
– Julie Christensen: background vocals ("Closing Time" and "Democracy")
– Vinnie Colaiuta: drums ("Democracy")
– Jim Cox: piano ("Always")
– Steve Croes: synclavier ("Tacoma Trailer") and synclavier programming ("Light As The Breeze")
– Brandon Fields: tenor saxophone ("Always")
– Michael Finnigan: organ pad ("Always")
– Jeff Fisher: keyboards ("Democracy")
– Bob Furgo: violin ("Waiting For The Miracle," "Closing Time," and "Light As The Breeze")
– James Gadson: drums ("Be For Real")
– Bill Ginn: synclavier ("Tacoma Trailer"), synclavier programming ("Light As The Breeze")
– Bob Glaub: bass ("Closing Time")
– Jacquelyn Gouche-Farris: background vocals ("Be For Real")
– Ed Greene: drums ("Always")
– Dennis Herring: electric guitar ("Always")
– Paul Jackson Jr.: guitar ("Be For Real")
– Jean Johnson: background vocals ("Always")
– Randy Kerber: additional keyboards ("Democracy")
– LA Mass Choir: choir vocals ("Anthem")
– Steve Lindsey: organ, Wurlitzer piano, and mellotron ("Be For Real"), additional keyboards ("Democracy"), ice-rink organ ("Always")
– Steve Meador: drums ("The Future" and "Anthem")
– Bob Metzger: acoustic and electric guitars ("The Future," "Closing Time," "Anthem," and "Light As The Breeze"), pedal steel ("Be For Real"), and bass ("Anthem")
– David Morgan: background vocals ("Democracy")
– Dean Parks: mandolin ("Waiting For The Miracle" and "Democracy"), guitars ("Democracy" and "Always"), and Weissenborn slide guitar ("Always")
– Greg Phillinganes: piano ("Be For Real")
– Valerie Pinkston-Mayo: background vocals ("Be For Real")
– Lon Price: tenor saxophone ("Always")
– Lee Sklar: bass ("Always")
– Greg Smith: baritone saxophone ("Always")
– Anjani Thomas: background vocals ("Waiting For The Miracle")
– Lee R. Thornburg: trumpet, trombone, horn arrangements ("Always")
– Jennifer Warnes: background vocals ("Democracy"), background vocals and arrangement ("Light As The Breeze")
– Tony Warren: background vocals ("Be For Real")
– Freddie Washington: bass ("Be For Real")
– Edna Wright: background vocals ("Always")

Additional string musicians
– David Campbell, Ron Clark, Larry Corbett, Joel Derouin, Bruce Dukov, Donald Ferrone, Berj Garabedian, Suzie Katayama, Sid Page, Daniel Smith, Thomas Tally, and Raymond Tischer II

Additional choir singers
– Laythan Amot, Evette Andrews, Gigi Bailey, Jeralynthia Banks, Cynthia Bass, Perla Batalla, Steve Berkley, Julie Christensen, Lavan Davis, Lashana Dendy, Brenda Eager, Aladrian Elmore, Patricia Finnie, Jimmie Frazier, Sonya Griffin, Raven Kane, Nysa Larry, Stephen Lively, Roseland Parker, Kevin Shoates, Dana Stockard, Carmen Twillie, Theresa Walker, Julia Walters, Maxine Waters, Oren Waters, and Mona Lisa Young

Cover art
– Dianne Lawrence: original hummingbird drawing
– Michael Petit: cover design

Side one
"The Future"
"Waiting For The Miracle"
"Be For Real"
"Closing Time"
"Anthem"

Side two
"Democracy"
"Light As The Breeze"
"Always"
"Tacoma Trailer"

Release date
November 24, 1992

Label and catalogue numbers
Vinyl: UK COL 472498 1
CD: US/Canada Columbia CK 53226, UK COL 472498 2
MiniDisc: Columbia COL 472498 3

Highest chart position on release
US/Canada DNC, UK 36

Notes
All songs written by Leonard Cohen except "Waiting For The Miracle" (by Leonard Cohen and Sharon Robinson); "Be For Real" (by Frederick Knight); and "Always" (by Irving Berlin). All song lyrics and musician credits

printed on the vinyl rear cover and in the CD booklet.

The finale is an instrumental and the only track on the album, and indeed in the entire Leonard Cohen canon of studio recordings, that does not feature either his vocal or instrumental talents.

A colour promo video of "The Future," directed by Curtis Wehrfritz, and a black-and-white promo video of "Closing Time" (co-directed with Wehrfritz and re-edited by Leonard's then fiancée Rebecca De Mornay) both came out in late 1992, the latter winning a Juno award for Best Video.

Vinyl reissued in Europe in 2012 (Music on Vinyl MOVLP 503).

Dedication: "And before I had done speaking in mine heart, behold, Rebecca came forth with her pitcher on her shoulder; and she went down unto the well, and drew water; and I said unto her, Let me drink, I pray thee. And she made haste, and let down her pitcher from her shoulder, and said, Drink, and I will give thy camels drink also: so I drank, and she made the camels drink also." Genesis 24

Ten New Songs, 2001

Recorded at Leonard's home studio (Still Life), Los Angeles, and Sharon Robinson's home studio (Small Mercies), Hollywood, California

Produced by Sharon Robinson

Personnel
– Leonard Cohen: vocals
– Sharon Robinson: vocals, arrangements, programing

Additional musicians
– David Campbell: string arrangements ("A Thousand Kisses Deep")
– Bob Metzger: guitar ("In My Secret Life")

Cover art
– Leonard Cohen: front-cover photography
– Nancy Donald: art direction
– Bob Ludwig: back-cover photography

Side one
"In My Secret Life"
"A Thousand Kisses Deep"
"That Don't Make It Junk"
"Here It Is"
"Love Itself"

Side two
"By The Rivers Dark"
"Alexandra Leaving"
"You Have Loved Enough"
"Boogie Street"
"The Land Of Plenty"

Release date
October 9, 2001

Label and catalogue numbers
Vinyl: Canada Columbia C 85953, UK COL 501202 1
CD: US/Canada Columbia CK 85953, UK COL 501202 2

Highest chart position on release
US 143, Canada 4, UK 26

Notes
All songs written by Leonard Cohen and Sharon Robinson. "Alexandra Leaving" is based on "The God Abandons Antony," a poem by the Greek poet Constantine P. Cavafy (1863–1933).

CD booklet includes lyrics and musician credits. The colour promo video of "In My Secret Life," directed by Floria Sigismondi, received a Juno nomination for Best Video.

"A Thousand Kisses Deep" is a new version of the song first seen and heard, sung by Leonard to his own keyboard accompaniment, in Armelle Brusq's 1996 documentary *Leonard Cohen: Portrait, Spring 1996*. And in the concerts of the 2008–2010 and 2012–2013 tours, "A Thousand Kisses Deep" was transformed again, this time into a poem recitation by Leonard, with a keyboard accompaniment composed and performed by Neil Larsen.

Vinyl reissued in Europe in 2009 (Music on Vinyl MOVLP 033).

Dedication: "Sharon, Leanne and Leonard dedicate this record to our friend Kyozan Joshu, Roshi."

Dear Heather, 2004

Recorded at Leonard's home studio (Still Life), Los Angeles, and Sharon Robinson's home studio (Small Mercies), Hollywood, California

Produced by Leonard Cohen ("Tennessee Waltz"), Henry Lewy (co-producer "The Faith"), Sharon Robinson ("Go No More A-Roving," "The Letters," and "There For You"), Ed Sanders (co-producer "Nightingale"), Anjani Thomas ("On That Day" and co-producer "Nightingale"), and Leanne Ungar ("Because Of," "Undertow," "Morning Glory," "Villanelle For Our Time," "Dear Heather," "To A Teacher" and co-producer "The Faith")

Personnel
– Leonard Cohen: vocals, guitars, Jew's harp ("On That Day" and "Nightingale")

– Johnny Friday: drums ("On That Day" and "Nightingale")
– Sarah Kramer: trumpet ("Dear Heather")
– Sharon Robinson: vocals ("Go No More A-Roving," "The Letters," and "There For You")
– Stan Sargent: bass ("On That Day" and "Nightingale")
– Bob Sheppard: tenor sax ("Go No More A-Roving")
– Anjani Thomas: vocals, piano ("On That Day" and "Nightingale")

"The Faith" only
– Roscoe Beck: bass
– John Bilezikjian: oud
– Bill Ginn: piano
– Raffi Hakopian: violin
– Garth Hudson: accordion
– Jeremy Lubbock: string arrangements
– Paul Ostermayer: flute
– Mitch Watkins: guitar

"Tennessee Waltz" only
– Richard Crooks: drums
– John Crowder: bass, vocals
– Ron Getman: steel guitar, vocals
– Anjani Thomas: piano, vocals
– Mitch Watkins: electric guitar, vocals

Cover art
– Leonard Cohen: drawings
– Michael Petit: design
– Anjani Thomas: photos
– Tina Tyrell: photos

Track listing
"Go No More A-Roving"
"Because Of"
"The Letters"
"Undertow"
"Morning Glory"
"On That Day"
"Villanelle For Our Time"
"There For You"
"Dear Heather"
"Nightingale"
"To A Teacher"
"The Faith"
"Tennessee Waltz" (Live, 1985)

Release date
October 26, 2004

Label and catalogue numbers
CD: US/Canada Columbia CK 92891, UK CBS 514768 2

Highest chart position on release
US 131, Canada 5, UK 34

Notes
All songs written by Leonard Cohen except: "The Letters" and "There For You" (by Leonard Cohen and Sharon

Robinson); "On That Day" and "Nightingale" (by Leonard Cohen and Anjani Thomas); and "Tennessee Waltz" (by Redd Stewart and Pee Wee King, with an additional verse by Leonard Cohen). CD booklet includes all lyrics and musician credits.

The words for "Go No More A-Roving" are by English poet Lord Byron (1788–1824). "On That Day" is a response to the events of September 11, 2001. The words for "Villanelle For Our Time" are by Canadian poet F. R. Scott (1899–1985). "The Faith" is based on an old Québécois folk song and uses an outtake track rescued from the 1979 *Recent Songs* sessions. The last song is taken from a concert in Montreux, Switzerland, on July 9, 1985.

Anjani Thomas would later include her own version of the song "Nightingale" on her 2006 album *Blue Alert* (co-written with and produced by Leonard). Leonard's daughter, Lorca, directed a promo video for the song "Because Of" in 2005.

Reissued on vinyl in Europe in 2012 (Music on Vinyl MOVLP 502) excluding the final live track.

The album is "in memory of Jack McClelland 1922–2004" (Leonard's Canadian publisher).

Old Ideas, 2012

Recorded/edited/mixed in various Los Angeles home studios: Still Life (Leonard's), Small Mercies (Sharon Robinson's), Two Word Music (Patrick Leonard's), Lars Nova (Neil Larsen's), Thread Telegraph Office (Dino Soldo's), and Street Sound (Ed Sanders').

Produced by Patrick Leonard ("Going Home," "Show Me The Place," "Anyhow," and "Come Healing"), Anjani Thomas ("Crazy To Love You"), Ed Sanders ("Amen," "Lullaby," and "Different Sides" and co-producer "Darkness"), Mark Vreeken (co-producer "Darkness"), and Dino Soldo ("Banjo").

Personnel
– Leonard Cohen: vocals, acoustic guitar ("Amen," "Crazy To Love You," and "Lullaby"), arrangements and programing ("Amen," "Lullaby," and "Different Sides")
– Jordan Charnofsky: guitar ("Amen")
– Dana Glover: vocals and female vocal arrangements ("Going Home," "Anyhow," "Come Healing," and "Different Sides")
– Robert Korda: violin ("Amen")
– Neil Larsen: Hammond B3, piano, synth bass, percussion ("Different Sides"), cornet ("Banjo")

– Patrick Leonard: arrangements and programing ("Going Home," "Show Me The Place," "Anyhow," and "Come Healing")
– Sharon Robinson: vocals and female vocal arrangements ("Amen," "Banjo," and "Lullaby"), synth bass ("Amen" and "Lullaby")
– Ed Sanders: vocals and male vocal arrangements ("Lullaby"), guitar ("Lullaby")
– Bela Santelli: violin ("Going Home," "Show Me The Place," and "Come Healing")
– Dino Soldo: all the instruments on "Banjo" except cornet
– Chris Wabich: drums ("Amen")
– Jennifer Warnes: vocals and female vocal arrangements ("Show Me The Place")

"Darkness" only

Unified Heart Touring Band
– Leonard Cohen: guitar and vocals
– Roscoe Beck: bass, musical director
– Rafael Bernardo Gayol: drums
– Neil Larsen: keyboards
– Javier Mas: archilaud
– Bob Metzger: guitars
– Sharon Robinson: vocals
– Dino Soldo: horns
– Charley Webb: vocals
– Hattie Webb: vocals

Cover art
– Leonard Cohen: cover design and drawings
– Kezban Özcan: photography
– Michael Petit: booklet design

Track listing
"Going Home"
"Amen"
"Show Me The Place"
"Darkness"
"Anyhow"
"Crazy To Love You"
"Come Healing"
"Banjo"
"Lullaby"
"Different Sides"

Release date
January 31, 2012 (US)
January 27, 2012 (rest of the world)

Label and catalogue numbers
US/Europe Columbia 8869798671 2

Highest chart position on release
US 3, Canada 1, UK 2

Notes
All songs written by Leonard Cohen except: "Going Home," "Show Me The Place," "Anyhow," and "Come Healing"

(by Leonard Cohen and Patrick Leonard); and "Crazy To Love You" (by Leonard Cohen and Anjani Thomas).

Also released in the US and Europe on vinyl (Columbia 8869798671 1) with the package containing a copy of the standard album on CD, bundled with an exclusive, limited-run lithograph (by Leonard). Vinyl copies included insert with lyrics and musicians credits; CD booklet contained the same.

Shortly before the album's official release, it was streamed online by NPR (US) on January 22, and by the *Guardian* (UK) on January 23, 2012.

Leonard's Unified Heart Touring Band was already playing the songs "Lullaby" and "Darkness" in its concerts in 2009 and 2010, well before the album was released. Anjani Thomas had released her own version of "Crazy To Love You" back in 2006 on *Blue Alert*. And Leonard himself was also in the habit of quoting several lines from this song during his own concert-concluding song "Closing Time" in 2012 and 2013.

A colour promo video of "Show Me The Place" appeared in 2012, directed by Aaron Hymes.

LIVE ALBUMS

Live Songs, 1973

Recorded at various venues in Europe from August 1970 to April 1972

Produced by Bob Johnston

Personnel
1970 songs
– Leonard Cohen: vocals, acoustic guitar
– Ron Cornelius: electric guitar
– Charlie Daniels: electric bass, fiddle
– Aileen Fowler: vocals
– Elkin "Bubba" Fowler: guitar, banjo
– Corlynn Hanney: vocals
– Bob Johnston: acoustic guitar, harmonica

1972 songs
– Leonard Cohen: vocals, acoustic guitar
– Ron Cornelius: acoustic and electric guitars
– Bob Johnston: organ
– Peter Marshall: stand-up and electric bass
– David O'Connor: acoustic guitar
– Jennifer Warnes: vocals
– Donna Washburn: vocals

Cover art
– S. B. Elrod: front cover photograph
– "from the work of Daphne Richardson (1939–1972)": back cover text/artwork

Side one

"Minute Prologue"
  (London, March 23, 1972)
"Passing Through"
  (London, March 23, 1972)
"You Know Who I Am"
  (Brussels, March 16, 1972)
"Bird On The Wire"
  (Paris, April 18, 1972)
"Nancy"
  (London, March 23, 1972)
"Improvisation"
  (Paris, April 18, 1972)

Side two

"Story Of Isaac"
  (Berlin, April 8, 1972)
"Please Don't Pass Me By (A Disgrace)"
  (London, May 10, 1970)
"Tonight Will Be Fine"
  (Isle of Wight, August 31, 1970)
"Queen Victoria"

Release date
April 1, 1973

Label and catalogue numbers
US Columbia KC 31724, Canada
Columbia C 31724, UK/Europe CBS 65224

Highest chart position on release
US 156, Canada/UK DNC

Notes
All songs written by Leonard Cohen
except: "Passing Through" (by Richard
Blakeslee, 1921–2000); the sleeve notes
say "R. Blakeslee arr. L. Cohen."

The photographer S. B. Elrod is
Suzanne Elrod, mother of Leonard's
two children, Adam and Lorca, and
not the Suzanne of the song (that was
Suzanne Verdal). Daphne Richardson's
"writing" on the back cover is called
"Transfiguration." Aileen Fowler (partner
of Elkin Fowler) was formerly Susan
Musmanno and appears under this latter
name in the credits on both *Songs of Love
and Hate* and *Live at the Isle of Wight 1970*.
Jennifer Warnes is credited under her
stage name, Jennifer Warren, which she
abandoned soon after (Warnes is her
birth name). Donna Washburn is not
credited here on vocals, though she
is credited on the later *Live at the Isle
of Wight 1970*.

"Improvisation" is a three-minute
instrumental around the song melody
of "You Know Who I Am." A slightly
longer "Tonight Will Be Fine" was
included on the three-disc vinyl album
*The First Great Rock Festivals of the
Seventies/Isle of Wight/Atlanta Pop Festival*
in 1971 (US/Canada G3X 30805; UK/
Europe CBS 66311). Unlike the other
tracks, the final song, "Queen Victoria,"

was not recorded live in front of an
audience, but in a small cabin in
Franklin, Tennessee, on a basic home-
recorder (similar in nature to Bruce
Springsteen's home recordings for his
1982 album *Nebraska*).

The 1970 Isle of Wight concert was
later released in 2009 on vinyl/CD/
DVD/BluRay (see overleaf). The 1972
tour was filmed by Tony Palmer and
first released in 1974 as *Bird on a Wire*;
a revised version was issued on DVD
in 2010 (Isolde Films TPDVD166).

Reissued on CD in 1996 (Canada
Columbia CK 80236; Europe CDCBS
65224).

Remastered US/Canada vinyl
(gatefold sleeve) reissued in 2009 (US
Sundazed Music LP 5285); and in Europe
in 2011 (Music on Vinyl MOVLP 327).

Cohen Live: Leonard Cohen in Concert, 1994

Recorded at various venues in Canada,
US, and Europe in 1988 and 1993

Produced by Leanne Ungar and
Bob Metzger

Personnel
1988 songs
– Leonard Cohen: vocals, acoustic guitar
– Perla Batalla: vocals
– Roscoe Beck: musical director
– John Bilezikjian: oud, mandolin
– Julie Christensen: vocals
– Bob Furgo: keyboards, violin
– Tom McMorran: keyboards
– Steve Meador: drums
– Bob Metzger: guitars, pedal steel guitar
– Stephen Zirkel: bass, keyboards, trumpet

1993 songs
– Leonard Cohen: vocals, acoustic guitar
– Perla Batalla: vocals
– Jorge Calderon: bass, vocals
– Julie Christensen: vocals
– Bob Furgo: keyboards, violin
– Bill Ginn: keyboards
– Steve Meador: drums
– Bob Metzger: guitars, pedal steel guitar
– Paul Ostermayer: saxophones, keyboards

Cover art
– Leonard Cohen: artwork
– Dianne Lawrence: hummingbird drawing
– Scott Newton: photo (Austin City Limits)
– Michael Petit: *The Future* logo design
– James Water: *I'm Your Man* logo design

Some elements in the cover collage are
based on details in the painting *The Last
Angel* by Nicholas Roerich.

Track listing

"Dance Me To The End Of Love"
  (Toronto, June 17, 1993)
"Bird On The Wire"
  (Toronto, June 17, 1993)
"Everybody Knows"
  (Vancouver, July 29, 1993)
"Joan Of Arc"
  (Toronto, June 17, 1993)
"There Is A War"
  (Toronto, June 17, 1993)
"Sisters Of Mercy"
  (Toronto, June 18, 1993)
"Hallelujah"
  (Austin, October 31, 1988)
"I'm Your Man"
  (Toronto, June 17, 1993)
"Who By Fire"
  (Austin, October 31, 1988)
"One Of Us Cannot Be Wrong"
  (San Sebastian, May 20, 1988)
"If It Be Your Will"
  (Austin, October 31, 1988)
"Heart With No Companion"
  (Amsterdam, April 19, 1988)
"Suzanne"
  (Vancouver, July 29, 1993)

Release date
June 28, 1994

Label and catalogue numbers
US Columbia CK 66327,
Canada Columbia CK 80188,
Europe Columbia COL 477171 2
MiniDisc: Columbia COL 477171 8

Highest chart position on release
US/Canada DNC, UK 35

Notes
All songs written by Leonard Cohen
except: "Everybody Knows" (by Leonard
Cohen and Sharon Robinson). CD booklet
includes lyrics and musician credits.

A colour promo video for "Dance Me
To The End Of Love" (using the Toronto
June 17, 1993 concert audio) came out
in 1994.

The French division of Sony Music
released a CD-sized hardback book
in 1997 in their "CD Livres" series (COL
487268-2) to accompany the CD – forty-
eight pages full of colour and black-and-
white photographs and a biography of
Leonard by two French journalists,
Alain-Guy Aknin and Philippe Crocq.

Field Commander Cohen: Tour of 1979, 2001

Recorded at the Hammersmith Odeon,
London, December 4–6, 1979; and Dome
Theatre, Brighton, December 15, 1979

Produced by Leanne Ungar (from the live recordings by Henry Lewy)

Personnel
– Leonard Cohen: vocals, acoustic guitar
– John Bilezikjian: oud, mandolin
– Raffi Hakopian: violin
– Sharon Robinson: vocals
– Jennifer Warnes: vocals

Passenger
– Roscoe Beck: bass
– Bill Ginn: keyboards
– Steve Meador: drums
– Paul Ostermayer: saxophone, flute
– Mitch Watkins: electric guitar
– John Wood: technical

Cover art
– Nancy Donald: art direction
– Hazel Field: cover photo, additional band photos
– Roger Moore: photo of Passenger

Track listing
"Field Commander Cohen"
"The Window"
"The Smokey Life"
"The Gypsy's Wife"
"Lover Lover Lover"
"Hey, That's No Way To Say Goodbye"
"The Stranger Song"
"The Guests"
"Memories"
"Why Don't You Try"
"Bird On The Wire"
"So Long, Marianne"

Release date
February 20, 2001

Label and catalogue numbers
US/Canada Columbia CK 66210, Europe Columbia COL 501225 2

Highest chart position on release
US/Canada DNC, UK 195

Notes
All songs written by Leonard Cohen except: "Memories" (lyrics by Leonard Cohen, music by Phil Spector).

"Field Commander Cohen" includes a brief rendition of part of "Rum And Coca-Cola" (by Morey Amsterdam, Jeri Kelli Sullivan, and Paul Girlando). CD booklet includes lyrics and musician credits.

Dedication: "to the memory of John Wood (1950–1983), the technical member of Passenger, 'wounded in the line of duty.' We have not forgotten his courage."

Reissued in Europe as a two-disc vinyl LP in 2014 (Music on Vinyl MOVLP 1012).

Live in London, 2009

Recorded at the O2 Arena, London, July 17, 2008

Executive producer: Robert Kory; Producer: Edward Sanders; Co-producer: Steve Berkowitz

Personnel
– Leonard Cohen: vocals, acoustic guitar, keyboard
– Roscoe Beck: musical director, electric bass, stand-up bass, background vocals
– Rafael Bernardo Gayol: drums and percussion
– Neil Larsen: keyboards (including Hammond B3)
– Javier Mas: bandurria, laud, archilaud, twelve-string guitar
– Bob Metzger: lead guitar, pedal steel guitar
– Sharon Robinson: background vocals
– Dino Soldo: wind instruments, harmonica, keyboard, background vocals
– Charley Webb: background vocals, acoustic guitar
– Hattie Webb: background vocals, harp

Cover art
– Lorca Cohen: still photographer, graphic design
– James Cumpsty: still photographer
– Michael Petit: graphic design
– Robert Yager: still photographer

Disc one
"Dance Me To The End Of Love"
"The Future"
"Ain't No Cure For Love"
"Bird On The Wire"
"Everybody Knows"
"In My Secret Life"
"Who By Fire"
"Hey, That's No Way To Say Goodbye"
"Anthem"
"Tower Of Song"
"Suzanne"
"The Gypsy's Wife"

Disc two
"Boogie Street"
  (featuring Sharon Robinson)
"Hallelujah"
"Democracy"
"I'm Your Man"
"Recitation" (with Neil Larsen)
"Take This Waltz"
"So Long, Marianne"
"First We Take Manhattan"
"Sisters Of Mercy"
"If It Be Your Will"
  (performed by the Webb Sisters)
"Closing Time"
"I Tried To Leave You"
"Whither Thou Goest"

Release date
March 31, 2009

Label and catalogue numbers
CD: Canada/Europe Columbia 8869740502 2
DVD: Europe Columbia 8869740503 9 and 8869748716 9

Highest chart position on release
US 76, Canada 7, UK 19

Notes
All songs written by Leonard Cohen except: "Everybody Knows," "In My Secret Life," and "Boogie Street" (by Leonard Cohen and Sharon Robinson); "Take This Waltz" (lyrics by Leonard Cohen, which he translated from the original Spanish poem "Pequeño vals vienés" by Federico García Lorca); "Recitation" (words by Leonard Cohen, music by Neil Larsen); and "Whither Thou Goest" (by Guy Singer, arr. Leonard Cohen). "Recitation" is best known as the poem "A Thousand Kisses Deep."

Released in foldout digipack form. CD booklet includes a newspaper review of the concert (by John Aizlewood, London *Evening Standard*), and musician credits. The DVD booklet has several different photographs.

Reissued in Europe as a three-disc vinyl LP in 2014 (Music on Vinyl MOVLP 1013).

Live at the Isle of Wight 1970, 2009

Recorded at East Afton Farm, Isle of Wight Festival, August 31, 1970

CD producer: Steve Berkowitz
DVD producer and director: Murray Lerner; Executive producer: Steve Berkowitz

Personnel
– Leonard Cohen: vocals, acoustic guitar
– Ron Cornelius: electric guitar
– Charlie Daniels: electric bass, fiddle
– Bob Johnston: organ, piano, guitar, harmonica
– Elkin "Bubba" Fowler: bass, banjo
– Corlynn Hanney: background vocals
– Susan Musmanno: background vocals
– Donna Washburn: background vocals

Cover art
– Mandy Eidgah: product direction
– Adam Farber: product direction
– Lowry Digital: cover-image enhancement
– Jim Marshall: photography

– MLF Films: film stills
– Brian Moody: photography
  (Rex Features)
– Edward O'Dowd: art direction, design
– Col Underhill: photography

Track listing
"Bird On The Wire"
"So Long, Marianne"
"You Know Who I Am"
"Lady Midnight"
"They Locked Up A Man" (poem)
"A Person Who Eats Meat" (poem)
"One Of Us Cannot Be Wrong"
"The Stranger Song"
"Tonight Will Be Fine"
"Hey, That's No Way To Say Goodbye"
"Diamonds In The Mine"
"Suzanne"
"Sing Another Song, Boys"
"The Partisan"
"Famous Blue Raincoat"
"Seems So Long Ago, Nancy"

Release date
October 20, 2009

Label and catalogue numbers
Vinyl: US Columbia/Legacy 8869757070 1
CD/DVD: US/Canada Columbia/Legacy
8869757067 2, Europe 8869757916 2
BluRay: 8869758829 9

Highest chart position on release
US/Canada DNC, UK 169

Notes
All songs written by Leonard Cohen
except: "The Partisan" (by A. Betoulinsky/
H. Zaret/J. Roussel). A. Betoulinsky is
Anna Betulinskaya (born 1917, St.
Petersburg) but is best known as Anna
Marly (see credits for *Songs from a
Room*). This particular *triple* credit also
appears on *Songs from the Road* and *The
Essential Leonard Cohen* (2010 version),
but on no other previous Cohen album.
Leonard sings the song in both English
and French. His reciting of poems during
concerts was common practice on his
1970, 1972, and 1976 tours, as were his
several improvisations, including the
1974 concerts.

Released in foldout digipack form,
this is Leonard's first simultaneous CD/
DVD release.

The album was originally announced
under the title *My Sad and Famous Songs:
Leonard Cohen Live at the Isle of Wight 1970*,
but released without the first part of the
title. Most of the available promotional
acetate CDRs and DVDRs show the
complete original title.

The twenty-page CD booklet
includes an essay by Sylvie Simmons,
and an explanatory note each from

director Murray Lerner and producer
Steve Berkowitz, and musician credits.

The DVD, described on the cover
as "concert film and documentary,"
presents twelve of the fourteen songs,
though not in concert order: Those
missing are "You Know Who I Am" and
"Lady Midnight." The DVD also contained
interviews (filmed in 2009) with Bob
Johnston, Judy Collins, Joan Baez, and
Kris Kristofferson.

Some of the Isle of Wight song
performances appear on other albums:
"Tonight Will Be Fine" was originally
included on *The First Great Rock Festivals
of the Seventies/Isle of Wight/Atlanta Pop
Festival* (1971), and then on *Live Songs*;
"Sing Another Song, Boys" on *Songs
of Love and Hate*; "Suzanne" on *Message
to Love: The Isle of Wight Festival 1970*
released in 1995 (on CD/VHS/laserdisc)
to celebrate the festival's twenty-fifth
anniversary; the DVD was released in 2000.

Reissued on vinyl in Europe in 2009
(Music on Vinyl MOVLP 005).

Songs from the Road, 2010

Recorded at various venues in Europe,
US, and Canada from October 2008
to November 2009

CD producer: Edward Sanders;
Co-producer: Steve Berkowitz; Executive
producer: Robert Kory; Additional
production: John Van Nest
DVD producer and director: Edward
Sanders; Co-producer: Richard Alcock;
Executive producers: Steve Berkowitz
and Robert Kory

Personnel
– Leonard Cohen: vocals, acoustic guitar,
  keyboard
– Roscoe Beck: musical director, electric
  bass, stand-up bass, background vocals
– Rafael Bernardo Gayol: drums and
  percussion
– Neil Larsen: keyboards (including
  Hammond B3)
– Javier Mas: bandurria, laud, archilaud,
  twelve-string guitar
– Bob Metzger: lead guitar, pedal steel
  guitar, background vocals
– Sharon Robinson: background vocals
– Dino Soldo: instruments of wind,
  harmonica, keyboard, background
  vocals
– Charley Webb: background vocals,
  acoustic guitar
– Hattie Webb: background vocals, harp

Cover art
– Lorca Cohen: art direction,
  photography

– Mike Curry: design
– Mandy Eidgah: product direction
– Adam Farber: product direction
– Dominique Issermann: photography
– Edward O'Dowd: art direction, design

Track listing
"Lover Lover Lover"
  (Tel Aviv, September 24, 2009)
"Bird On The Wire"
  (Glasgow, November 6, 2008)
"Chelsea Hotel"
  (London/Royal Albert Hall,
  November 17, 2008)
"Heart With No Companion"
  (Oberhausen, Germany,
  November 2, 2008)
"That Don't Make It Junk"
  (London/O2 Arena, November 13, 2008)
"Waiting For The Miracle"
  (San Jose, California, November 13, 2009)
"Avalanche"
  (Gothenburg, October 12, 2008)
"Suzanne"
  (Manchester, November 30, 2008)
"The Partisan"
  (Helsinki, October 10, 2008)
"Famous Blue Raincoat"
  (London/O2 Arena, November 13, 2008)
"Hallelujah"
  (Coachella Festival, Indio, California,
  April 17, 2009)
"Closing Time"
  (London, Ontario, May 24, 2009)

Release date
September 14, 2010

Label and catalogue numbers
Vinyl: US Columbia 8869777112 1,
Europe Music on Vinyl MOVLP 193
CD/DVD: US/Canada/Europe Columbia/
Legacy 8869776839 2
CD: Canada/Europe Columbia/Legacy
8869775916 2
BluRay: 8869775909 9

Highest chart position on release
US 112, Canada 10, UK 68

Notes
All songs written by Leonard Cohen
except: "That Don't Make It Junk" and
"Waiting For The Miracle" (by Leonard
Cohen and Sharon Robinson); and
"The Partisan" (by A. Betoulinsky/
H. Zaret/J. Roussel – see *Live at the Isle
of Wight 1970* for credits clarification).
"Chelsea Hotel" is "Chelsea Hotel #2."

Released in foldout digipack form.
The twelve-page CD booklet includes
an essay by Leon Wieseltier and producer
Ed Sanders' notes on all the songs, and
musician credits.

The DVD contains a bonus feature:
"Backstage Sketch," a short film (22 mins

in colour and black and white) by Lorca Cohen, including interviews with band members and technicians, and rehearsal and concert footage, etc.

Live in Fredericton, 2012

Recorded at the Fredericton Playhouse, Fredericton, New Brunswick, Canada on May 11, 2008

Personnel
Unified Heart Touring Band
- Leonard Cohen: lead vocal, guitar, keyboard
- Roscoe Beck: musical director, electric bass, stand-up bass, background vocals
- Rafael Bernardo Gayol: drums and percussion
- Neil Larsen: keyboards
- Javier Mas: bandurria, laud, archilaud, twelve-string guitar
- Bob Metzger: lead guitar, pedal steel guitar
- Sharon Robinson: background vocals
- Dino Soldo: wind instruments, harmonica, keyboard, background vocals
- Charley Webb: background vocals and guitar
- Hattie Webb: background vocals and harp

Cover art
- Lorca Cohen: front photograph
- Michael Petit: graphic design
- Robert Yager: back photograph

Side one
"Dance Me To The End Of Love"
"In My Secret Life"
"Heart With No Companion"

Side two
"Bird On The Wire"
"Who By Fire"

Release dates
January 6, 2012 and April 21, 2012

Label and catalogue number
Vinyl EP: Columbia 8869196115 7

Highest chart position on release
US/Canada/Europe DNC

Notes
All songs written by Leonard Cohen except "In My Secret Life" (by Leonard Cohen and Sharon Robinson).

An mp3 download was offered by Canadian newspaper the *Ottawa Citizen* in conjunction with iTunes for a period of twenty-four hours on January 6, 2012. The mini-set of five songs was released on a vinyl EP for one day only to mark Record Store Day, April 21, 2012.

Fredericton was the opening concert of the 2008 tour – Leonard's first live concert since July 1993, and the first of what turned out to be 247 concerts across Canada, Europe, Australia, New Zealand, and the US, ending in Las Vegas on December 11, 2010. After the release of his twelfth studio album, *Old Ideas*, in January 2012, Leonard and the band went back on tour in August 2012 for another "125 shows, again across Europe, US, Canada, Australia, and New Zealand, concluding on December 21 in Auckland, New Zealand. No official releases have been issued from the 2012–2013 concerts.

COMPILATION ALBUMS

The Best of (US/Canada) / Greatest Hits (UK/Europe)

Released January 1, 1975
Vinyl: US COL JC 34077, Canada ES 90334, UK CBS 69161
MiniDisc: COL 032644 8
Chart: US/Canada DNC, UK 88

Side one
"Suzanne"
"Sisters Of Mercy"
"So Long, Marianne"
"Bird On The Wire"
"Lady Midnight"
"The Partisan"

Side two
"Hey, That's No Way To Say Goodbye"
"Famous Blue Raincoat"
"Last Year's Man"
"Chelsea Hotel #2"
"Who By Fire"
"Take This Longing"

Notes
All songs written by Leonard Cohen except: "The Partisan" (credited here as by A. Marly/H. Zaret/Bernard, though credits on other albums sometimes include the names Emmanuel d'Astier de la Vigerie and J. Roussel, and sometimes omit "Bernard," an alias for d'Astier de la Vigerie – there is no consistency).

Leonard chose the songs and wrote the sleeve notes. Some vinyl back covers have the last three songs on side one listed in the wrong order.

Reissued on CD in 1988 (Canada WCK34077), in 1989 (Europe COL 32644), and in 1990 (US CK34077).

Remastered vinyl reissued in Europe in 2010 (Music on Vinyl MOVLP 124).

So Long, Marianne

Released 1989, and thereafter at irregular intervals worldwide
US COL 460500 2, Europe CBS 460500 2, UK Columbia 983319 2, Australia Columbia 471144 2
Chart: DNC

Track listing
"Who By Fire"
"So Long, Marianne"
"Chelsea Hotel"
"Lady Midnight"
"Sisters Of Mercy"
"Bird On The Wire"
"Suzanne"
"Lover Lover Lover"
"Winter Lady"
"Tonight Will Be Fine"
"The Partisan"
"Diamonds In The Mine"

Notes
All songs written by Leonard Cohen except: "The Partisan" (credited here as by A. Marly and H. Zaret – see *The Best of/Greatest Hits* regarding the credits for this song). Several countries' releases had a different colour CD cover photo of Leonard. "Chelsea Hotel" is "Chelsea Hotel #2." The cassette tape release (CBS 466209 4) contains four additional songs: "You Know Who I Am," "Is This What You Wanted," "I Tried To Leave You," and "Please Don't Pass Me By (A Disgrace)" (Live, 1970).

This is the most notable example of the many "greatest hits" compilations on vinyl issued by different CBS concerns, especially in Europe (e.g. France, Germany, Italy) in the late 1970s and into the 1980s, in such series as "Top Artists of Pop Music" and "Golden Highlights." The compilation that became best known as *So Long, Marianne* was originally released on vinyl in 1983 as a half-speed mastered edition in the "Starsound Collection" (CBS Memory/Starsound Collection 296 947-270), before its reissue on CD in 1989.

More Best of

Released October 7, 1997
CD: US/Canada COL CK 68636, UK CBS 488237 2
MiniDisc: 488237 8
Chart: US DNC, Canada 90, UK 82

Track listing
"Everybody Knows"
"I'm Your Man"
"Take This Waltz"
"Tower Of Song"

"Anthem"
"Democracy"
"The Future"
"Closing Time"
"Dance Me To The End Of Love"
  (Live, 1993)
"Suzanne"
  (Live, 1993)
"Hallelujah"
  (Live, 1988)
"Never Any Good"
"The Great Event"

Notes

All songs written by Leonard Cohen except: "Everybody Knows" (by Leonard Cohen and Sharon Robinson); and "Take This Waltz" (lyrics by Leonard Cohen, which he translated from the original Spanish poem "Pequeño vals vienés" by Federico García Lorca).

The album was released to celebrate the thirtieth anniversary of Leonard having signed to Columbia in 1967. The last two tracks were newly recorded and previously unreleased, although a demo version of "Never Any Good," sung by Billy Valentine, had featured at the end of Armelle Brusq's 1996 documentary *Leonard Cohen: Portrait, Spring 1996*. The final track is not really a song; it consists of a computerized mix of Leonard's voice, synthesized out of all recognition (reflecting his continuing interest in computers and technology), set to part of Beethoven's Piano Sonata Op.27 No.2 ("The Moonlight") played backwards! The album is "to the memory of Victor R. Cohen 1926–1994" (Leonard's brother-in-law).

The Essential Leonard Cohen

Released October 22, 2002
US COL C2K 86884 (remastered), Canada TV2K 86884, UK COL 497995 2
Chart: US/Canada DNC, UK 70

Disc one
"Suzanne"
"The Stranger Song"
"Sisters Of Mercy"
"Hey, That's No Way To Say Goodbye"
"So Long, Marianne"
"Bird On A Wire"
"The Partisan"
"Famous Blue Raincoat"
"Chelsea Hotel #2"
"Take This Longing"
"Who By Fire"
"The Guests"
"Hallelujah"

"If It Be Your Will"
"Night Comes On"
"I'm Your Man"
"Everybody Knows"
"Tower Of Song"

Disc two
"Ain't No Cure For Love"
"Take This Waltz"
"First We Take Manhattan"
"Dance Me To The End Of Love"
  (Live, 1993)
"The Future"
"Democracy"
"Waiting For The Miracle"
"Closing Time"
"Anthem"
"In My Secret Life"
"Alexandra Leaving"
"A Thousand Kisses Deep"
"Love Itself"

Notes

All songs written by Leonard Cohen except: "The Partisan" (credited here as by H. Zaret and A. Marly – see *The Best of/Greatest Hits* regarding the credits for this song); "Everybody Knows," "Waiting For The Miracle," "In My Secret Life," "Alexandra Leaving," "A Thousand Kisses Deep," and "Love Itself" (by Leonard Cohen and Sharon Robinson); and "Take This Waltz" (lyrics by Leonard Cohen, which he translated from the original Spanish poem "Pequeño vals vienés" by Federico García Lorca). "Bird On A Wire" is "Bird On The Wire." Booklet with credits, photos etc., and a short essay by Pico Iyer.

Reissued with a bonus disc in August 2008 as *The Essential Leonard Cohen 3.0 Limited Edition* (Columbia/Legacy 8869730996 2). The bonus disc contained the following tracks: "Seems So Long Ago, Nancy," "Love Calls You By Your Name," "A Singer Must Die," "Death Of A Ladies' Man" (Cohen/Spector), "The Traitor," "By The Rivers Dark" (Cohen/Robinson), and "The Letters" (Cohen/Robinson).

Reissued without the bonus disc and with a slightly different track listing in September 2010 (Columbia/Legacy 8869777364 2). Four tracks – "The Stranger Song," "Dance Me To The End Of Love" (Live, 1993), "Alexandra Leaving," and "Love Itself" – were replaced by "Dance Me To The End Of Love" (album version), "Boogie Street" (Cohen/Robinson), "The Letters" (Cohen/Robinson), and "Tennessee Waltz" (Live, 1985) (Redd Stewart/Pee Wee King, with an additional verse by Leonard Cohen). The photo of Leonard on the front cover and disc one is back to front.

MOJO presents ... an introduction to LEONARD COHEN

Released September 22, 2003
US/UK Columbia 512852 2
Chart: DNC

Disc one
"Suzanne"
"Sisters Of Mercy"
"One Of Us Cannot Be Wrong"
"The Old Revolution"
"Seems So Long Ago, Nancy"
"Bird On The Wire"
"Joan Of Arc"
"Famous Blue Raincoat"
"Diamonds In The Mine"
"Chelsea Hotel #2"
"I Tried To Leave You"
"Who By Fire"
"Iodine"

Disc two
"The Smokey Life"
"Dance Me To The End Of Love"
"Hallelujah"
"If It Be Your Will"
"I'm Your Man"
"Take This Waltz"
"Tower Of Song"
"Light As The Breeze"
"The Gypsy's Wife"
  (Live, 1979)
"That Don't Make It Junk"

Notes

All songs written by Leonard Cohen except: "Iodine" (lyrics by Leonard Cohen, music by Phil Spector); "Take This Waltz" (lyrics by Leonard Cohen, which he translated from the original Spanish poem "Pequeño vals vienés" by Federico García Lorca); and "That Don't Make It Junk" (by Leonard Cohen and Sharon Robinson).

The booklet contains credits, photos etc., and a short essay/album notes by Sylvie Simmons.

Greatest Hits

Released July 13, 2009
UK Columbia 8869755613 2
Chart: UK 29

Track listing
"Suzanne"
"So Long, Marianne"
"Sisters Of Mercy"
"Famous Blue Raincoat"
"Everybody Knows"
"Waiting For The Miracle"
"Who By Fire"

"Chelsea Hotel #2"
"Hey, That's No Way To Say Goodbye"
"Bird On The Wire"
"A Thousand Kisses Deep"
"The Future"
"Closing Time"
"Dance Me To The End Of Love"
"First We Take Manhattan"
"I'm Your Man"
"Hallelujah"

Notes
An expanded and updated version of the original 1975 compilation.

All songs written by Leonard Cohen except: "Everybody Knows," "Waiting For The Miracle," and "A Thousand Kisses Deep" (by Leonard Cohen and Sharon Robinson).

"Waiting For The Miracle" is cut to 3'24" (the original is 7'42"). Similar booklet to the 1975 version with lyrics and credits, and some extra photos, but without any of Leonard's comments on his songs.

BOXED SETS

Songs and Poems

Released in 1980 in Australia
Vinyl: S4BP 220602

Contains the first four studio albums including a booklet with black-and-white photos and all the lyrics.

Songs and Poems

Released in 1981 in the Netherlands
Vinyl: CBS 66373

Contains the first three studio albums including a booklet with black-and-white photos and all the lyrics.

The CBS Collection, 5 CDs

Released 1989
UK/Europe CBS 465883 2

Contains *Songs from a Room* (1969), *Songs of Love and Hate* (1971), *New Skin for the Old Ceremony* (1974), *Death of a Ladies' Man* (1977), and *Various Positions* (1984).

The Collection, 5 CDs

Released June 30, 2008
UK/Europe Columbia 8869731272 2

Contains *Songs of Leonard Cohen* (1967), *Various Positions* (1984), *I'm Your Man* (1988), *The Future* (1992), and *Ten New Songs* (2001). Booklet containing album credits and photos. "Tacoma Trailer" is mistakenly listed twice on *The Future* credits page, and "Always" is not listed. Each CD is housed in a cardboard sleeve reproduction of the original.

Hallelujah: The Essential Leonard Cohen Album Collection, 8 CDs

Released 2009
The Netherlands Sony Music Entertainment 8869761557 2

Contains the first eight studio albums, from *Songs of Leonard Cohen* (1967) to *I'm Your Man* (1988). The bonus tracks issued with the first three remastered studio albums (in 2007) are included. Twelve-page booklet with essay (in Dutch) by Henk Hofstede, photos, song credits (excluding musicians), etc.

The Complete Studio Albums Collection, 11 CDs

Released October 10, 2011
US/Canada/Europe Columbia Legacy 8869796177 2

Contains the first eleven studio albums, from *Songs of Leonard Cohen* (1967) to *Dear Heather* (2004), each remastered. The bonus tracks issued with the remastered first three studio albums in 2007 are not included. Each CD is housed in a cardboard sleeve reproduction of the original. Twenty-four-page booklet with individual album credits, photos, and essay by Pico Iyer.

The Complete Columbia Albums Collection, 18 CDs

Released October 11, 2011
US/Canada/Europe Columbia Legacy 8869787184 2

Contains the first eleven studio albums, from *Songs of Leonard Cohen* (1967) to *Dear Heather* (2004), and the first six live albums, from *Live Songs* (1973) to *Songs from the Road* (2010), each remastered. (*Live in London* [2009] takes up two CDs.) The bonus tracks issued with the remastered first three studio albums in 2007 are not included. "Greatest hits"

compilations are also not included. Each CD is housed in a cardboard sleeve reproduction of the original. Thirty-six-page booklet with individual album credits, photos, and essay by Pico Iyer.

7" AND 12" VINYL SINGLES
EPs AND CD-SINGLES

This selection is not exhaustive and does not include every promo, demo, reissue or alternative B-side.

All US/Canada releases are on Columbia and all UK/Europe/Australia releases on CBS except where noted. Japan releases are on CBS/Sony. All singles are 7" vinyl except where noted. A large majority of 7" singles issued in UK/Europe have picture sleeves, very often with each different country having a different picture for the same single. All 12" singles, EPs, and CD-singles have picture sleeves.

The only song to make a significant impression on the US *Billboard*/UK Top 40 charts was "Hallelujah" in 2008.

1968

"Suzanne" / "So Long, Marianne" (UK/Europe 3337)

"So Long, Marianne" / "Hey, That's No Way To Say Goodbye" (Canada C4 2785)

1969

"Suzanne" / "Teachers" (Greece 301323)

"Bird On The Wire" / "Seems So Long Ago, Nancy" (UK/Europe 4245)

"The Partisan" / "Bird On The Wire" (Europe 4262)

"The Partisan" / "Suzanne" (Europe 4651)

1971

"Joan Of Arc" / "Diamonds In The Mine" (UK/Europe 7292)

"So Long, Marianne" / "Pajaro En El Alambre" (trans. "Bird On The Wire") (Spain 7522)

This Spanish single was rereleased in 2007 in US/Europe (Sony LC02523) to promote the first set of remastered studio albums.

1972

"Suzanne" / "Bird On The Wire"
(UK/Europe 8353)

McCabe & Mrs Miller (EP): "Sisters Of
Mercy" / "Winter Lady" / "The Stranger
Song" (US 7684; UK 9162)

McCabe & Mrs Miller (EP): "Winter Lady" /
"Sisters Of Mercy" / "The Stranger
Song" (Europe 7684)

"Stranger Song" / "Sisters Of Mercy"
(Germany 7762)

1973

"Passing Through" (Live, 1972) / "Nancy"
(Live, 1972) (US 45852; Europe 1544)

1974

"Bird On The Wire" (Live, 1972) /
"Tonight Will Be Fine" (Live, 1970)
(UK 2494)

"Bird On The Wire" (Live, 1972) / "Nancy"
(Live, 1972) (UK 8140)

"Lover Lover Lover" / "Who By Fire"
(UK/Europe 2699)

1975

"Tonight Will Be Fine" / "Why Don't
You Try" (Germany S 3524)

1976

"Suzanne" / "Who By Fire"
(Spain 3938)

"Suzanne" / "Take This Longing"
(UK/Europe S 4306)

"Do I Have To Dance All Night" (Live,
1976) / "The Butcher" (Live, 1976)
(Europe 4431)

*The two songs on this single have still not
been released on any official Leonard
Cohen album.*

1977

"Memories" / "Don't Go Home With Your
Hard-On" (UK/Europe S 5882)

"True Love Leaves No Traces" / "I Left A
Woman Waiting" (UK/Europe 6095)

"True Love Leaves No Traces" / "Iodine"
(US Warner Bros 8527)

1979

"The Guests" / "The Lost Canadian
(Un Canadien Errant)" (Europe S 7938)

1983

Leonard Cohen (EP): "Bird On The Wire" /
"Lady Midnight" / "Joan Of Arc" /
"Suzanne" / "Hey, That's No Way To
Say Goodbye" / "Paper Thin Hotel"
(UK Pickwick Scoop 7SR 5022)

1985

"Dance Me To The End Of Love" /
"The Law" (UK 6052)

"Dance Me To The End Of Love" /
"Coming Back To You" (Europe A4895)

"Dance Me To The End Of Love" /
"If It Be Your Will" (Japan 07SP 873)

"Hallelujah" / "The Law"
(Europe A4918)

*In the UK Christmas charts of 2008,
Leonard's version of "Hallelujah" actually
reached #36, clearly due to the popularity
of Alexandra Burke's cover, which was at #1,
having become the fastest-selling single
ever by a female solo artist, after she won
the UK TV show The X Factor. The late Jeff
Buckley's cover was at #2 – the last time
that the same song occupied both top
positions was in 1957 with "Singin' The
Blues" by Tommy Steele and Guy Mitchell. A
third "Hallelujah" cover, by Kate Voegele,
also charted, meaning that the song held
four chart positions at the same time.*

1986

"Take This Waltz" (Leonard Cohen) /
"Grido A Roma" (Angelo Branduardi) /
"Asesinato" (Paco de Lucia y Pepe de
Lucia) (Europe 650210 7)

*This single was released to tie in with the
Lorca tribute album* Poetas en Nueva York
/ Poets in New York. *Leonard features in
the song's promo video, shot on location in
and around the house in Granada, Spain,
where Lorca was born. The single went to
#1 in Spain. A new remix of this track was
later included, with additional vocals and
instrumentation, on Leonard's 1988 album*
I'm Your Man.

1987

"First We Take Manhattan" / "Sisters
Of Mercy" / "Bird On The Wire" /
"Suzanne" (Europe: 12" 651352 6;
CD-single 651352 2)

1988

"First We Take Manhattan" /
"Bird On The Wire" / "Suzanne"
(Europe: 12" 651352 6)

"First We Take Manhattan" / "Sisters
Of Mercy" (UK/Europe 651352 7)

"Ain't No Cure For Love" / "Jazz Police" /
"Hey, That's No Way To Say Goodbye" /
"So Long, Marianne" (UK: 12" 651599 6;
CD-single 651599 2)

"Ain't No Cure For Love" / "Jazz Police"
(UK/Australia 651599 7)

"I'm Your Man" / "Chelsea Hotel #2" /
"Who By Fire" (Holland: 12" 651522 6;
CD-single 651522 2)

"I'm Your Man" / "Chelsea Hotel #2"
(Europe 651522 7)

"Everybody Knows" / "The Partisan"
(Holland 652881 7)

1989

"First We Take Manhattan" / "Suzanne" /
"So Long, Marianne" (UK 3" mini CD-
single 654565 3)

"I Can't Forget" / "Hey, That's No Way
To Say Goodbye" (Holland 654734 7)

1992

"Closing Time" / "Everybody Knows"
(Europe 658760 7)

"Closing Time" / "Everybody Knows" /
"Hallelujah" (US CD-single 658760 2)

"Closing Time" / "Waiting For The
Miracle" / "Ain't No Cure For Love" /
"First We Take Manhattan"
(Europe CD-single 658942 2)

"Democracy" / "First We Take
Manhattan" / "I'm Your Man"
(US CD-single 44K 74778)

*The European version of the "Democracy"
CD-single contains a radio edit/album
version of the title track (659402 1).*

1993

"The Future" / "Be For Real"
(US/Europe CD-single 658948 1)

"The Future" / "Be For Real" /
"Ain't No Cure For Love"
(US/Europe CD-single 658948 2)

"Closing Time" / "First We Take
Manhattan" / "Famous Blue Raincoat" /
"Winter Lady" (UK CD-single 659299 2)

*The "Closing Time" single contains
four album prints in a cardboard box
"to commemorate Cohen's 1993 Royal
Albert Hall shows."*

1994

"Dance Me To The End Of Love"
(Live, 1993) / "I'm Your Man" (Live, 1993)
(US CD-single 660724 1)

1997

"Never Any Good" / "Suzanne"
(Live, 1993)
(Europe CD-single 665072 1)

"Never Any Good" / "Suzanne"
(Live, 1993) / "Everybody Knows"
(Spain CD-single 665072 2)

2012

"Hallelujah" (Leonard Cohen) /
"Hallelujah" (Jeff Buckley) (Columbia
Legacy/Music on Vinyl MOV 7017)

*This single was released as a "numbered
collector's edition" to celebrate Record
Store Day, November 23, 2012, and to
support the publication of Alan Light's book
about the song,* The Holy or the Broken
(New York: Atria Books, 2012).

VARIOUS ARTISTS AND GUEST APPEARANCES

This list includes Leonard Cohen
recordings available only on albums
by various artists or on albums by
other individual artists.

1957
Six Montreal Poets

Leonard reads eight of his own poems:
"For Wilf and His House," "Beside the
Shepherd," "Poem," "Lovers," "The
Sparrows," "Warning," "Les Vieux,"
and "Elegy."

Vinyl: Folkways Records and Service
Corporation, FL 9805.

Reissued in 1991 on cassette tape by the
Smithsonian Institute, on Smithsonian
Folkways 09085. The other poets on
the disc are: F. R. Scott, Louis Dudek,
A. M. Klein, Irving Layton, and A. J. M.
Smith. Leonard's setting of F. R. Scott's
"Villanelle for Our Time" appeared
on *Dear Heather* in 2004.

1966
Canadian Poets 1

Leonard reads seven of his own poems:
"What I'm Doing Here," "You Have the
Lovers," "Now of Sleeping," "Style,"
"Two Went to Sleep," "Nothing Has
Been Broken," and "These Heroics."

Double vinyl: *Canadian Poets 1*,
Canadian Broadcasting Corporation
(no catalogue number on album sleeve).

The other poets on the disc are:
Earle Birney, George Bowering,
Irving Layton, Gwendolyn Macewen,
John Newlove, Alfred Purdy, and
Phyllis Webb.

1975
The Earl Scruggs Revue Anniversary Special: Volume 1

Leonard contributes shared lead vocal
on "Passing Through" (with Joan Baez,
Buffy Sainte-Marie, Ramblin' Jack Elliott,
and the Pointer Sisters).

Vinyl: US Columbia PC 33416,
Canada Columbia KC 33416,
UK/Europe CBS 80821

Reissued in 2005 on CD: GottCD021
(licensed from Sony BMG Music Ltd)

The song was written by Richard Blakeslee
and credited on the disc label as
"R. Blakeslee – Arr. Leonard Cohen."
Other musicians on the album include
Ron Cornelius, Charlie Daniels, and Bob
Johnston, who had recorded and toured
with Leonard on previous albums and tours.

1986
Poetas en Nueva York / Poets in New York

"Take This Waltz"

Vinyl: Spain (*Poetas en Nueva York*)
CBS 450307 1; Netherlands/UK
(*Poets in New York*) CBS 450286 1

CD: *Poetas en Nueva York* COL 477773 2;
Poets in New York CBS 450286 2

All the tracks recorded in 1986, the
fiftieth anniversary of the death of
Federico García Lorca. "Take This Waltz"
is Leonard's translation into English of
Lorca's original Spanish poem "Pequeño
vals vienés." The album contains lyrics
to all the songs and the original Lorca
poems in both Castilian and English.
Other contributors include Lluis Llach,
Angelo Branduardi, Donovan, and
Patxi Andion.

1987
Jennifer Warnes: Famous Blue Raincoat

"Joan Of Arc"
(duet with Jennifer Warnes)

Vinyl: US Cypress 661 111-1, Canada
Attic LAT 1227, UK Cypress PL90048

CD: US Private Music 01005-82092-2,
Canada Attic ACD 1227,
UK Cypress PD90048

Also released as B-side of 12" vinyl
single, c/w: "First We Take Manhattan" /
"Famous Blue Raincoat" (Cypress
Records PT 49710)

(see also Tributes section overleaf)

1988
The Prince's Trust Rock Gala

"Tower Of Song" (Live, London,
June 6, 1988)

Video: Europe MSD V9122

Reissued in 1999 on DVD
(as Prince's Royal Trust Gala Volume 3):
Germany TDK DV-PTRU88

The album does not contain the complete performance of the song; it has been edited down to just under four minutes. Leonard also plays keyboard, and is backed by Julie Christensen and Perla Batalla. Other musicians in these two concerts include Peter Gabriel, Phil Collins, Elton John, Eric Clapton, and Mark Knopfler.

1990
Was (Not Was): are you okay?

"Elvis' Rolls Royce" (lead vocals)

Vinyl: Europe/UK Fontana 846 351 1

CD: US Chrysalis F2 21778, UK/Europe Phonogram/Fontana 846 351 2

The song was written by David and Don Was. Iggy Pop is one of the background vocalists.

1992
Weird Nightmare: Meditations on Mingus

Leonard reads Charlie Mingus's song lyric "The Chill Of Death," set to some of Mingus's music, on the Diamanda Galás track "Eclipse."

CD: US Columbia CK 52739, Europe Columbia 472467 2

The album was produced by Hal Willner, who was to bring his Leonard Cohen tribute Came So Far for Beauty to the public in the mid-2000s (see Tributes section overleaf).

1993
Paul Shaffer & the Party Boys of Rock 'n' Roll: The World's Most Dangerous Party

Leonard speaks a few words on the track "1999."

Double CD: US SBK Records K2 89786

"1999" is the song by Prince, first issued in 1982 on the album of the same title.
Paul Shaffer was the house-band leader on the US TV Late Show with David Letterman; Leonard had sung his song "The Future" on this same show in early February 1993. Other singers on the album include Tony Bennett, Joan Jett, and Aaron Neville. Sid McGinnis plays guitars – he'd toured with Leonard in Europe back in 1976 and played on Various Positions (1984).

Elton John: Duets
"Born To Lose" (duet with Elton John)

Double vinyl: UK Rocket Records 518 478 1

CD: US MCA Records MCAD 10926, Canada MCASD 10926, UK/Europe Rocket Records 518 478 2

A promo "special edition CD singles box" was also issued with each duet in its own CD sleeve. The song was written by Ted Daffan (1943) and was a minor hit for Ray Charles in 1962. Other duettists on the album include Little Richard, Tammy Wynette, and Gladys Knight.

Vintage Voices

Leonard reads passages from his 1966 novel Beautiful Losers.

Promotional cassette tape, produced by Vintage Books, New York, Autumn 1993 edition.

Other authors on the tape include Rita Dove, Gloria Naylor, Mark Leyner, and Michael Ondaatje – author of Leonard Cohen (Toronto: McClelland & Stewart, 1970), the first serious study in book form of Leonard's poetry and novels.

1994
Rare on Air, Volume One

Leonard reads his own "Poem."

CD: Mammoth Records MR0074-2

Recorded November 1993 at the KCRW studios in Los Angeles during an interview with Chris Douridas on the "Morning Becomes Eclectic" show, and broadcast on December 3. "Poem" was one of six poems read that morning. It begins with the words "I heard of a man" and was first published in Let Us Compare Mythologies, in 1956. The album also includes performances by Tori Amos, Mark Isham, and John Cale.

The Tibetan Book of the Dead

Leonard is the narrator throughout the two-part ninety-five-minute film, a co-production between NHK (Japan), Mistral Films (France), and the NFB (Canada). The history of the book is explained and connected to its contemporary usage. The film also includes an interview with the Dalai Lama. First broadcast on Canadian TV, December 1994.

DVD: Wellspring Media WSP773

1996
The United States of Poetry

Leonard reads his own song lyric "Democracy."

Video: The original PBS special, titled U.S. Poetry, was issued by KOED Books and Video.

CD: The soundtrack CD was issued in 1996 by Mercury Records/Mouth Almighty Records 314 532 139-2. (Thirty-seven poems recited by the authors with original music by Tomandandy).

PBS broadcast the five-part series The United States of Poetry in February and March 1996. Leonard's reading is at the beginning of part three: "The American Dream."

In Their Own Voices: A Century of Recorded Poetry

Leonard reads his own song lyric "Story Of Isaac" (from the studio album Songs from a Room, 1969).

Four-CD boxed set: US WEA/Atlantic/ Rhino Records R2 72408

The project was created by Rebekah Presson, who also wrote the included notes along with Erica Jong and Al Young. Other poets reading their work include Robert Frost, e e cummings, Robert Lowell, Allen Ginsberg, and Sylvia Plath.

2006
Hommage à Paul Simon / Tribute to Paul Simon

Leonard reads Paul Simon's song lyric "The Sound Of Silence."

CD: Du Rêve et de la Musique 766937105 2

The original version of the song issued in 1966 on Simon & Garfunkel's album Sounds of Silence. Other musicians on the tribute album include Elvis Costello, Jim Cuddy, Colin James, and Ariane Moffatt. Leonard's is the bonus track.

I'm Your Man (motion picture and CD soundtrack)

"Tower Of Song" (with U2)

CD: US Verve Forecast B0007169-02, UK Verve Forecast 0602517024083

DVD: Lionsgate LG93896

(see also Tributes section overleaf)

2007
Philip Glass / Leonard Cohen: Book of Longing

Leonard reads his own poems from *Book of Longing*.

Double CD: Orange Mountain Music OMM0043

Book of Longing was published in 2006 – a collection of poems, prose pieces, and drawings; Glass made his own selection and set the texts to music. Live concert performances, with Leonard's pre-recorded spoken vocals, followed in 2007 including in Toronto (world premiere), Chicago, Stanford, Cardiff, London, and Wellington.

Herbie Hancock: River: The Joni Letters

Leonard reads Joni Mitchell's song lyric "The Jungle Line."

Double vinyl: US Verve 0602517468344

CD: US Verve B0009791-02, Europe Verve B0602517448261

The original version of the song issued in 1975 on Joni Mitchell's album *The Hissing of Summer Lawns*. This tribute album to Joni Mitchell won the Grammy for Album of the Year in 2008 – only the second jazz album ever to win the overall award (the first was Stan Getz and João Gilberto's *Getz/Gilberto* in 1965). Other contributors include Norah Jones, Tina Turner, and Joni Mitchell herself.

2008
Born to the Breed: A Tribute to Judy Collins

Leonard reads Judy Collins' song lyric "Since You've Asked."

CD: US Wildflower WFL 1313

The original version of the song was issued in 1967 on Judy Collins' album *Wildflowers* (which also contained covers of three of Leonard's songs, "Sisters Of Mercy," "Priests," and "Hey, That's No Way To Say Goodbye"). Other singers on the album include Chrissie Hynde, Jimmy Webb, Rufus Wainwright, and the Webb Sisters (Leonard's backing vocalists in concerts 2008–2013).

SELECTED TRIBUTE ALBUMS

1987
Jennifer Warnes: Famous Blue Raincoat

Vinyl: US Cypress 661 111-1, Canada Attic LAT 1227, UK Cypress PL90048

CD: US Private Music 01005-82092-2, Canada Attic ACD 1227, UK Cypress PD90048

Side one
"First We Take Manhattan"
"Bird On The Wire"
"Famous Blue Raincoat"
"Joan Of Arc" (duet with Leonard Cohen)

Side two
"Ain't No Cure For Love"
"Coming Back To You"
"Song Of Bernadette"
"A Singer Must Die"
"Came So Far For Beauty"

Notes
"Joan Of Arc" was issued as a B-side on Warnes' 12" single of "First We Take Manhattan" (Cypress Records PT 49710).

The album was remastered and reissued on CD in 2007 as a twentieth-anniversary edition with four previously unreleased tracks: "Night Comes On," "Ballad Of The Runaway Horse," "If It Be Your Will," and "Joan Of Arc" (live in concert).

Also reissued in a three-LP boxed set (limited/numbered edition), playing at 45rpm, with one extra vinyl-exclusive track, "A Singer Must Die" (demo) (Porch Light/Cisco Music CLP7060-45).

1991
I'm Your Fan

Double-vinyl: UK EastWest Records 9031-75598-1, Europe Columbia COL 469032 1

CD: US Atlantic 7 82349-2, Canada EastWest Records CD75598, Europe EastWest Records 9031-77598-2

Side one
"Who By Fire" – The House of Love
"Hey, That's No Way To Say Goodbye" – Ian McCulloch
"I Can't Forget" – Pixies
"Stories Of The Street" – That Petrol Emotion
"Bird On The Wire" – The Lilac Time

Side two
"Suzanne" – Geoffrey Oryema
"So Long, Marianne" – James
"Avalanche IV" – Jean-Louis Murat
"Don't Go Home With Your Hard-On" – David McComb & Adam Peters

Side three
"First We Take Manhattan" – R.E.M.
"Chelsea Hotel" – Lloyd Cole
"Tower Of Song" – Robert Forster
"Take This Longing" – Peter Astor
"True Love Leaves No Traces" – Dead Famous People

Side four
"I'm Your Man" – Bill Pritchard
"A Singer Must Die" – Fatima Mansions
"Tower Of Song" – Nick Cave and the Bad Seeds
"Hallelujah" – John Cale

Notes
Produced by the French music magazine *Les Inrockuptibles*, editor Christian Fevret.

1995
Tower of Song

CD: US/Canada A&M 31454 0259 2, UK A&M 540 259-2

Track listing
"Everybody Knows" – Don Henley
"Coming Back To You" – Trisha Yearwood
"Sisters Of Mercy" – Sting with the Chieftains
"Hallelujah" – Bono
"Famous Blue Raincoat" – Tori Amos
"Ain't No Cure For Love" – Aaron Neville
"I'm Your Man" – Elton John
"Bird On A Wire" – Willie Nelson
"Suzanne" – Peter Gabriel
"Light As The Breeze" – Billy Joel
"If It Be Your Will" – Jann Arden
"Story Of Isaac" – Suzanne Vega
"Coming Back To You" – Martin Gore

Notes
Originally planned to celebrate Leonard's sixtieth birthday in 1994, but not released until the following year. The front cover of the US CD has the same "Anima Sola" image (of a chained woman, enveloped in flames, looking heavenward) that first appeared on the back of Leonard's debut album, *Songs of Leonard Cohen*, in 1967.

2004
Judy Collins Sings Leonard Cohen: Democracy

CD: Elektra/Rhino 8122-76510-2

Track listing
"Democracy" (new recording)
"Suzanne" (1966)
"A Thousand Kisses Deep"
 (new recording)
"Hey, That's No Way
 To Say Goodbye" (1967)
"Dress Rehearsal Rag" (1966)
"Priests" (1967)
"Night Comes On" (new recording)
"Sisters Of Mercy" (1967)
"Story Of Isaac" (1968)
"Bird On The Wire" (1968)
"Famous Blue Raincoat" (1971)
"Take This Longing" (1976)
"Song Of Bernadette" (Live, 1999)

Notes
This disc gathers together Judy Collins' previously released Leonard Cohen recordings together with three newly recorded songs.

2006
I'm Your Man (motion picture and CD soundtrack)

CD: US Verve Forecast B0007169-02,
UK 0602517024083

DVD: Lionsgate LG93896

Track listing
"Tower Of Song" – Martha Wainwright
"Tonight Will Be Fine" – Teddy Thompson
"I'm Your Man" – Nick Cave
"Winter Lady" – Kate McGarrigle,
 Anna McGarrigle, Martha Wainwright
"Sisters Of Mercy" – Beth Orton
"Chelsea Hotel #2" – Rufus Wainwright
"If It Be Your Will" – Antony
"I Can't Forget" – Jarvis Cocker
"Famous Blue Raincoat"
 – The Handsome Family
"Bird On A Wire" – Perla Batalla
"Everybody Knows" – Rufus Wainwright
"The Traitor" – Martha Wainwright
"Suzanne" – Nick Cave, Julie Christensen,
 Perla Batalla
"The Future" – Teddy Thompson
"Anthem" – Perla Batalla,
 Julie Christensen
"Tower Of Song" – Leonard Cohen and U2

Notes
All songs recorded live at performances of Hal Willner's *Came So Far For Beauty: An Evening Of Leonard Cohen Songs* at the Brighton Dome (England) as part of the Brighton Festival in May 2004 and at the Sydney Opera House (Australia) as part of the Sydney Festival in January 2005, except "Tower Of Song" featuring Leonard Cohen and U2 with background vocals by Anjani – recorded in New York, May 2005.
The DVD-film (directed by Lian Lunson) is built around coverage of the Sydney concert. Special features include additional songs, rehearsal footage, and "A Conversation with Leonard Cohen."

2007
Perla Batalla: Bird on the Wire

CD: Mechuda Music 25346 90882

Track listing
"If It Be Your Will"
"Seems So Long Ago, Nancy"
"Coming Back To You"
"Dance Me To The End Of Love"
 (featuring Bill Gable)
"So Long, Marianne"
"Came So Far For Beauty"
"Ballad Of The Absent Mare"
 (featuring David Hidalgo)
"Famous Blue Raincoat"
"Bird On The Wire"
"Suzanne" (featuring Eva Batalla-Mann)

Notes
Julie Christensen sings backing vocals on a couple of tracks; she and Perla were Leonard's backing vocalists on the 1988 and 1993 tours and both also featured on *The Future* and the *I'm Your Man* tribute film and album.

NOTE FROM THE COMPILER

My most reliable and important source of information was:

www.leonardcohenfiles.com
Full and comprehensive details of all the studio albums, live albums, compilation albums, singles (including promos, demos, picture sleeves, cassette tapes, etc.), more than eighty tribute albums, reissues, limited editions, picture discs, videos, DVDs, and every other Leonard Cohen recording (including TV, radio, films, poems, interviews, documentaries, etc.), and more.

It also shows links to many other excellent websites including:

www.leonardcohencroatia.com
Visuals, lists, and information on a wide variety of Leonard Cohen topics especially *Dear Heather* (2004) and *Old Ideas* (2012)

www.maartenmassa.be
All the piano/guitar chords of all the songs on all the albums (and more), all the concert set-lists 2008–2010

www.webheights.net/speakingcohen
Articles, analysis, opinions, interview transcripts, album and concert reviews, all the song lyrics, and more

And I consulted **www.discogs.com** for almost everything else.

FURTHER READING

COMPLETE LIST OF PUBLISHED
WORKS BY LEONARD COHEN

1956
Let Us Compare Mythologies
Toronto: Contact Press (McGill Poetry Series).
Poetry collection. Republished in 1966 by
McClelland & Stewart, and in 2007, as a facsimile
of the 1956 edition, by HarperCollins (Ecco Books).

1961
The Spice-Box of Earth
Toronto: McClelland & Stewart. Poetry.

1963
The Favourite Game
London: Secker and Warburg. Novel. Not published
in the United States until 1964 (by Viking) and in
Canada until 1970 (by McClelland & Stewart).

1964
Flowers for Hitler
Toronto: McClelland & Stewart. Poetry.

1966
Beautiful Losers
Toronto: McClelland & Stewart. Novel.

Parasites of Heaven
Toronto: McClelland & Stewart. Poetry.

1968
Selected Poems: 1956–1968
Toronto: McClelland & Stewart. An anthology
drawn from the first four poetry collections.
An abridged edition was published in the UK
in 1969 by Jonathan Cape.

1972
The Energy of Slaves
Toronto: McClelland & Stewart /
New York: Viking. Poetry.

1978
Death of a Lady's Man
Toronto: McClelland & Stewart / London & New
York: Viking. Poetry and prose.

1984
Book of Mercy
Toronto: McClelland & Stewart.
Meditations, prayers, and psalms.

1993
Stranger Music: Selected Poems and Songs
Toronto: McClelland & Stewart /
New York: Pantheon Books.
An anthology of poetry and song lyrics, including
rewrites of some works – particularly those from
Death of a Lady's Man.

2006
Book of Longing
Toronto: McClelland & Stewart /
New York: HarperCollins.
Poetry, artworks, and line drawings.

2011
Poems and Songs
New York: Random House (Everyman's Library,
Pocket Poets). An anthology of poems and song
lyrics from throughout Leonard's career.

2012
Fifteen Poems
New York: Random House (Everyman's Library,
Pocket Poets). An eBook-only selection of poems
from throughout Leonard's career accompanied
by twenty-four of his drawings.

SELECTED BOOKS ABOUT
LEONARD COHEN

Burger, Jeff. *Leonard Cohen on Leonard Cohen: Interviews and Encounters.*
Chicago: Chicago Review Press, 2014.

Devlin, Jim. *Leonard Cohen: In Every Style of Passion.*
London: Omnibus Press, 1996.

Devlin, Jim. *Leonard Cohen in His Own Words.*
London: Omnibus Press, 1998.

Light, Alan. *The Holy or the Broken: Leonard Cohen, Jeff Buckley, and the Unlikely Ascent of "Hallelujah".*
New York: Atria Books, 2012.

Nadel, Ira. *Leonard Cohen: A Life in Art.*
Toronto: ECW Press, 1994.

Nadel, Ira. *Various Positions: A Life of Leonard Cohen.*
Toronto: Random House of Canada, 1996 (revised 2006) / London: Bloomsbury, 1997 / Austin, Texas: University of Texas Press, 2007.

Ondaatje, Michael. *Leonard Cohen.*
Toronto: McClelland & Stewart, 1970.

Rasky, Harry. *The Song of Leonard Cohen.*
Oakville, Ontario: Mosaic Press, 2001 & 2010 / London: Souvenir Press, 2010.

Reynolds, Anthony. *Leonard Cohen: A Remarkable Life.*
London: Omnibus Press, 2010.

Scobie, Stephen. *Leonard Cohen.*
Vancouver: Douglas & McIntyre, 1978.

Simmons, Sylvie. *I'm Your Man: The Life of Leonard Cohen.*
Toronto: McClelland & Stewart, 2012 / New York: HarperCollins, 2012 / London: Jonathan Cape, 2012.

SELECTED WEBSITES

Diamonds in the Lines: Leonard Cohen in His Own Live Words
www.leonardcohen-prologues.com

Heck of a Guy: The Other Leonard Cohen Site
1heckofaguy.com

Leonard Cohen: The Official Leonard Cohen Site
www.leonardcohen.com

Leonard Cohen: Poeta Nascitur, Non Fit (includes the Cohen Chords Archive)
www.maartenmassa.be

Leonard Cohen Concordance
www.webheights.net/cohenconcordance

Leonard Cohen Files
www.leonardcohenfiles.com

Leonard Cohen Forum
www.leonardcohenforum.com

Speaking Cohen: A Tribute to Leonard Cohen and His Words
www.webheights.net/speakingcohen

QUOTE SOURCES

All quotes come from previously unpublished interviews by Harvey Kubernik except for those listed below.

6 "The artist, and …" Federico García Lorca, quoted in *Lorca: A Dream of Life* by Leslie Stainton, New York: Farrar, Straus and Giroux, 1999
7 "I studied the …" LC, from his "How I Got My Song" speech, Prince of Asturias awards ceremony, 2011
14 "If you happen …" LC interview with Michael C Ford, *Los Angeles Free Press*, 1975
16 "Some say that …" LC, from *The Favourite Game*, London: Secker & Warburg, 1963
17 "I first wrote …" LC speaking in 1972 in Tony Palmer's *Bird on a Wire* documentary, 1974
19 "In the early …" LC interview with Harvey Kubernik, *Melody Maker*, 1975
19 "E. J. Pratt. …" LC interview with Michael C Ford, *Los Angeles Free Press*, 1975
20 "Yeats' father said …" LC interview with Nigel Williamson, *Sunday Times* magazine (UK), 1997
20 "I met Leonard …" Ruth R. Wisse, from *My Life Without Leonard Cohen*, Commentary magazine, 1995
22 "I was always …" LC, quoted in *Various Positions: A Life of Leonard Cohen* by Ira B. Nadel, New York: Pantheon Books, 1996
26 "The years are …" LC, quoted in *Various Positions: A Life of Leonard Cohen* by Ira B. Nadel, New York: Pantheon Books, 1996
30 "When I got …" LC interview with Diego A. Manrique, *Rockdelux* (Spain), 1985
33 "unhappy people who've …" LC television interview with Stuart Smith, *Youth Special*, CBC, 1963
36 "How can I …" LC, from *Beautiful Losers*, Toronto: McClelland & Stewart, 1966
37 "I've been on …" LC, quoted in an ad for his debut LP in *KRLA Beat*, 1968
40 "I came to …" LC radio interview in *The John Hammond Years*, BBC, 1986
42 "Although my books …" LC radio interview in *The John Hammond Years*, BBC, 1986
42 "I had a …" Judy Collins television interview with Tavis Smiley, *Tavis Smiley Show*, PBS, 2010
43 "The writing of …" LC radio interview in *The John Hammond Years*, BBC, 1986
44 "So, I listened …" John Hammond radio interview in *The John Hammond Years*, BBC, 1986
44 "Hammond was extremely …" LC interview with Harvey Kubernik, *Melody Maker*, 1976
45 "I met Leonard …" Judy Collins, from *Trust Your Heart: An Autobiography*, Boston: Houghton Mifflin, 1987
49 "I was really …" Clive Davis interview with Harvey Kubernik, 2007 (a portion published in *Goldmine* magazine, 2007)
49 "When I first …" LC radio interview in *The John Hammond Years*, BBC, 1986
49 "My first producer …" LC interview with Harvey Kubernik, *Melody Maker*, 1976

52 "Leonard Cohen, incredibly …" Ellen Sander, from "Leonard Cohen … The Man," *Sing Out!*, August/September 1967; Copyright © 1967 Ellen Sander (article and reproduction courtesy of Ellen Sander)
52 "There's something uncomfortable …" Buffy Sainte-Marie, from "Leonard Cohen … His Songs," *Sing Out!*, August/September 1967
53 "He [Simon] took …" LC interview with Harvey Kubernik, *Melody Maker*, 1976
55 "My lyrics are …" Joni Mitchell, quoted in *Both Sides Now* by Brian Hinton, London: Sanctuary Publishing, 1996
60 "So, the record …" John Hammond radio interview in *The John Hammond Years*, BBC, 1986
61 "I was handsome …" LC, "Teachers" from *Songs of Leonard Cohen*, 1967
63 "I know there …" LC interview with Michael C Ford, *Los Angeles Free Press*, 1975
67 "I used to …" LC interview with Harvey Kubernik, *Melody Maker*, 1975
68 "'Bird On The …" LC interview with Paul Zollo, *SongTalk*, 1992
68 "It was very …" LC interview with Paul Zollo, *SongTalk*, 1992
68 "Like a bird …" LC, "Bird On The Wire" from *Songs from a Room*, 1969
68 "I remember you …" LC, "Chelsea Hotel #2" from *New Skin for the Old Ceremony*, 1974
76 "I liked the …" LC interview with Harvey Kubernik, *Melody Maker*, 1976
80 "I don't think …" LC interview with Paul Zollo, *SongTalk*, 1992
86 "With each record …" LC interview with Harvey Kubernik, *Melody Maker*, 1976
88 "'Famous Blue Raincoat' …" LC interview with Paul Zollo, *SongTalk*, 1992
88 "It's four in …" LC, "Famous Blue Raincoat" from *Songs of Love and Hate*, 1971
90 "There's an interesting …" LC interview with Harvey Kubernik, *Melody Maker*, 1976
92 "I was already …" Jennifer Warnes, quoted in a Cypress Records media release, 1987
97 "I have occasionally …" LC interview with Harvey Kubernik, *Melody Maker*, 1975
99 "The album *Live* …" LC interview with Harvey Kubernik, *Melody Maker*, 1975
99–100 "For a while …" LC interview with Harvey Kubernik, *Melody Maker*, 1975
102 "I must say …" LC interview with Harvey Kubernik, *Melody Maker*, 1975
109 "A Zen monastery …" LC interview with Jordi Saládrigas, *ABC* (Spain), 2001
112 "I can really …" LC interview with Harvey Kubernik, *Melody Maker* and *Phonograph Record Magazine*, 1977
115 "I'm feeling more …" LC interview with Ritchie Yorke, 1985
115 "Phil is not …" LC interview with Harvey Kubernik, *Melody Maker* and *Phonograph Record Magazine*, 1977
115 "In those songs …" LC interview with Harvey Kubernik, *Melody Maker* and *Phonograph Record Magazine*, 1977
115 "Do not be …" LC, from "How to Speak Poetry" in *Death of a Lady's Man*, Toronto: McClelland & Stewart/ New York: Viking, 1978

116 "Working with Phil …" LC interview with Harvey Kubernik, *Melody Maker* and *Phonograph Record Magazine*, 1977
118 "Gold Star was …" Stan Ross interview with Harvey Kubernik, 2001 (a portion published in *Goldmine* magazine, 2001)
118 "When you see …" Phil Spector interview with Harvey Kubernik, *Melody Maker*, 1977
118 "On the Cohen …" Don Randi interview with Harvey Kubernik, 2008 (a portion published in *Goldmine* magazine, 2001)
119 "One day he …" LC interview with Nick Paton Walsh, *Observer* (UK), 2001
125 "I have never …" LC interview in *El Mundo* (Spain), 2001
131 "The poem is …" LC, from "How to Speak Poetry" in *Death of a Lady's Man*, Toronto: McClelland & Stewart/New York: Viking, 1978
136 "Suddenly, I knew …" LC interview with Judith Fitzgerald, *Globe and Mail*, 2000
136 "If It Be …'" LC interview with Paul Zollo, *SongTalk*, 1992
137 "[The songs on …]" LC interview with Ritchie Yorke, 1985
140 "Jennifer helped me …" LC interview with Dave DiMartino, *Billboard* magazine, 1988
140 "I'm guided by …" LC, "First We Take Manhattan" from *I'm Your Man*, 1988
141 "Like a lot …" Jennifer Warnes interview with Michael Segell, *Cosmopolitan*, 1987
141 "When I signed …" Jennifer Warnes, quoted in a Cypress Records media release, 1987
144 "I felt for …" LC interview with Paul Zollo, *SongTalk*, 1992
145 "I just fell …" Suzanne Vega on stage in Tel Aviv, 2009
146 "A poem takes …" LC interview with Richard Harrington, *Washington Post*, 1988
149 "I've seen the …" LC, "The Future" from *The Future*, 1992
149 "This last album …" LC interview with Paul Zollo, *SongTalk*, 1992
154 "I am not …" LC interview with Jordi Saládrigas, *ABC* (Spain), 2001
154 "There is a …" LC, "Anthem" from *The Future*, 1992
160 "[Anjani] seems to …" LC quote from Legacy/Columbia media relations press release, 2006
162 "There's a blaze …" and "I couldn't feel …" LC, "Hallelujah" from *Various Positions*, 1984
164 "Hallelujah is a …" LC interview, *Guitare et Claviers*, 1985
170 "It's a rigorous …" LC interview with Ritchie Yorke, 1985
175 "When I was …" LC, on stage, various venues, 2008/2009
179 "On the drums …" LC, on stage, various venues, 2010
182 "I was looking …" LC, on stage, various venues, 2012/2013
182 "I love to …" LC, "Going Home" from *Old Ideas*, 2012
184 "Writing in the …" review by Neil McCormick, *Telegraph* (UK), 2012
185 "Everything that you …" LC, from his "How I Got My Song" speech, Prince of Asturias awards ceremony, 2011

188 "There are always ..." LC interview with Paul Zollo, *SongTalk*, 1992
188 "I'm turning tricks ..." LC, "A Thousand Kisses Deep" from *Ten New Songs*, 2001
188 "I tried jeans ..." LC speaking in Lian Lunson's *Leonard Cohen: I'm Your Man* documentary, 2005
190 "As far as ..." LC interview with Michael C Ford, *Los Angeles Free Press*, 1975
191 "I've been a ..." Curtis Hanson interview with Harvey Kubernik, 2000 (a portion appeared in *HITS* magazine, 2000)
191 "I think Noel ..." LC interview with Ritchie Yorke, 1985
192 "If it be ..." LC, "If It Be Your Will" from *Various Positions*, 1984
195 "There's a kind ..." LC interview with Suzanne Nunziata, *Billboard* "30th Anniversary Tribute to Leonard Cohen," November 28, 1998
197 "I always had ..." LC interview with Paul Zollo, *SongTalk*, 1992
224 "The older you ..." LC quoting Joshu Sasaki Roshi in an interview with Jordi Saládrigas, *ABC* (Spain), 2001
224 "A love a ..." LC, "A Thousand Kisses Deep" from *Ten New Songs*, 2001

PICTURE CREDITS

Every effort has been made to trace and acknowledge the copyright holders. We apologize in advance for any unintentional omissions and would be pleased, if any such case should arise, to add appropriate acknowledgment in any future edition of the book. Please note that all sources for copyright are associated where applicable with the images used.

T: top; B: bottom; R: right; L: left

Getty Images: Endpapers (Josep Lago); 11, 116 (Michael Ochs Archives); 24–25, 27 L & R, 29, 30, 31 (James Burke); 38–39 (Michael Ochs Archives/Roz Kelly); 41 (AFP/Emmanuel Dunand); 46 BL & BR (Fred W. McDarrah); 53, 62–63, 69, 70–71 (The Estate of David Gahr); 66 (Redferns/Tony Russell); 78 T, 79 B, 103 T (Redferns); 79 T (Redferns/K & K Ulf Krüger/Günter Zint); 80–81 (Express Newspapers); 82–83, 194 (Michael Putland); 91 (Redferns/Stephanie Chernikowski); 93 TR & C (Redferns/Jan Persson); 96 (Redferns/K & K Ulf Krüger/Hans-Jürgen Dibbert); 97 (WireImage/Tom Hill); 110 (Jørgen Angel); 116–117 (CTS Images/Ray Avery); 122 (FilmMagic/BuzzFoto/Brad Elterman); 126–127 (Redferns/Frans Schellekens); 134–135 (Time & Life Pictures/Ian Cook); 149 B (Terry O'Neill); 166–167 (AFP/Miguel Riopa); 169 L, 175 (Film Magic/Jeff Kravitz); 169 C (Frederick M. Brown); 169 R (Songwriter's Hall of Fame/Larry Busacca); 171 (Ethan Hill/Contour); 173 (Frank Hönsch); 176–177 (Redferns/Gary Wolstenholme); 176 L (Jack Vartoogian); 176 R (AFP/Ben Stansall); 178 T (Scott Legato); 178 B (AFP/Nicolas Maeterlinck); 182 (AFP/Joël Saget); **Corbis:** 1 (Kipa/Alain Denize); 7 (Hulton-Deutsch); 12–13 (Ann Johansson); 17 (Outline/Tina Tyrell); 23 L (Allen Ginsberg); 44 B (Jeff Albertson); 47, 57 M (Steve Schapiro); 56, 57 TL (Bettman); 70 (National Geographic Society/Kike Calvo);

109 background (National Geographic Society/Prof. Ellerman); 125 T (Outline/Gary Moss); 125 B, 155 TL, 155 TR, 155 C, 155 BL, 156–157 (Neal Preston); 130 (Sygma/Stefani); 145 (Deborah Feingold); 172 (Axel Koester); 174 (Ann Johansson); 183 (ZUMA Press/Carlos Osorio); 184 (Pool); 196 (Outline/Darcy Hemley); 224 (Reuters/Eloy Alonso); © **Antonio Olmos:** 2–3; **Rex Features:** 6 (Sipa Press); 75 B (Ilpo Musto); 111 (Everett/CSU Archives); 112–113 (Max Malandrino); 181 (Richard Young); © **Platon/Trunk Archive:** 8; **TopFoto:** 15 TL (RIA Novosti); **Courtesy of the Dominique Boile Archives:** 18 R, 19 L & R, 21 T; **Rare Books and Special Collections, McGill University Library:** 18 L (McGill Yearbooks); 23 R (John Glassco Papers); **Concordia University Records Management and Archives:** 22; **Allan R. Leishman/Montreal Star/Library and Archives Canada/PA-190166:** 32, 35, 37; **NFBC:** 34 R; **Photograph by Jack Robinson, Jack Robinson Archive, LLC:** 43, 48, 51; ©**GuyWebster.com:** 45; © **Daniel Kramer:** 46 T; **Henry Diltz:** 55, 72, 150–151, 186–187; **Chris Darrow Archive:** 57 B, 58; **Globe Photos Inc:** 61; **Press Association Images:** 64–65, 82 R (Peter Kemp); 165 (Aaron Harris); **Lebrecht:** 74 (L. McAfee), 93 BR (Rocksign); **Courtesy of the Charlie Daniels Band:** 75 T; © **Danny Fields:** 77; **Photofest:** 81 (Columbia); **Photofeatures.com/Chris Walter:** 84–85; **Uri Dan/Courtesy of the Farkash Gallery, Israel:** 87 L, 98; **Photoshot:** 89, 106–107, 109 (Sunshine); 119 (Picture Alliance); 133 B (Idols); 162–163 (Retna/Marcel Hartmann); © **Estate of Arnaud Maggs, Courtesy: Susan Hobbs Gallery, Toronto:** 94–95, 114; **John Lissauer:** 102, 103 B; **Frank Lane Photo Agency/Laurens Van Houten:** 104; **John Miller:** 108; **Contrasto:** 120 (Giuseppe Pino); 138–139 (Guido Harari); © **Hazel Field:** 133, 133 T; **Sharon Weisz:** 137, 140 T & C, 142, 143 T, 195; **Eyevine:** 146 (Hollandse Hoogte/Roy Tee); 190 (*Toronto Star*/Andrew Stawicki); **Jillian Edelstein:** 158; **cpimages.com:** 161; **Gered Mankowitz** © **BOWSTIR Ltd. 2012/mankowitz.com:** 189 **Camera Press, London:** 193 (Agence VU/Eric Mulet); © **Paul Zollo:** 198.

Printed ephemera
Courtesy of the collection of J. Brouwer: 15 B; **Courtesy of Linda and Dick Straub:** 21 B (Contact Press); 27 C (Secker & Warburg, London); 28, 34 L, 36 R (McClelland & Stewart Ltd., Toronto); 87 R (Jonathan Cape Ltd., London); **Jarkko Arjatsalo, Finland, founder and webmaster of the Leonard Cohen Files and Leonard Cohen Forum:** 36 L (McClelland & Stewart Ltd., Toronto); 93 BL; **Courtesy of the collection of Maarten Massa:** 78 B; **The Kobal Collection:** 90 L (FISA); **Courtesy of the Dominique Boile Archives:** 93 TL (Tony Palmer); 149 T (Jonathan Cape Ltd., London); **Private Collections:** 15 TR (Johnson Smith & Company); 52 (Sing Out! Corporation); 99 B (*Playbill* Magazine); 82 L (Fiery Creations Ltd.).

Album covers
Courtesy of the Dominique Boile Archives: 15 TC (Folkway Records); 60 T, 60 B, 76 T & B, 90 R, 99 T, 105, 123, 161 B, 164, 181 insets T & B (Columbia); **Jarkko Arjatsalo, Finland, founder and webmaster of the Leonard**

Cohen Files and Leonard Cohen Forum: 90 C (CBS); 100, 148, 159 B (Columbia); **Private Collections:** 44 T (Elektra); 57 TR (Polydor); 32, 136, 143 B, 159 T (Columbia); 140 B (Cypress Records).

ACKNOWLEDGMENTS

I am extremely grateful to Colin Webb, the Publisher at Palazzo Editions, for his initiation of this endeavor and constant support during this book's creation, and to Palazzo editor James Hodgson for his subject-specific suggestions and well-informed guidance.

My team in California greatly enhanced my assembled collective prose and multi-voice narrative. I'm especially thankful to my Los Angeles–based editorial director, Kenneth Kubernik, who provided game-changing literary observations, writing and ESPN-like first-round draft analysis during *The Long Season*. I'm also deeply indebted to my San Francisco–located copy editor Joseph McCombs, and Studio City archivist Gary Strobl. Much appreciation to James Cushing in San Luis Obispo and Claremont's Chris Darrow for their joint wisdom.

UGMAA (Union of God's Musicians and Artists Ascension) avatar Horace Tapscott often described the organization's credo as "contributive, not competitive." Previously published Leonard Cohen biographers and chroniclers were extremely generous with their library items, sources and information on Leonard's creative life. These valued contributors include: Jarkko Arjatsalo, Jeff Burger, Ray Coleman, Karl Dallas, Jim Devlin, Henry Diltz, Ira Nadel, Anthony J. Reynolds, Ellen Sander, Allan Showalter, Ritchie Yorke, and Paul Zollo.

Plus a very special thanks to my pal and Cohen scholar Sylvie Simmons.

I'd also like to cite the contributions of Peter Asher, Izzy Chait, Tom Cording, Rodel Delfin, Mark Ellen, Michael C Ford, Gabriela Gibb, Jeff Goldman, Randy Haecker, Stephen J. Kalinich, David Kann, Dan Kessel, Al Kooper, Elliott Lefko, John Leland, S. Ti Muntarbhorn, Morgan Neville, Andrew Loog Oldham, Open Door Church, Justin Pierce, Nancy Rose Retchin, Daniel Weizmann, Rachel Willis, and Wyline and Scott. And always, Hilda and Marshall Kubernik.

And, of course, gratitude is extended to Leonard Cohen for his offerings. Namaste.

Om Mani Padme Hum

Harvey Kubernik

Palazzo Editions thanks David Costa at Wherefore Art? for his initial presentations and constant design inspiration.

Overleaf: Prince of Asturias Award ceremony, Oviedo, Spain, October 21, 2011.

"The older you get, the lonelier you
become and the deeper the love you need."
– Joshu Sasaki Roshi

"A love a thousand kisses deep."
– Leonard Cohen